Applied Financial Econometrics

Moinak Maiti

Applied Financial Econometrics

Theory, Method and Applications

Moinak Maiti
Department of Finance
National Research University
Higher School of Economics
St. Petersburg, Russia

ISBN 978-981-16-4062-9   ISBN 978-981-16-4063-6   (eBook)
https://doi.org/10.1007/978-981-16-4063-6

This Palgrave Macmillan imprint is published by the registered company Springer Nature
Singapore Pte Ltd.
The registered company address is: 152 Beach Road, #21-01/04 Gateway East, Singapore
189721, Singapore

To my parents: Mr. Lakshmi Kanta Maiti and Mrs. Sandhya Maiti.

—Moinak Maiti

PREFACE

Every year while teaching Financial Econometrics course at the Master level. I find that most of the candidates are quite interested to take up the Financial econometrics course but many of them do not dare to take up the course primarily due to the fear of complex mathematics and notations. Candidates do come from different backgrounds and for most of them mathematics is just a night mare. Most of the candidates those who have taken advance econometrics course earlier is usually get enrolled for my financial econometrics course. Most of such candidates share that advanced econometrics courses are usually based on mathematical derivations, notations and at the end any how they just manage to clear the subject. That makes it really a challenging task for any instructor to deliver the course in a very simple way (without much complex mathematical notations). Next issue arises due to the reason that many of them have no background in the programming. Altogether it makes somewhat more difficult to deliver a course successfully. Financial econometrics course that I teach, the syllabus is built in such a way that it starts with some basics but ends with advanced concepts. The primary aim of the course is to give students an updated knowledge of the econometrics techniques so that they can implement it with confident in solving the real-world problems. After completion of my course, some of the comments that students share are as follows:

Thanks for all the helps you given to me during the lecture. And all the lecture materials we used in the class are associated with most current researches and study, that are very useful and practical. I personally benefited from this.

I would like to continue my studies for both the subjects because I learned a lot, it would be great. In any case, I want to say thank to you for your passion and teaching.

I would want to take this opportunity to express my heartfelt appreciation for your contribution to the publication of my term paper and other assistance you have given me. It was a great beginning for my research career.

Thank you professor for the course! It was very useful and practical oriented.

What's next? Student says it is very difficult to find an econometrics book that covers all important topics that you teach altogether. Then most of the books available either talks too much on theory or mathematical modelling. In such case there is real demand for a financial econometrics book that is written from the students point of view that makes pleasure in learning. A book that explains theory in the simplest way. My students ask me "professor why do not you write a book that will help the learning community in a greater extent". I am very encouraged by my beloved students' statements. So, I decided to write a book that will fulfil all such needs. This book has real-world examples with software execution and finally clear cut explanation of the obtained results. All examples are executed either by EViews or R programming with stepwise explanation in a visual format wherever necessary. EViews and R programming both are chosen due to two reasons: (1) EViews is simple to use and even though it is a paid software but both student and tutor versions are available for free. (2) On the other hand, R is free and programming oriented. By this students will learn both the techniques together and they can choose either of them for applications as required. This book will be beneficial for both students and instructors who are associated with econometrics subjects at the undergraduate and postgraduate levels. Finally, I appreciate all comments and suggestions for further improvement of the book. As nothing is perfect in this world.

St. Petersburg, Russia   Moinak Maiti

ACKNOWLEDGEMENTS

First of all I would like to express my sincere gratitude to my family and friends for their support, directly or indirectly in making this book a reality. I am thankful to the commissioning and production team at the Palgrave Macmillan publications for their sincere support and consideration. I am also grateful to the three anonymous reviewers for their valuable comments and suggestions for establishment of this book. I give thanks to the almighty god for protection and ability to do work.

Special thanks to the learners, students, and colleagues. Lastly I am thankful to everyone who are directly or indirectly associated in making this book a reality.

Moinak Maiti

About This Book

The title of the book is "Applied Financial Econometrics". The content of the book is put to practical use as opposed to being just theoretical. The present edition of this book is intended to cover different topics related to the financial econometrics ranging from basic to advanced spectrums. The organization and chapter-wise distribution includes up to date topics. This book is written keeping in mind to ease the problem of students and most importantly practical examples are included throughout from the financial backgrounds. It discusses not only about the financial econometric applications in the real world but it also conveys how one should approach practical problem solving in finance. Throughout the book, I have made all sincere efforts introducing the complex topics in a very simplistic manner and keeping the language too simple. This book has nine chapters as mentioned below.

1. Introduction
2. Random Walk Hypothesis
3. Geometric Brownian Motion
4. Efficient Frontier & Portfolio Optimization
5. Introduction to Asset Pricing Factor Models
6. Risk Analysis
7. Introduction to Fat Tails
8. Threshold Autoregression
9. Introduction to Wavelets

Every chapter starts with a detailed background of the topic followed by stepwise software implementation of the real-world problems with comprehensive interpretations. Then every chapter has "Finance in Action" and "Analyst/Investor Corners" sections. At the end of each chapter, numerous practise exercises are included namely MCQs, fill in the blanks, long answer questions, real-world tasks, and case studies. Moreover the scope of this book is not only limited to the financial econometric course but many of these chapters listed above could also be useful in other courses such as asset pricing, theory of finance, risk management, and others. Last few decades have seen significant increase in the interest for econometrics in allied fields as well, especially in the management and technological fields apart from the regular economics or finance. There are no prerequisites for reading this book. Though a basic knowledge of finance, statistics, or any programming language is a plus. This book will be useful for both the students and instructors who are associated with econometrics courses at the undergraduate and postgraduate levels.

Moinak Maiti

PRAISE FOR *APPLIED FINANCIAL ECONOMETRICS*

"Moinak Maiti's book "Applied Financial Econometrics" provides a great introduction to a couple of highly relevant topics in empirical finance. The hands-on approach is a particular strength and guides students how to DO econometrics rather than just to know the concepts. While the book focuses on under- and postgraduate students, also young empirical researchers will benefit from it. A superb book for students and instructors."

—Professor Michael Frömmel, *Finance Professor, Ghent University*

"The present book in Applied Financial Econometrics introduces relevant topics using econometrics to deal with financial problems. It is practically oriented and includes practical examples in every chapter showing the reader how to solve in a stepwise manner real cases. For all that I highly recommend it."

—Professor Angel Barajas, *Head, Department of Finance, Higher School of Economics*

"This is a must-read for anyone interested in entering the world of finance with quantitative focus. The author explains the theories with practical examples. Furthermore, I see very little need for any prerequisites. I recommend everyone interested in financial analytics in general to benefit from this book."
—Dr. Badri Narayanan Gopalakrishnan, *Consultant Economists, McKinsey & Company*

"Moinak always had a knack of simplifying the most complex of problems, and that is exactly what he has very successfully done through this book. This is a must read for anyone wanting to understand the application of Econometrics to everyday problems."
—Kartik Palaniappan, *South Asia Head, Buyside Order Management Solution, Bloomberg LP*

"Author in his book titled "Applied Financial Econometrics" presents a new way of thinking about machine learning that gives its own place in the econometric toolbox through appropriate examples. The detailed deliberation on "Fat tailed distribution" will immensely help and guide investors in the money market, business entrepreneurs of all sectors. I recommend this book as a must read for all students aspiring to pursue Finance & Management Courses. I wish! Many more editions of this book will be published with the latest updates in years to come."
—Dilip Kumar Bardhan, *Additional General Manager (Retd.), NTPC Limited, Ministry of Power, Government of India*

"The book "Applied Financial Econometrics" will be aimed for theorists, practitioner, as well as for advanced students, from a wide range of econometrics, financial markets and institutions, corporate finance, and digital finance. This book develops insights on an innovative approach, in order to underpin practice and research in the area of financial econometrics."
—Dr. Darko Vukovic, *Head, International Laboratory for Finance and Financial Markets, People's Friendship University of Russia "RUDN"*

"In "Applied financial econometrics", this fantastic author guides us through the financial econometrics, a relative complicated issue even with finance students and lecturers, in a very simplistic but helpful manner. I enjoy reading his wonderful approach to include practical examples, software implementation, real world tasks, and also case studies. Notably, I am surprising with the update of this book as it has included current latest development in financial econometrics such as fat tails, threshold regression, and Wavelets analysis. I confidently recommend "Applied financial econometrics" and I trust that it would provide huge benefits for finance students but also promoting their future development."

—Dr. Canh Phuc Nguyen, *Senior Lecturer, University of Economics Ho Chi Minh City*

"Dr. Maiti's "Applied Financial Econometrics" is an interesting read for students and professionals alike. The topics, although difficult, are nicely described and deal with real word applications."

—Dr. Cornel Nesseler, *Postdoctoral Fellow, University of Zurich, & NTNU Business School*

"This book is a sophisticated beautiful integration of Econometrics and real world use of it…written in plain English, based on simplified notation and full of case studies. An important and practical combination for both academic and professionals. Highly recommended."

—Sattwik Das, CFA, FRM, *Independent Model Review Manager, HSBC*

"This book is a complete balance between the theory and the practice. It is a comprehensive book with excellent features."

—Dr. Saakshi, *Assistant Professor, Indian Institute of Management Ranchi*

"Today health economics is emerging as one of the challenging and interesting field to deal with especially for the applied econometricians. The COVID-19 pandemic raises several questions on the risk management related to healthcare, social insurance, spatial health econometrics and others. The author in this book has covered several important topics such as how to deal with the nonlinearity, fat tails, and heterogeneity existing in the data using the highly sophisticated techniques. Overall I find this book is very helpful and highly recommended in the field of applied health econometrics."

—Dr. Mousam Maiti, MS-Otorhinolaryngology, Head & Neck Surgery, *Resident Doctor, All India Institute of Medical Sciences Bhopal*

"Dr. Maiti's reader-friendly illustrations provide an amazing insight and wonderful learning platform on the real world applications in Financial Econometrics. Definitely, this book is going to inspire many students not only to enhance their technical knowhow but also foster a desire to pursue it as a career to work in the finance industry."

—Mihir Kumar Parial, *Director (Retd.), Directorate General of Training, Ministry of Skill Development and Entrepreneurship, Government of India*

"This book on "Applied Financial Econometrics" enables students with real life problem solving skills in financial markets while giving intuitive grasp on the underlying concepts. The author has put in sincere efforts to keep the content practical, industry oriented and data driven to keep the students involved."

—Satya Venkata Chalapathi, *Former Vice President of Singapore Mercantile Exchange*

"Prof. Maiti's well-written textbook represents a novel and refreshing treatment of financial econometrics and should have be seen as bridge between theoretical econometrics and applied financial econometrics. Moreover, it is a practitioner friendly textbook. Even so complicated topics such as Wavelet analysis are treated at an accessible level. I consider it as a gift to graduate students in terms of discussing the terms, presenting topics and showing how to apply each method to real life data. Thus, I strongly advice the adaptation of Maiti's book to my colleagues."

—Professor Mustafa Özer, *Economics Professor, Anadolu University*

"I have not seen a more thorough resource dedicated specifically to the practical aspects of financial econometrics. It will transform your understanding of topics related to financial econometrics ranging from basic to advanced spectrums. I would recommend this book to both the students and instructors of econometrics at different levels and for anyone looking to advance their knowledge and expand their scope of practice."

—Professor B. Charumathi, *Head, Department of Management studies, Pondicherry University*

"Dr. Maiti has written a must-read primer for anyone considering financial econometrics... This book has several real world examples that take us towards the data sciences ... such as examples on forecasting, non-linear data series, predictive modelling etc..."

—Dr. Amrit Mukherjee, *Postdoctoral Fellow, Zhejiang University*

"I have had the pleasure of knowing Moinak since his student days when he was an offsite intern for Bloomberg LP at Pondicherry University. He consistently impressed me with his rigor and tenacity. He brings the same spirit to the title "Applied Financial Econometrics". His work considers existing econometric theory and aspires to juxtapose it against emerging research and practice."

—Joel Pannikot, *Head, India at CMT Association; Former Head of Asia-Pacific Strategy-Education, Bloomberg LP*

"The author's proactive approach implies the active participation of the reader through solving tasks and various case studies. The multidisciplinary of the books is reflected in the usefulness that this material provides for risk analysis, asset management options, and financial theory in general. The book has significant use value at all levels of study in areas related to econometrics."

—Dr. Duško Ranisavljević, *Assistant Professor, Health and Business Studies, Singidunum University*

"This book has a lucid representation and relevant content for the 21st century financial econometrician. Highly recommended to all students, academicians and working professionals in this area as the book provides both theoretical as well as pragmatist insights."

—Dr. Abhijeet Lele, *Assistant Professor, Symbiosis Institute of Business Management Pune*

"An indefatigable effort has been taken by the author to provide practical knowledge on trending topics of finance. This book going to make a difference."

—Srividya Mortha, *Data Management Consultant, Wells Fargo*

"The book "Applied Financial Econometrics" deals with relevant and contemporary topics related to financial econometrics. The author gave a detailed and satisfactory literature dealing with this subject. The objective of the book sets the tone and expectations. This book guides thinking."

—Dr. Marko D. Petrović, *Honorary Fellow, University of Wisconsin–Madison*

CONTENTS

About the Author

Dr. Moinak Maiti is Associate Professor in the Department of Finance, National Research University-Higher School of Economics, Saint Petersburg. He is an Active Speaker and invited to share the World renowned platforms of World Bank, United Nations, World Trade Organisation (WTO Studies), SAS®, Bloomberg LP, Max Plank Society, PEP Canada, Ivy League Universities, and many others. He holds university Gold Medal along with several other notable awards throughout in his timeline. Several eminent research grants from World renowned institutions like World Bank, Max Plank Society Germany, PEP Canada, World Trade Organisation (WTO Studies), Ivy League Universities, and others are added to his account.

He is in the editorial board members of several International Journals published by Elsevier, Emerald, Wiley, and other reputed publishing house. His article regularly published as Research articles, Book chapters, Cases, Blogs, Newspapers and Reviews, etc., by renowned publishing house.

His area of interest and expertise is Finance, more specifically in Asset Pricing, Financial Econometrics, Fintech, IoT, and Neuroscience. He is open to collaborate and discuss interesting consultancy projects.

ABBREVIATIONS

ACF	Autocorrelation Function
ADF Test	Augmented Dickey-Fuller Test
APT	Arbitrage Pricing Theory
AR	Auto-Regressive
ARCH	Autoregressive Conditional Heteroskedasticity
ARIMA	Auto-Regressive Integrated Moving Average
ARMA	Autoregressive Moving Average
BDS Independence Test	Brock, Dechert, and Scheinkman Independence Test
BE/ME	Book to Market ratio
BSE	Bombay Stock Exchange
CAPM	Capital Asset Pricing Model
CCAPM	Consumption Capital Asset Pricing Model
CCM	Constant Coefficients Model
CMA	Conservative Minus Aggressive
CML	Capital Market Line
CWT	Continuous Wavelet Transform
DJIA	Dow Jones Industrial Average
DWT	Discrete Wavelet Transform
EMH	Efficient Market Hypothesis
ESTAR	Exponential Smooth Transition Autoregressive
GARCH	Generalized Autoregressive Conditional Heteroskedasticity
GBM	Geometric Brownian Motion
GMM	Generalized Method of Moments
GRS Test	Gibbons, Ross, & Shanken Test
HML	High Minus Low

HPR	Holding Period Returns
ICAPM	Intertemporal Capital Asset Pricing Model
IDE	Integrated Development Environment
IID	Independently and Identically distributed
KPSS Test	Kwiatkowski–Phillips–Schmidt–Shin Test
LOESS	Locally Estimated Scatterplot Smoothing
LP	Linear Programming
LSTAR	Logistic Smooth Threshold Autoregression
MA	Moving Average
MMV	Multifactor Mean Variance
MODWT	Maximal Overlap Discrete Wavelet Transform
NSE	National Stock Exchange of India
NYSE	New York Stock Exchange
OLS	Ordinary Least Square
PACF	Partial Autocorrelation Function
P/B	Price to Book ratio
PDL	Program Design Language
PP Test	Phillips-Perron test
RBI	Reserve Bank of India
RMW	Robust Minus Weak
RWH	Random Walk Hypothesis
SETAR	Self-Exciting Threshold Autoregressive
SMB	Small Minus Big
SML	Security Market Line
SoFiE	Society for Financial Econometrics
SSR	Sum of Squared Residuals
STAR	Smooth Threshold Autoregression
STL	Seasonal and Trend decomposition using LOESS
TAR	Threshold Autoregression
VAR	Vector autoregression
VECM	Vector Error Correction Model
VIX	Volatility Index
WML	Winners Minus Losers

LIST OF FIGURES

LIST OF TABLES

CHAPTER 1

Introduction

Key Topics Covered

- *What is Applied Financial Econometrics?*
- *The essential steps to conduct the applied financial econometrics study*
- *Type I and Type II errors*
- *Importance of Stochastic specification (ε) in the model*
- *Basic data types that are used in financial econometrics study*
- *Introduction to Econometric software packages: EViews and R programming*

1.1 BACKGROUND

The term "econometrics" was emphasized by Ragnar Frisch in the inaugural issue of the Journal of the Econometric Society (Econometrica) editorial note[1] published in the year 1933. Even though Pawel Ciompa have used the term *"Oekonometrie"* (Econometrics in German) in the year 1910, almost two decades beforehand Frisch. Modern economists favour Frisch version of econometrics that *"aims at a unification of the theoretical quantitative and the empirical-quantitative approach to*

---

[1] Frisch, R. (1933). Editor's note. *Econometrica, 1*(1), 1–4. Retrieved March 20, 2021, from http://www.jstor.org/stable/1912224.

© The Author(s), under exclusive license to Springer Nature Singapore Pte Ltd. 2021
M. Maiti, *Applied Financial Econometrics,*
https://doi.org/10.1007/978-981-16-4063-6_1

economic problem" in contrast to the Pawel's conception of econometrics which is entirely descriptive. Frisch stressed that to understand the quantitative relationships of the real complex economic environment, only single viewpoint of statistics, economic theory, or mathematic is not sufficient rather it demands the union of three. Hereafter econometrics as a distinct branch of economics began to emerge and it further gains momentum with the foundation of entities namely *"Cowles Commission for Research in Economics"* and others. Foremost methodological debate in econometrics initiated with the article titled "The Probability Approach in Econometrics" by Trygve Haavelmo (1944)[2] and hereafter other areas of econometrics seen significant developments. Subsequently, notably Gerhard Tintner (1953)[3] defines origin of the word "econometrics" as the neology of two Greek words, "oikonomia" (administration or economics) and "metron" (measure). Hence, factually meaning of the term econometrics appears to be as the "measurement in economics". Gerhard made an attempts to provide an expressive definition for: what is econometrics? To do so, Gerhard in his study quoted several viewpoints of "econometrics" as defined by the several noteworthy researchers. In conclusion Gerhard argues that the definition of econometrics as defined by the earlier studies is somewhat sketchy in nature. It is really a difficult and challenging task to define econometrics with just a single characterization as the space of econometrics is very vast. It is true that "measurement" is one of the important component of econometrics but likewise nowadays the scope of econometrics is much wider than that.

Thereafter, in a relatively short period of time studies in the field of econometrics have seen significant development holistically. To support the increase in demand for the econometrics studies development of several supportive econometrics software packages began to progress. Some of the notable econometrics software packages that are developed over a period of time is represented in Fig. 1.1.

Studies in econometrics could be grouped into two groups: theoretical and applied econometrics. Theoretical econometrics explore the properties of existing statistical tests and procedures for estimating unknown

---

[2] Haavelmo, T. (1944). The probability approach in econometrics. *Econometrica: Journal of the Econometric Society*, iii–115.

[3] Tintner, G. (1953). The definition of econometrics. *Econometrica, 21*(1), 31–40. https://doi.org/10.2307/1906941

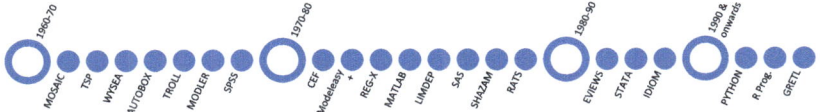

Fig. 1.1   Evolution of various econometrics software packages

variables in the model. Whereas applied econometrics combines the theoretical econometrics and real-world data for evaluating economic theories, constructing innovative econometric models, and forecasting models. Today the applications of econometrics are just not only limited to the field of economics but it is well adapted in the other allied fields such as business and management. Sir Clive William John Granger during in his noble prize speech quoted the following.

> We econometricians love numbers… which I view as a healthy local trend.[4]—Clive W.J. Granger

In practice, there exists the ambiguities and overlaps between "econometrics, data science, machine learning and others" in the way different people see these terms. The fundamental difference between econometrics and other terms such as data science and machine learning lies with the different approaches for problem solving. Econometrics focuses more on the casual relationship between the variables under study. In contrast data science and machine learning focuses more on the reverse engineering and curve fitting problems. Nonetheless knowledge of econometrics would be a treat for the data scientists as both shares a lot of common interests, such as Regressions, ARIMA & VAR models, and others. Having a strong foundation of econometrics, data scientists would be able to interpret the obtained results and understand the causality better among the variables. That is how the knowledge of econometrics could make the data scientists influential.

Financial econometrics is a subset of the financial economics (subset of economics) that deals with the application of statistical methods to financial market data. The field of financial econometrics has seen significant developments in the last few decades. Today financial econometrics

---

[4] Granger, C. W. (2004). Time series analysis, cointegration, and applications. *American Economic Review, 94*(3), 421–425.

is considered being one among the fast growing fields in economics. To promote the global network of academics and practitioners dedicated to sharing research and ideas in the field of financial econometrics, Society for Financial Econometrics (SoFiE)[5] is co-founded by Robert F. Engle and Eric Ghysels. Top academic journals namely Journal of Finance, Econometrica, Journal of Econometrics, Journal of Financial Economics, Journal of Financial Econometrics, and others publish studies on financial economics frequently. Studies in applied financial econometrics typically include the following topics but are not limited to

- Analysis of high-frequency time series
- Asset pricing dynamics
- Optimal asset allocation
- Non-linear time series
- Fund performance analysis
- Derivative structuring
- Volatility estimation techniques
- Risk analysis
- Coherence and co-movements
- Forecasting models
- Portfolio optimisation and theory
- Test of market efficiency
- Causation and effect
- Identification of shocks and thresholds estimation
- Random walk models
- Fixed Income, equities, commodities, currencies & others asset classes
- Intraday trading
- Modelling financial markets.

1.2   STEPS TO BE FOLLOWED IN APPLIED FINANCIAL ECONOMETRICS STUDY

Seven key steps that have to be followed to conduct applied financial econometrics study successfully are as follows:

---

[5] http://sofie.stern.nyu.edu/.

- Problem definition or statement
- Selection of variables
- Model description
- Selection of methods or techniques
- Result Estimation
- Interpretation and Validation
- Conclusion and research implications.

1.2.1 Problem Definition or Statement

Problem definition or statement is the very first step for conducting any financial econometrics study. It is very important to identify the clear-cut research problem or what study is going to address? For an instant let's define the study statement as "To examine the performance of Capital Asset Pricing Model (CAPM) in Indian context". Based on the study problem following hypotheses are framed:

Null Hypothesis (Ho): CAPM regression intercept is equal to zero.

Alternative Hypothesis (Ha): CAPM regression intercept is not equal to zero.

As the entire study centres around the framed hypotheses and a minor mistake in framing the hypotheses could result into an absolute disaster. So, any financial econometrics study requires in-depth understanding of the hypotheses testing for the different statistical methods and econometrics models used. Testing of hypothesis concludes either with rejection of the null hypothesis or acceptance of the alternative hypothesis. Rejection of the null hypothesis indicates that the null hypothesis is not true and alternative hypothesis could be accepted or vice versa. Decision of acceptance or rejection of the null hypothesis is based on the obtained p-values or t-values.

Wrongly rejecting the null or alternative hypothesis could give rise to the circumstances of Type I (alpha) and Type II (beta) errors. Rejection of null hypothesis even when that's true would result into Type I error. Likewise fail to reject the null hypothesis even when that's false would result into Type II error. Type I errors largely arise due to scepticisms and by selecting the correct critical values it could be eliminated to a greater degree. In practice depending on the type of datasets different critical values that are being used are based on the 1, 5 or 10% statistical significance level. In contrast Type II errors could be prevented mostly using large sample size. Second approach might be the choosing higher level of significance. The impact of Type I and Type II errors ruling can be accessed through determining the appropriate level of statistical significance. This is how the appropriate level of statistical significance is powerful. Next crucial question is "Which type of the errors are the worst: Type I or II"? Well, both Type I and II errors could be worst depending upon the context. By and large Type I errors are more serious than Type II errors.

1.2.2   Selection of Variables

Based on the study statement wisely selects the study variables. Selection of variables is the another important task in financial econometrics study. Most of the financial econometrics study deals with the closest proxy variables available as it is very difficult to obtained the real variables data. For example, it is very difficult to obtain the real estimates for the market returns. Influential Stock Index benchmarks (S&P 500; BSE 30; NSE 50, and others) are often used as the proxy for market returns. For the study statement "To examine the performance of Capital Asset Pricing Model (CAPM) in Indian context", study variables could be as follows: individual stocks or portfolio excess returns (dependent variable); risk free rate (91 days T-bills); market returns (BSE 30 or BSE-200 index monthly excess returns). For financial econometrics studies, data could be obtained from both paid and unpaid databases or data sources. Bloomberg, Thomson Reuters Eikon, Capitaline, Compustat, Datastream, CMIE Prowess, and others are some of the leading providers of financial data or databases based on subscriptions. Likewise Yahoo finance, central banks, World bank, IMF, Stock exchanges, Google finance, SEC, CoinMarketCap (Cryptocurrency), and others are some of the leading providers of public or free financial data or databases. Once variables are chosen next study period and frequency of data (daily, weekly, monthly, yearly or others) has to be specified.

1.2.3 Model Description

Once the study variables are identified based on it develop the financial econometric model. Mathematically represent the developed financial econometric model taking into account all possible factors or variables that could affect the dependent variable(s). For example, the CAPM illustrates the relationship between market (systematic risk) and expected return for assets. Here the relationship between market (systematic risk) and expected return for assets is not exact and deterministic, rather a typical or stochastic one. Moreover in financial econometrics study the relationship between the variables often has two way causality. These types of situations demand for a stochastic specification in the model. And that is possible by inserting "stochastic terms" or "Error terms" or "noise terms" or "disturbance terms" or "residuals terms" in the model. Other justification for inclusion of the stochastic specification (ε) in the model could take into account the erratic human behaviour, influence of omitted variables, measurement errors if any and others. To examine the performance of CAPM in Indian context following model is developed as shown below in Eq. 1.1:

$$R_{\text{pit}} - R_{\text{ft}} = \alpha + \beta(R_{\text{mt}} - R_{\text{ft}}) + \varepsilon_{\text{it}} \qquad (1.1)$$

where

$R_{\text{pit}} - R_{\text{ft}}$ = Individual stocks or excess portfolio returns
$R_{\text{mt}} - R_{\text{ft}}$ = excess market returns
R_{ft} = Risk free rate
α = alpha
β = beta coefficient
ε = "Error terms" or "noise terms" or "disturbance terms" or "residuals terms".

Stochastic specification (ε) in the above model is not readily observable like the other variables. Often study in applied financial econometrics makes some reasonable assumptions about the shape of the distribution of each (ε).
Which are as follows:

- Error terms (ε) are normally distributed
- Mean of the error terms (ε) is zero
- Error terms (ε) have uniform variance (σ^2) or homoscedastic
- Error terms (ε) are independent or uncorrelated to each other.

1.2.4 Selection of Methods or Techniques

Once the model has been described based on it appropriate econometric method or techniques selection should be carried out. For an instant performance of CAPM in Indian context could be tested using the linear regression.

1.2.5 Result Estimation

Before running the developed financial econometric model (regression or others), it is worthwhile to look into the details characteristics of the study variables. Preliminarily plot different graphs of the chosen study variables to look at glance the nature of the variables. Look for the unusual spikes and try to find out the cause-and-effect of it. Check to see for the descriptive statistics of the study variables whether they follow central limit theorem or not? Thereafter check for covariances and correlations among the explanatory variables. Financial econometrics study generally deals with the different time series, and it is always necessary to verify whether the time series is stationary or not. Besides unit root test, several other tests are available to check the quality and reliability of the data. For any financial econometrics study quality and reliability of the data is essential as all estimated outputs are based on the selected data. All possible necessary checks should be done to justify quality and reliability of the study data. When all of the above-mentioned necessary checks are performed then run the above regression model (or other chosen models) using available econometrics software packages and obtained the results from it. Commonly all available econometrics software packages provide much details of the estimated results. Include only the necessary information of the estimated results as obtained from the econometrics software packages such as values of the coefficients, t statistics, R^2 value and others.

1.2.6 Interpretation and Validation

It is worthwhile to begin the discussion with the explanatory variables. Include a short interpretation on all of the necessary information obtained from the graphical plots, descriptive statistics, covariance and correlation analysis, unit root testing, and other necessary estimations. Subsequently critically interpret the estimated outputs obtained from the developed financial econometric model. Further it is desirable to check the robustness of the developed financial econometric model. For robustness check of the financial econometric model different tests are available such as GRS, GMM, Boot strapping, and others could be implemented. Even one could go one step ahead later with the forecasting models.

1.2.7   Conclusion and Research Implications

Although it is the last step it is very important in terms of real contribution of the study/research taken. Study results or findings should convey about the direct policy implications or key message for the future studies.

1.3   FUNDAMENTAL DATA TYPES USED IN FINANCIAL ECONOMETRICS STUDY

Financial econometrics study primarily deals with the four data types namely cross sectional, time series, pooled, and panel data. Usually based on the data types different methods or techniques are selected for the financial econometrics study/research. Hence, it is very important to have the knowledge of these various data types used in the financial econometrics study/research.

1.3.1   Cross-Sectional Data

Cross-sectional data consists of data gathered from the multiple subjects (individuals, firms, countries, or regions) at the one particular point or period of time. Table 1.1 shows cross-sectional data of country wise chosen by the largest banks interest incomes for the year 2006. In this illustration of the cross-sectional data, period is fixed (Year is 2006) whereas remaining factors (Country and Interest Incomes) changes.

Table 1.1 Illustration of cross-sectional data

Country	Year	Interest income (in millions, EUR)
Romania	2006	209.44
Serbia	2006	43.85
Slovenia	2006	129.65

Table 1.2 Illustration of time series data

Year	Interest income (in millions, EUR)
2006	209.44
2007	218.13
2008	283.85
2009	318.00
2010	360.07

Table 1.3 Illustration of pooled data

Country	Year	Interest income (in millions, EUR)
Romania	2006	209.44
Serbia	2006	43.85
Romania	2007	218.13
Serbia	2007	77.28
Slovenia	2007	148.10

1.3.2   Time Series Data

Time series data consists of data points of the single subject (individuals, firms, countries, or regions) over a period of time or at regular intervals. Table 1.2 shows time series yearly data of chosen by the Romanian largest banks interest incomes for a period of five years (2006–2010). In this illustration of the time series sectional data period, country is fixed (Romania) whereas time period (Year) varies between 2006 and 2010.

1.3.3   Pooled Data

Pooled data is combination of the both cross-sectional and time series data. It is sometimes referred to as "time series of cross sections" in which the data points contained in each of the cross section necessarily do not refer to the same subject(s). Table 1.3 shows pooled data of country wise chosen by the largest banks interest incomes for the year 2006 and 2007. In this illustration of the pooled data the number of subject elements in cross section is not identical for the year 2006 and 2007. In the year 2007, Slovenia is in addition to the Romania and Serbia. Pooled data is used often to see how the key relationship between the variables has altered over a period.

1.3.4   *Panel Data*

Panel data is often referred as the longitudinal data. Panel data consists of the repeated data points of the same multiple subjects over the short or long periods of time. Panel data is of two types namely balanced and unbalanced panel data. Table 1.4a shows balanced panel data of country wise chosen by the largest banks interest incomes for the year 2006 and 2007. In this illustration of the balanced panel data number of period (2006 and 2007) are identical for the each cross-sectional units.

Likewise Table 1.4b shows unbalanced panel data of country wise chosen by the largest banks interest incomes for the year 2006, 2007, and 2008. In this illustration of the unbalanced panel data number of period (2006, 2007, and 2008) are not identical for Romania and Serbia.

1.4   SOFTWARE PACKAGES

Today various econometrics software packages are available to users for carrying out studies in financial econometrics. Here in this section two commonly used econometrics software packages are discussed namely EViews and R programming. All the discussions and interpretations that are made either with the EViews 11 (Student Version Lite) or R programming outputs in this text book are merely for knowledge sharing purposes of greater interest.

Table 1.4 Illustration of balanced panel data

Country	Year	Interest income (in millions, EUR)
(a)		
Romania	2006	209.44
Romania	2007	218.13
Serbia	2006	43.85
Serbia	2007	77.28
(b)		
Romania	2006	209.44
Romania	2007	218.13
Serbia	2006	43.85
Serbia	2007	77.28
Serbia	2008	83.6

1.4.1   EViews

EViews econometrics software is currently being promoted by the IHS Markit. It is a window based and user friendly econometrics software that offers basics to advanced statistical forecasting and modelling tools for interaction. Today EViews is well accepted by the practitioners and academics in practice. Users include 600⁺ central banks, financial institutions, IMF, Federal reserves, United Nations, World bank, 1,600⁺ university's economics and business departments, over 50% of Fortune's Top 100 Companies, and others. EViews provides user with three choices for the interface: first graphical user interface, second single commands, and third program files.

EViews offers several product and pricing options for the users namely Standard, Enterprise, University Edition, Student Version Lite, and others. EViews Student Version Lite is a free version available to the students and faculty members for usage. EViews Student Version comes with various limitations such as length of use (1 year), image only copy paste options, limit in total observations (15,000), only available for 64-bit devices, and many others. Presently EViews 11 Student Version Lite version is available to download in their official website.[6] First download the EViews 11 Student Version Lite software. Then register yourself with EViews by providing basic information (such as name, university, email, and others) to request a serial number. Upon successful registration EViews will send the 24-character serial number to the registered email. This 24-character serial number is required as a part of the installation and product activation/registration. Then get installed the EViews 11 Student Version Lite software in your system to use. EViews also provides several useful resources for knowledge purpose under the section "Learning Resources" could be accessed from their official websites.

1.4.1.1   EViews in Action

Graphical user interface is the most preferred interface by the users to work with the EViews. By clicking on the EViews 11 Student Version Lite (Hereafter EViews) shortcut icon, EViews interface will open as shown in Fig. 1.2. Here some of the basic estimations that could be performed using EViews software are discussed. To do so following datasets are used:

---

[6] http://www.eviews.com/home.html.

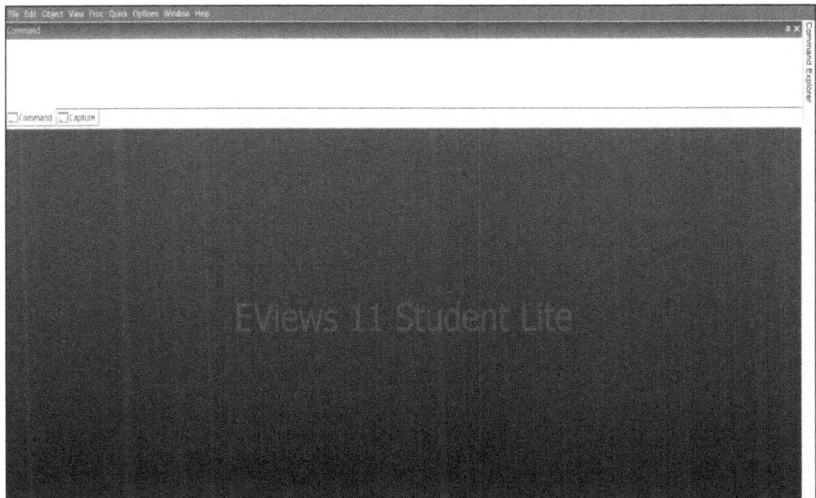

Fig. 1.2 EViews 11 Student Lite Main Window

EUR_USD, and GBP_USD exchange rates daily closing price between 1 January 2020 and 31 March 2020 (Data source: Yahoo Finance).

Importing Data

EViews can read several types of available data formats such as MS Excel, SPSS, SAS, txt, csv, and many others. Basically there are two ways by which data that can be imported into the EViews.

First approach:
File → Import → select the file → Finish

Second approach:
File → New → Workfile → The "Workfile Create" new window will appear as shown in Fig. 1.3.

It provides users with three choices of workfile structure and thirteen choices of data frequency. Once details are chosen then click OK button, and a new "workfile" window will be displayed. Right click on the workfile window, then select paste and finish. Final output after importing the data (EUR_USD, and GBP_USD exchange rates daily closing price)

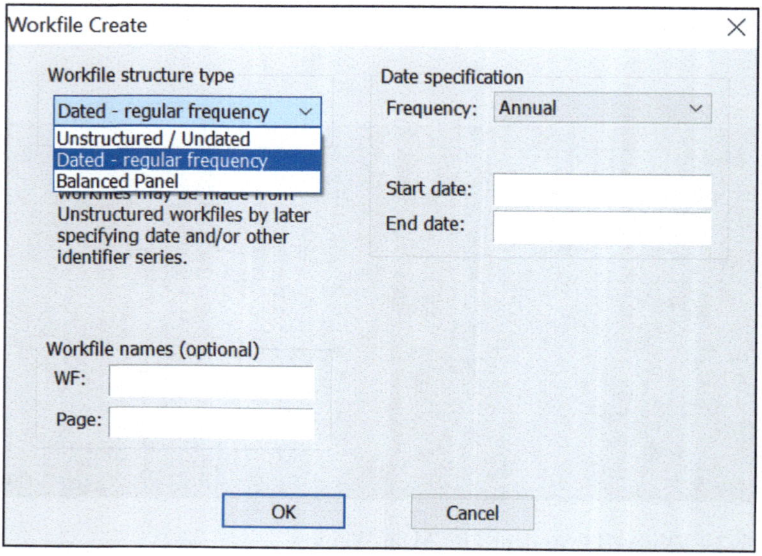

Fig. 1.3   Workfile create window

into the EViews interface following any one of the above-mentioned two approaches is shown in Fig. 1.4.

Plotting Graphs

User can plot several type of graphs using EViews.

For plotting the multiple series into a single graph: select the series variables (eur_usd and gbp_usd) and open as "Group". A new workfile window will be displayed with the titled "Group". Then click on the View → Graph → A new window with "Graph Options" will appear as shown in Fig. 1.5.

After selecting the details and clicking OK button in the Graph Options window. Likewise, to plot the individual series graph simply click on any of the series variables (eur_usd) in the workfile window and follow the remaining steps as stated above. Final output for both cases (group and individual) is displayed in Fig. 1.6. The sharp decline pattern of EUR_USD & GBP_USD pairs in the figure is during the global lockdown period of the COVID pandemic.

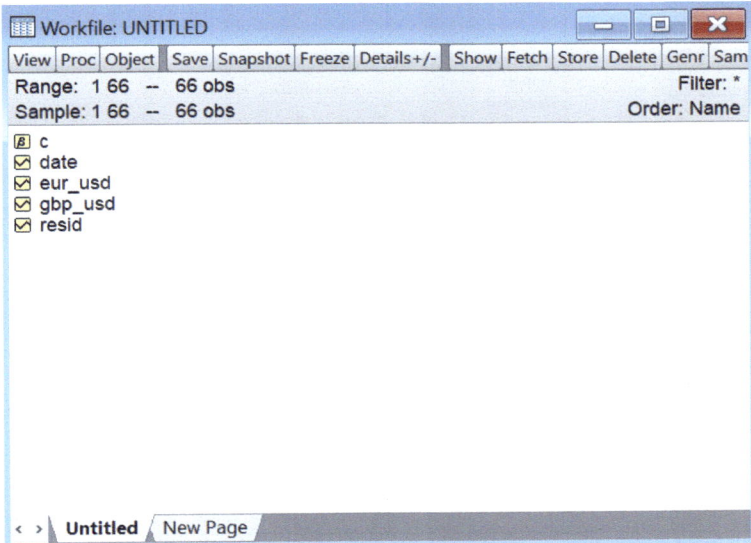

Fig. 1.4   Imported data in the workfile window

Descriptive Statistics

To estimate the descriptive statistics of the two series variables eur_usd and gbp_usd, perform the following steps: Open Group workfile window → View → Descriptive Stats → Individual Samples.

Then the final output with descriptive statistics looks as illustrated in Fig. 1.7. Jarque-Bera test statistics indicate that EUR_USD series follows normal distribution among the two series. GBP_USD series is more volatile (Standard deviation value is higher) and have heavy tails (Kurtosis value is higher) as compared to the EUR_USD series.

Histogram and descriptive statistics of the individual series variables (eur_usd) may also be plotted as shown in Fig. 1.8 by doing the following: Open EUR_USD workfile window → Descriptive Statistics & Tests → Histogram and Stats.

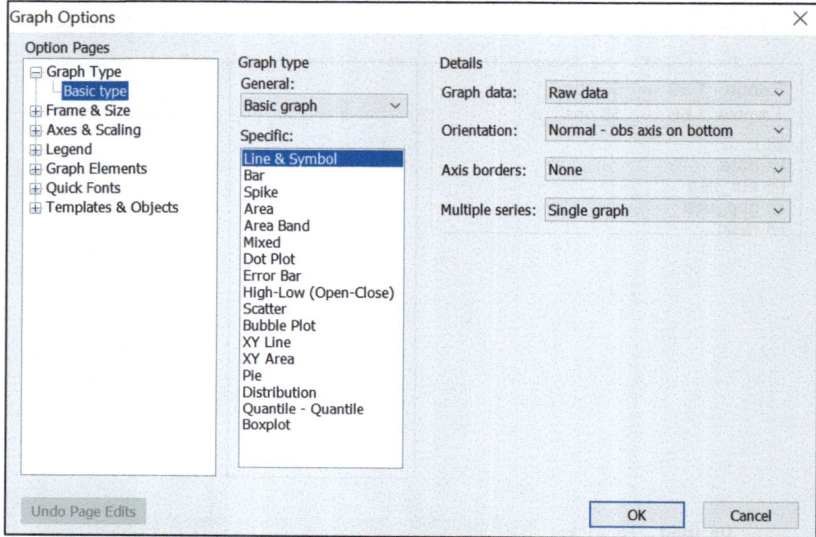

Fig. 1.5 Graph options window

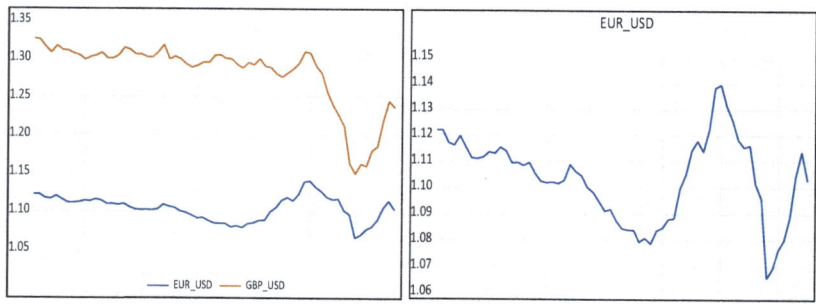

Fig. 1.6 Multi and single series output

	EUR_USD	GBP_USD
Mean	1.103688	1.281412
Median	1.105131	1.299714
Maximum	1.139796	1.326260
Minimum	1.065735	1.149439
Std. Dev.	0.015976	0.043912
Skewness	-0.203787	-1.793153
Kurtosis	2.692283	5.114089
Jarque-Bera	0.706349	46.93801
Probability	0.702455	0.000000
Sum	71.73975	83.29179
Sum Sq. Dev.	0.016335	0.123411
Observations	65	65

Fig. 1.7 Descriptive statistics estimates

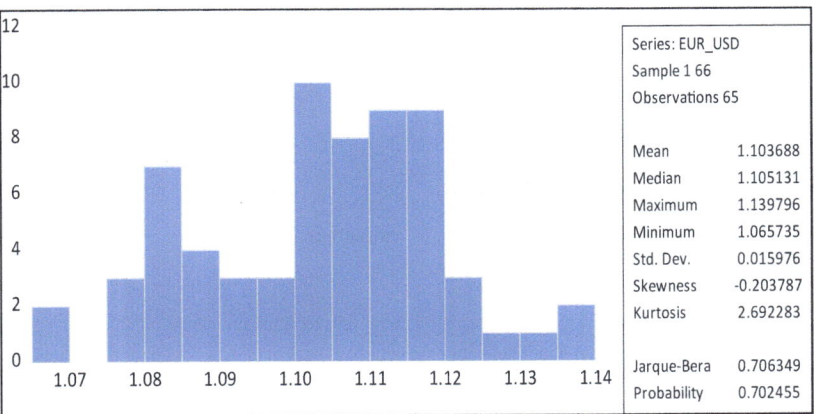

Fig. 1.8 Histogram and descriptive statistics output

Correlation Analysis

Correlation analysis among the two series variables "eur_usd and gbp_usd" can be estimated by following steps.

Open Group workfile window → View → Covariance analysis → Covariance Analysis window will appear as shown in Fig. 1.9. Interface offers several methods to choose namely ordinary, Spearman rank-order and Kendall's tau for estimating correlations among the variables.

Upon selecting the necessary fields and clicking the OK button. The correlation analysis output will appear as shown in Fig. 1.10. Estimation shows that the correlation coefficient value (0.434079) among the variables is within the acceptable limit.

Unit Root Test

Stationarity is an important property of the time series. Stationary time series are the ones whose statistical properties do not change over time.

Stationary time series do not have a unit root. Unit root test can be performed in EViews by performing the following steps:

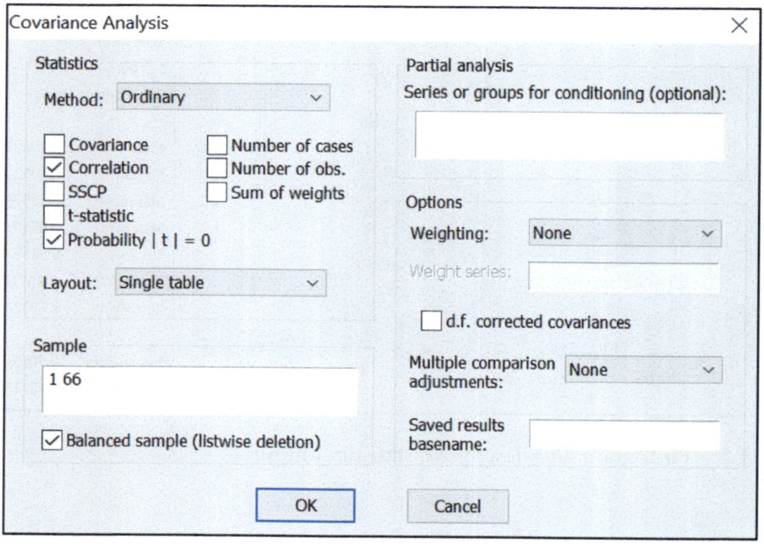

Fig. 1.9   Covariance Analysis window

```
Covariance Analysis: Ordinary
Date: 03/24/21   Time: 11:08
Sample: 1 65
Included observations: 65
Balanced sample (listwise missing value deletion)

Correlation
Probability         EUR_USD      GBP_USD
    EUR_USD         1.000000
                     -----

    GBP_USD         0.434079      1.000000
                    0.0003         -----
```

Fig. 1.10   Correlation analysis estimates

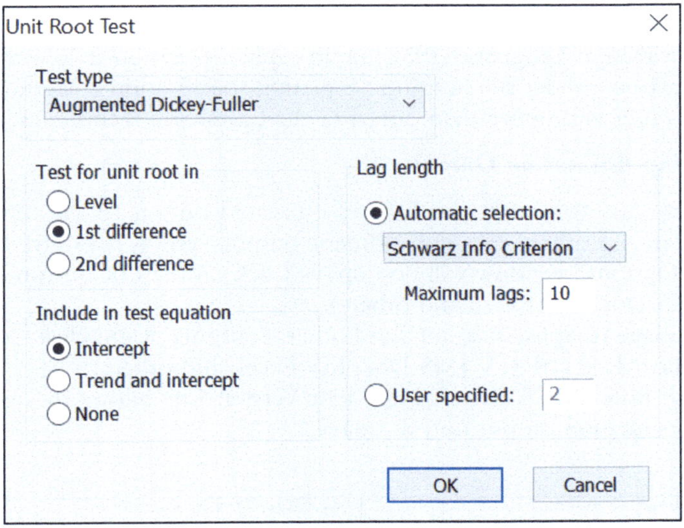

Fig. 1.11   Unit root test window

Open EUR_USD workfile window → View → Unit Root Tests → Standard Unit Root Test → Unit Root Test window will appear as shown in Fig. 1.11.

First test for the presence of unit root in the original series (EUR_USD). The results obtained from unit root testing are shown in

Fig. 1.12. Augmented Dickey-Fuller test statistics clearly indicate that the EUR_USD series has a unit root. Then reperform unit root test for the 1st differential of original series [D(EUR_USD)]. Unit root test estimates for the 1st differentiation of original series [D(EUR_USD)] is shown in Fig. 1.12.

Augmented Dickey-Fuller test statistics clearly indicate that [D(EUR_USD)] series has no unit root.

Equation Estimation

EViews provides very easy with an interactive interface to specify the developed financial econometrics model for quantitative analysis. Follow these steps to open the "Equation Estimation".

EViews Main Window → Estimate Equation → The Equation Estimation window will appear as shown in Fig. 1.13. Describe your developed financial econometrics model for quantitative analysis in the form of Program Design Language (PDL) or an explicit equation style within the white text box under the heading "Equation specification". Method field provides user with more than dozen of the estimation techniques.

Exporting Estimation Output

It is very easy to export the EViews estimated output to the MS Doc, MS Excel, and others. For alphanumeric outputs: ctrl + A → ctrl + C → "Copy Options" window will pop up → Click on the OK button → ctrl + V (MS Doc, MS Excel, and others).

For image (graphs, diagrams, and others) outputs: Right click → Copy to Clipboard → ctrl + V (MS Doc, MS Excel, and others).

Please note that EViews 11 Student Version Lite allows the users to export estimation output only as image.

Null Hypothesis: EUR_USD has a unit root Exogenous: Constant Lag Length: 1 (Automatic - based on SIC, maxlag=10)		t-Statistic	Prob.*
Augmented Dickey-Fuller test statistic		-2.507821	0.1185
Test critical values:	1% level	-3.538362	
	5% level	-2.908420	
	10% level	-2.591799	
*MacKinnon (1996) one-sided p-values.			

Null Hypothesis: D(EUR_USD) has a unit root Exogenous: Constant Lag Length: 0 (Automatic - based on SIC, maxlag=10)		t-Statistic	Prob.*
Augmented Dickey-Fuller test statistic		-5.711042	0.0000
Test critical values:	1% level	-3.538362	
	5% level	-2.908420	
	10% level	-2.591799	
*MacKinnon (1996) one-sided p-values.			

Fig. 1.12 Unit root test estimates for the original series and first differentiation

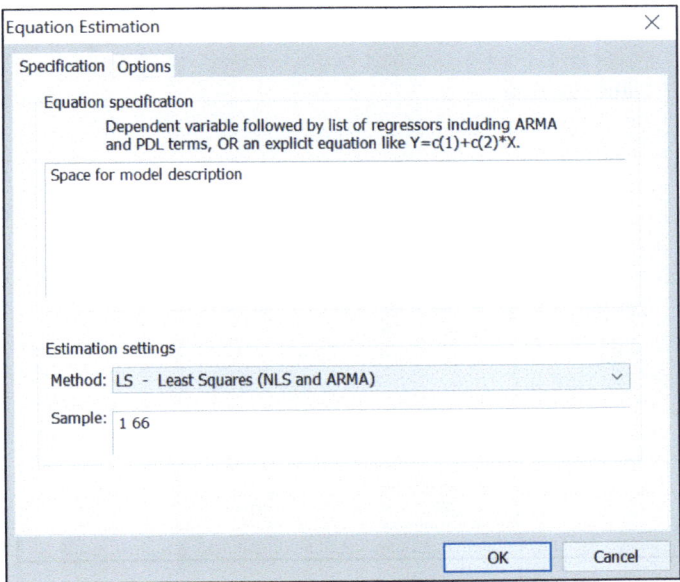

Fig. 1.13   Equation Estimation window

Generating a new series

User can generate a new series from the original in EViews. For generating a new series click on the "Genr" in the workfile window and a new window will appear as shown in Fig. 1.14.

Then under the field "Enter equation" in the white space write simple equations to generate the new series.

Basic syntax is as follows

New_Data_Series_Name = Build_in_functions(Data_series)

For example, to generate a new log series use the following:

New_Data_Series_Name = log(Data_series)

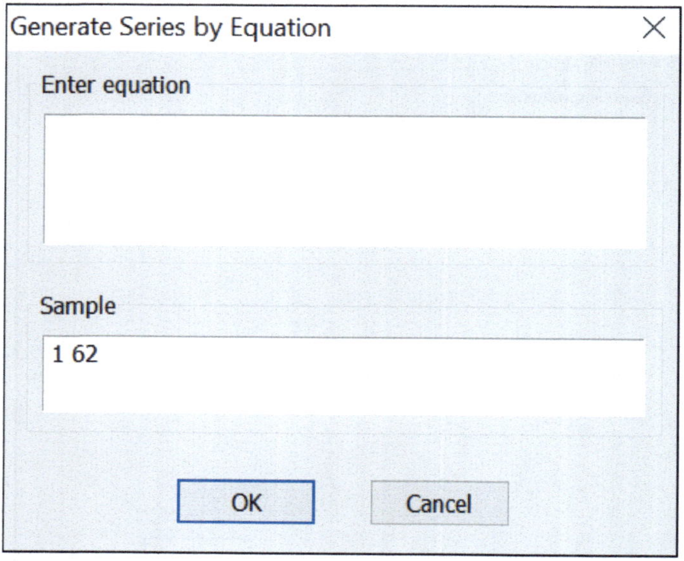

Fig. 1.14 Generate series by equation window

1.4.2   R Programming

R programming is an open source software package that offers user to perform basics to advanced statistical analysis. Currently R programming is being used by millions of users across the globe. It is being used extensively not only in finance sector but other sectors as well. The greatest advantage of the R programming interface is that it can be easily integrated with the other software packages. R software package installer can be downloaded from the CRAN[7] mirrors. R is often used with the RStudio. RStudio provides an Integrated Development Environment (IDE) environment for the R. RStudio is available in both versions open source and commercial. RStudio Desktop version is an open source version and can be downloaded from the RStudio official website.[8]

---

[7] https://cran.r-project.org.

[8] https://rstudio.com/.

R software package must be installed first in the system and then the RStudio Desktop version. The unified interface of RStudio Desktop version and R appears to be as displayed in Fig. 1.15. The unified interface provides users with four different window space namely: (1) attributes, (2) data information, (3) R console to write programs, and (4) visualization window to display graphs, diagrams, charts and others. R is an object-oriented programming. The heart of the R programming is R packages. Different R packages can be downloaded directly from the CRAN. Several resources are available free for learning the various applications of R. R community also encourage its users to develop their own R package and get it published on CRAN or GitHub, etc., as the community participation.

1.4.2.1   R in Action
Click on the R icon if you are using only R to start the application. Likewise for RStudio users click on the RStudio icon and begin the application.

Some of the Useful Codes to Begin with the R Programming Are as Follows
Setting up the R directory

setwd("include path of the directory")

Getting the list of all the packages installed

library()

Installing a package

First method: Download the required R packages from CRAN mirrors. Then run the following code:

install.packages(file_name_with_path, repos = NULL, type = "source") .

Second method: Write this following code in the R console and it must be connected to the internet:

install.packages("Package_Name").

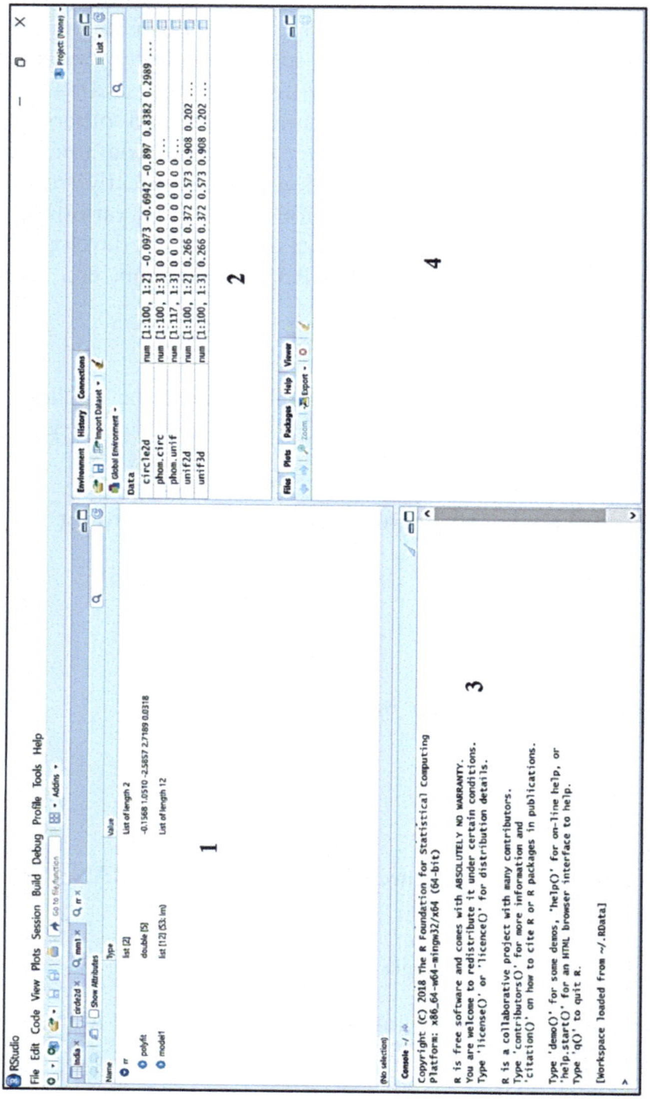

Fig. 1.15 RStudio interface with R console

Loading packages

library(package_name)

Importing data file

Txt files: df < - read.table("file_path/file_name.txt", header = FALSE).

CSV files: df < - read.csv("file_path/file_name.csv", header = FALSE).

Exporting data file

CSV files: write.csv(df, "file_name.csv").

Quit from the R interface

q()

Few Important Exercise with Data

Some of the basic finance exercises that could be performed using R programming are discussed here. To do so same datasets are used: EUR_USD and GBP_USD exchange rates daily closing price between 1 January 2020 and 31 March 2020 (Data source: Yahoo Finance).

View Data

Initiate by viewing the imported data into the R console. To view the begin and end of the imported data use these commands in R: head() and tail(). These commands will display the initial six and end six rows of the imported data as shown below.

head(dataframe_name)

	Date	EUR_USD	GBP_USD
1	01-01-2020	1.122083	1.326260
2	02-01-2020	1.122083	1.325030
3	03-01-2020	1.117144	1.315270
4	06-01-2020	1.116196	1.308010
5	07-01-2020	1.119799	1.317003
6	08-01-2020	1.115474	1.311372

Tail(dataframe_name)

	Date	EUR_USD	GBP_USD
60	24-03-2020	1.076461	1.159555
61	25-03-2020	1.080264	1.179204
62	26-03-2020	1.088957	1.185115
63	27-03-2020	1.104826	1.220063
64	30-03-2020	1.113908	1.245319
65	31-03-2020	1.103047	1.237164

To view the structure of the dataset use

str(dataframe_name)

and the output will appears as shown below. It shows that the dataset contains 65 observations and 3 variables.

```
'data.frame':    65 obs. of  3 variables:
 $ Date   : Factor w/ 65 levels "01-01-2020","02-01-2020",..
 $ EUR_USD: num  1.12 1.12 1.12 1.12 1.12 ...
 $ GBP_USD: num  1.33 1.33 1.32 1.31 1.32 ...
```

Descriptive statistics

To view the descriptive statistics of data as shown below, use R package "pastecs"[9] and execute following codes:

[9] https://cran.r-project.org/web/packages/pastecs/pastecs.pdf.

```
library(pastec)
stat.desc(dataframe_name, norm = TRUE).
```

The descriptive statistics shows mean, median, skewness, kurtosis, and normality test estimates.

Note that "Date" variable is not numeric. Hence, descriptive statistics cannot be computed and it is displayed as NA.

	Date	EUR_USD	GBP_USD
nbr.val	NA	65.0000000000	6.500000e+01
nbr.null	NA	0.0000000000	0.000000e+00
nbr.na	NA	0.0000000000	0.000000e+00
min	NA	1.0657350000	1.149439e+00
max	NA	1.1397960000	1.326260e+00
range	NA	0.0740610000	1.768210e-01
sum	NA	71.7397520000	8.329179e+01
median	NA	1.1051310000	1.299714e+00
mean	NA	1.1036884923	1.281412e+00
SE.mean	NA	0.0019815679	5.446651e-03
CI.mean	NA	0.0039586370	1.088094e-02
var	NA	0.0002552297	1.928290e-03
std.dev	NA	0.0159759114	4.391230e-02
coef.var	NA	0.0144750186	3.426868e-02
skewness	NA	-0.1991019480	-1.751932e+00
skew.2SE	NA	-0.3350579461	-2.948232e+00
kurtosis	NA	-0.3899195237	1.957943e+00
kurt.2SE	NA	-0.3325617588	1.669926e+00
normtest.W	NA	0.9782369598	7.185822e-01
normtest.p	NA	0.3074156497	7.429725e-10

Correlation

To estimate the Pearson's correlation between the variables use the following code:

```
ress < - cor.test(dataframe_name$variable_name_1, dataframe_name$variable_name_2, method = "pearson")
```

ress

On execution the above code following output will appears as shown below. The estimates show that the Pearson's correlation between the variables EUR_USD and GBP_USD is 0.4340795. Likewise to estimate the Kendall's tau and Spearman's rank correlation statistics replace method with "kendall" and "spearman", respectively, in the above-mentioned code.

```
Pearson's product-moment correlation

data:  variable_1 and variable_2
t = 3.8245, df = 63, p-value = 0.0003031
alternative hypothesis: true correlation is not equal to 0
95 percent confidence interval:
0.2126992 0.6130717
sample estimates:
cor
0.4340795
```

Graph Plotting

Different types of graphs can be plotted by using the R interface.

Line graphs

For dot plot as shown in Fig. 1.16, use the following code:

```
plot(dataframe_name$variable_name_1)
```

The basic R code to draw the line chart is as follows:

```
plot(v,type,col,xlab,ylab)
```

where

> v is the "dataframe_name" that contains the variables numeric values
> type can be p, l, o, or b : "p" for dot plot, "l" for line chart, "o" for overlap of both dot and line chart, and "b" for both the dot and line charts

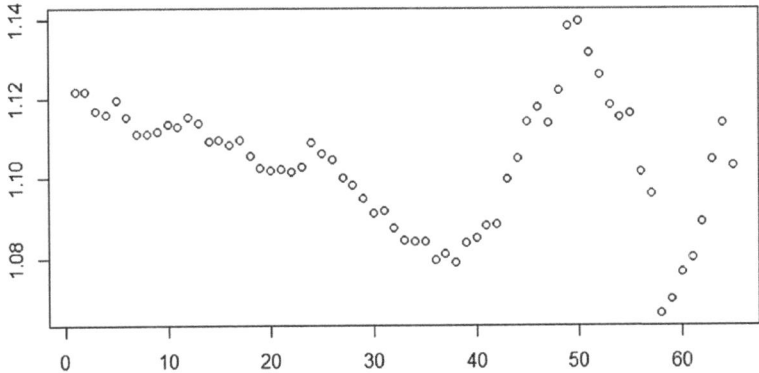

Fig. 1.16 Dot plot for EUR_USD series

col is used to give colours to both the points and lines
xlab: label for x axis
ylab: label for y axis
main: Title of the chart

Then plot the line graph with colour, labels and title by executing the following code:

plot(dataframe_name$variable_name_1, type = "o", col = "blue", xlab = "Daily", ylab = "Closing Price of EUR_USD",main = "Daily movement of EUR_USD")

Observe the main difference between the two graphs types "o" (Fig. 1.17) and "b" (Fig. 1.18). In case of "o" continuous line is plotted and overlaps with the dots, whereas in case of "b" either line or dot is plotted to display the whole series (EUR_USD) daily movement.

Histogram

Plot histogram (as shown in Fig. 1.19) using the following code:

hist(dataframe_name$variable_name_1, col = "green")

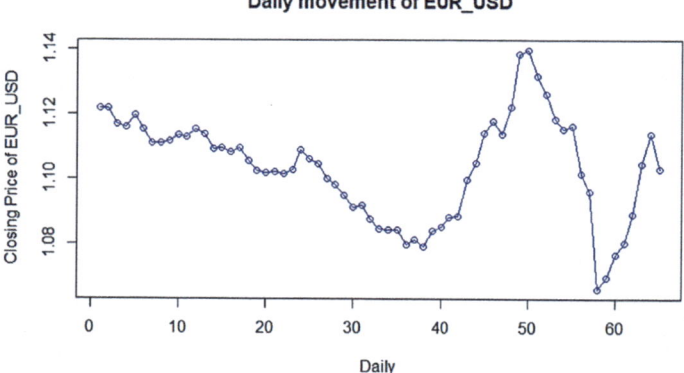

Fig. 1.17   Line and dot overlapped graph for EUR_USD series

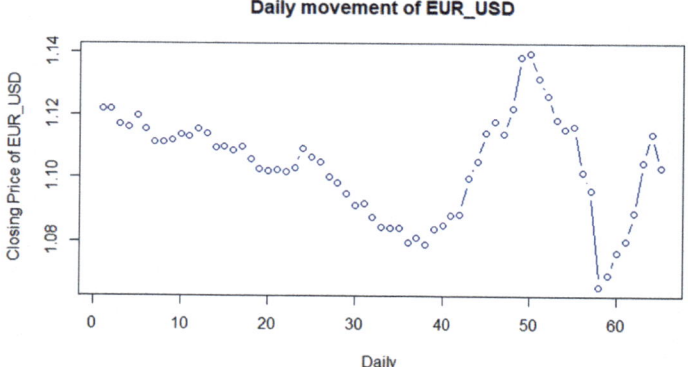

Fig. 1.18   Combination of either line and dot graph for EUR_USD series

Unit root test

R programming offers different methods to test for the presence of unit root in the time series. To do so *library(tseries)*[10] of R is used. Unit root test results for GBP_USD exchange rates daily closing price

---

[10] https://cran.r-project.org/web/packages/tseries/tseries.pdf.

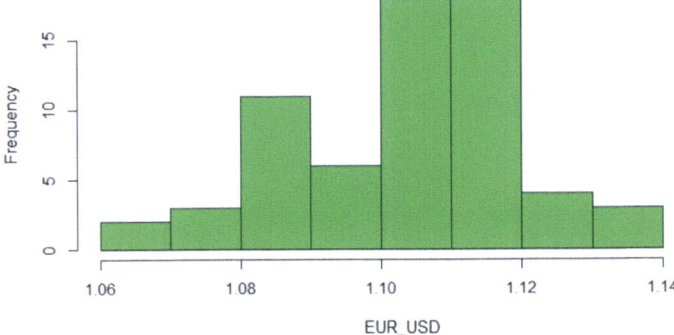

Fig. 1.19 Histogram plot for the EUR_USD series

time series applying different methods (Augmented Dickey-Fuller Test, Phillips-Perron test, and KPSS test) are shown below:
   Augmented dickey-fuller Test

Code: adf.test(dataframe_name$variable_name_1, k = 0) // Here k represents number of lags

```
           Augmented Dickey-Fuller Test

data:          GBP_USD
Dickey-Fuller = -1.5668, Lag order = 0, p-value = 0.7506
alternative hypothesis: stationary
```

Phillips-Perron test

Code: pp.test(dataframe_name$variable_name_1)

```
        Phillips-Perron Unit Root Test

data:        GBP_USD
Dickey-Fuller Z(alpha) = -9.2936, Truncation lag parameter = 3, p-value = 0.5641
alternative hypothesis: stationary
```

KPSS test (with a drift, and with a linear trend).

Code: kpss.test(dataframe_name$variable_name_1,"Level")

```
          KPSS Test for Level Stationarity

data:          GBP_USD
KPSS Level = 1.919, Truncation lag parameter = 1, p-value = 0.01
```

Code: kpss.test(dataframe_name$variable_name_1,"Trend")

```
          KPSS Test for Trend Stationarity

data:          GBP_USD
KPSS Trend = 0.38904, Truncation lag parameter = 1, p-value = 0.01
```

Null hypothesis for Augmented Dickey-Fuller Test, and Phillips-Perron test, is that the series (GBP_USD) has a unit root. Whereas KPSS test has a null hypothesis "the series is stationary". All of the above tests (Augmented Dickey-Fuller Test, Phillips-Perron test, and KPSS test) estimates show that the GBP_USD series has a unit root or non-stationary.

Next take the first-order differentiation of the original series GBP_USD and reperform the unit root test. Obtain the first-order differentiation series of the original series GBP_USD and assigned it a new name (z).

Use this following code to perform the above step.

z = diff(Original series_ GBP_USD)

Then estimate the unit root test estimates for the obtained first-order differentiation of the series GBP_USD (z). Unit root tests results obtained from the different methods used are shown below.

Augmented Dickey-Fuller Test

```
            Augmented Dickey-Fuller Test

data:  z
Dickey-Fuller = -5.6697, Lag order = 0, p-value = 0.01
alternative hypothesis: stationary
```

Phillips-Perron test

```
            Phillips-Perron Unit Root Test

data:  z
Dickey-Fuller Z(alpha) = -45.996, Truncation lag parameter = 3, p-value = 0.01
alternative hypothesis: stationary
```

KPSS test (with a drift and with a linear trend).

```
            KPSS Test for Level Stationarity

data:  z
KPSS Level = 0.087365, Truncation lag parameter = 1, p-value = 0.1
```

```
            KPSS Test for Trend Stationarity

data:  z
KPSS Trend = 0.061181, Truncation lag parameter = 1, p-value = 0.1
```

Above all tests (Augmented Dickey-Fuller Test, Phillips-Perron test, and KPSS test) estimates show that the obtained first-order differentiation of the GBP_USD series is stationary.

Basic R operators

R has several operators to perform the various mathematical, logical, relational, assignment, and other functions.

Mathematical operators

+ : Addition
−: Subtraction
*: Multiplication
/: Division
^: Exponent

Logical operators

!: NOT
&&: AND
||: OR

Relational operators

< : Less than
> : Greater than
< =: Less than equal to
> =: Greater than equal to
= =: Equal to
!=: Not equal to

Assignment operators

<-, = , < <-, -> , - > >

Some Basic Calculations Used in Finance

Basic calculations that are often used in the finance are shown using R.

Log return

Mathematically log return formula is represented by the below equation:

$ret = \log (P_t) - \log (P_{t-1}) = \log (P_t/P_{t-1})$ // where P_t is the current price

To estimate the log return in R use the following code:

```
ret < -diff(log(dataframe_name$variable_name_1))
ret
```

Log return of the series EUR_USD exchange rates daily closing price estimated by the above code in R is shown below.

```
[1]   0.0000000000 -0.0044113509 -0.0008489527  0.0032227291 -0.0038697782 -0.0037300289
[7]  -0.0001889822  0.0005002749  0.0017130741 -0.0004338331  0.0020731534 -0.0012936462
[13] -0.0040469297  0.0002108914 -0.0010206226  0.0009764653 -0.0037216215 -0.0027046407
[19] -0.0005071415  0.0002531493 -0.0005172550  0.0011131277  0.0054849108 -0.0024249856
[25] -0.0014156358 -0.0040789931 -0.0017584489 -0.0030703612 -0.0032795508  0.0005450497
[31] -0.0039880101 -0.0027585031 -0.0003910043 -0.0001512785 -0.0041330261  0.0013607648
[37] -0.0020464770  0.0047209485  0.0009359908  0.0030187035  0.0003574072  0.0101759677
[43]  0.0049055501  0.0083567502  0.0032815656 -0.0037276430  0.0075813327  0.0143453086
[49]  0.0010481049 -0.0071716707 -0.0048711166 -0.0068242682 -0.0026472367  0.0007034501
[55] -0.0133183625 -0.0049114926 -0.0281438999  0.0034695099  0.0065445967  0.0035266471
[61]  0.0080149017  0.0144674991  0.0081866963 -0.0097982024
```

Holding Period Return

Mathematically holding period return formula is represented by the below equation:

$$\text{hpr} = (P_t - P_{t-1})/P_{t-1} = (P_t/P_{t-1}) - 1 = e^{\text{hpr}-1} \text{ // where } P_t \text{ is}$$

the current price

To estimate the holding period return in R use the following code:

```
hpr < -exp(ret)-1 // ret is estimated above

hpr
```

Holding period return of the series EUR_USD exchange rates daily closing price estimated by the above code in R is shown below.

```
[1]   0.0000000000 -0.0044016352 -0.0008485925  0.0032279277 -0.0038623003 -0.0037230810
[7]  -0.0001889643  0.0005004001  0.0017145422 -0.0004337390  0.0020753039 -0.0012928098
[13] -0.0040387519  0.0002109136 -0.0010201020  0.0009769422 -0.0037147049 -0.0027009865
[19] -0.0005070129  0.0002531813 -0.0005171212  0.0011137475  0.0054999805 -0.0024220477
[25] -0.0014146343 -0.0040706853 -0.0017569038 -0.0030656525 -0.0032741789  0.0005451983
[31] -0.0039800685 -0.0027547019 -0.0003909279 -0.0001512671 -0.0041244969  0.0013616911
[37] -0.0020443844  0.0047321098  0.0009364289  0.0030232644  0.0003574711  0.0102279189
[43]  0.0049176020  0.0083917653  0.0032869558 -0.0037207039  0.0076101437  0.0144486963
[49]  0.0010486544 -0.0071460156 -0.0048592720 -0.0068010357 -0.0026437358  0.0007036976
[55] -0.0132300655 -0.0048994510 -0.0277515497  0.0034755357  0.0065660594  0.0035328730
[61]  0.0080471070  0.0145726599  0.0082202989 -0.0097503564
```

Average Return

Above paragraphs show how to estimate the returns (log return and holding period return) in R. Average return can easily be calculated from the obtained return series using the following R code as shown below:

```
mean(return_series_name)
```

Average return of the series EUR_USD exchange rates daily closing price estimated by the above code in R is shown below.

```
> mean(ret)
[1] -0.0002673505
> mean(hpr)
[1] -0.0002487948
```

The above estimates show that investment in the "EUR_USD" currency pair for the period (1 January 2020–31 March 2020) yields a negative mean return of (−0.0003).

Volatility

Standard deviation is the measure of volatility and higher volatile means higher risk. In finance study risk is an important component as it has a direct relationship with the returns. Daily volatility can be estimated using the following R code.

```
Sd(return_series_name)*100 // in percentage
```

Volatility of the "EUR_USD" daily average return series estimated by using the above R code is shown below.

```
> sd(ret)
[1] 0.006141502
> sd(hpr)
[1] 0.006120557
```

To estimate the monthly, yearly, and n period volatility use the following codes:

Monthly: sqrt(22)*sd(return_series_name)*100 // 22 trading days in a month

Yearly: sqrt(252)*sd(return_series_name)*100sqrt(252)*sd(return_series_name)*100 // 252 trading days in a year

n period: sqrt(n)*sd(return_series_name)*100

Exporting Estimation Output

R estimated outputs can be exported by using several methods, few of them are discussed below:

CSV files: write.csv(df, "file_name.csv").

Txt files: write.table(df, "file_name.txt").

Images: Copy to clipboard and then paste; direct export as image or pdf file.

Summary

This chapter briefly introduced "what is applied financial econometrics"? Discussed all the important steps to conduct any applied financial econometrics study successfully. Basic data types that are used in the applied financial econometric study are explained in detail with the help of suitable examples. Two widely used econometrics software packages namely EViews and R programming are introduced for the learners. "EUR_USD" and "GBP_USD" currency pairs daily datasets are used to explain the basic estimations that could be performed using both the EViews and R programming, respectively.

Analyst/Investor Corners

Reliable and quality data is the heart of any applied financial econometric study. As based on the data inputs econometric method or technique certainly yields outputs. Then considerable amount of knowledge in the application and output interpretation of any available "econometrics software packages" is desirable as they yield similar estimates (might be in a different format).

1.5   Exercises

1.5.1   Multiple Choice Questions

1. Which type of the errors are the worst: Type I or II"?

   (a) Type I errors
   (b) Type II errors
   (c) Both Type I and II: It depends on the context
   (d) None

2. Stochastic specification (ε) in the model is also known as

   (a) Error terms
   (b) Noise terms
   (c) "disturbance terms" or "residuals terms"
   (d) All of the above

3. Panel data often referred as the

   (a) Longitudinal data
   (b) Cross-sectional data
   (c) Time series data
   (d) All of the above

4. Daily mean excess return series of the stock "X" for five years is an example of

   (a) Panel data
   (b) Pooled data
   (c) Time series data
   (d) Cross-sectional data

5. Which of the following is an example of open source software?

   (a) EViews
   (b) SPSS

(c) SAS

(d) R programming

6. Which among the following is not a logical operator?

   (a) ! "NOT"
   (b) && "AND"
   (c) || "OR"
   (d) == "Equal"

7. Descriptive statistics estimates of a variable includes:

   (a) Mean
   (b) Median
   (c) Skewness & Kurtosis
   (d) All of the above

8. Which among the following is not used for testing the unit root ?

   (a) Augmented Dickey-Fuller Test
   (b) Phillips-Perron test
   (c) KPSS test
   (d) BDS independence test

9. Which among the following test is/are used for correlation analysis?

   (a) Kendall's tau
   (b) Spearman's rank correlation
   (c) Pearson correlation
   (d) All of the above

10. Which among the following test is not used for the time series normality test?

    (a) Shapiro-Wilk test
    (b) Jarque-Bera test
    (c) Phillips-Perron test
    (d) Anderson-Darling test

1.5.2   Fill in the Blanks

1. Rejection of null hypothesis even when that's true would result into _____.
2. Type II errors could be prevented mostly using _____.
3. Error terms (ε) have uniform variance (σ^2) or _____.
4. Pooled data is combination of the both _____ and _____ data.
5. Pooled data is often referred as the _____.
6. Stationary time series do not have a _____.
7. This mathematical model [$R_{Pit} - R_{Ft} = \alpha + \beta\,(R_{Mt} - R_{Ft}) + \varepsilon_{it}$] is often referred as the _____.
8. Higher value of Kurtosis in the data implies _____.
9. Decision of acceptance or rejection of the null hypothesis is based on the obtained _____.
10. _____ is the measure of central tendency.
11. If the values of mean, median and mode are all equal then the distribution is said to be _____.
12. The _____ is the value that appears most frequently in a data set.
13. A _____ time series is one whose properties do not depend on the time at which the series is observed.
14. _____ is the average value of set of given data.
15. _____ is the middle value when the data set is arranged in an order either ascending or descending.

1.5.3   Long Answer Questions

1. Define the term Applied Financial Econometrics?
2. How Applied Financial Econometrics is different from Machine Learning and Data sciences?
3. Explain in brief the importance of the error terms (ε) in Applied Financial Econometrics modelling?
4. What are basic assumptions of error terms (ε)?
5. What is the difference between a bar graph and histogram? Explain it with appropriate example.
6. Why stationary time series are often used for time series research?
7. Is there any difference between the pooled and panel data? Explain it with appropriate example.

8. What are Type I and Type II errors? How they are related with the hypothesis testing? Explain it with appropriate example.

9. Using different R operators define simple function(s) and execute it in R console?

10. Below there are two statements on credit scoring. Classify them into Type I or Type II errors with appropriate justification?

> Statement one : *Good credit is assigned to the wrong category as bad credit*
> Statement two: *Bad credit is assigned to the wrong category as good credit*

11. Below there are two statements on loan decision. Classify them into Type I or Type II errors with appropriate justification?

> Statement one : *Bank denied a loan to a creditworthy customer*
> Statement two: *Bank granted a loan to a financially indebted customer*

12. A researcher wants to conduct a study to understand the impact of financial crisis 2008 and COVID-19 on the US and UK financial markets? But the researcher does not know from where to begin. So, help him/her in the following to begin with:

   (a) Framing study Hypotheses
   (b) Selecting the study variables
   (c) Model description and others.

1.5.4   Real-World Tasks

1. A professor ask his/her student to do a basic comparative analysis of the COVID-19 first and second phase impact on the Asian stock markets ? Assume yourself as the student and perform the task. Then prepare a detailed report of the analysis to be submitted to the professor.

2. A researcher want to conduct elementary analyse on the performance of cryptocurrencies during the noble Coronavirus pandemic. Assume yourself as the researcher: perform the mentioned task in details and develop the analysis report.

3. A Financial analyst want to study the elementary performances of the world indices before, during, and after the first phase of COVID-19. Help him/her to perform the said analysis and prepare the report.

4. A student need to perform descriptive examination on the major three currency pairs exchange rate for the last three years as his/her project dissertation. Help the student to complete his/her project dissertation successfully and satisfactorily.

5. A senior manager of the Reserve bank of India (RBI) asked an intern working under him/her to prepare a detailed report on the total amount of paperless transactions done in India through the various medium before and during the COVID-19 first phase. Help the intern in analysing and developing the final report for timely submission to the senior RBI manager.

1.5.5   Case Studies

1. Descriptive statistics and correlation analysis for the daily average returns of Gold and Silver between the period 2 January 2020 and 18 June 2020 are shown below (Data source: Yahoo Finance).

   Based on the given information, comment on the characteristics of the two series (Gold and Silver) daily average returns.

	GOLD	SILVER
Mean	0.001085	0.000223
Median	0.000947	0.000113
Maximum	0.076411	0.110799
Minimum	-0.046281	-0.122183
Std. Dev.	0.015898	0.026674
Skewness	0.793323	-0.632424
Kurtosis	7.821080	10.24003
Jarque-Bera	144.9014	303.8501
Probability	0.000000	0.000000
Sum	0.146476	0.030083
Sum Sq. Dev.	0.033868	0.095343
Observations	135	135

Covariance Analysis: Ordinary
Date: 03/28/21   Time: 09:58
Sample: 1 135
Included observations: 135

Correlation Probability	GOLD	SILVER
GOLD	1.000000	

SILVER	0.730016	1.000000
	0.0000	-----

2. Below figure shows the Volatility Index or "VIX" daily movements over the period 2 January 2020 and 31 March 2020 (Data source: Yahoo Finance). To represent the daily open, high, low and close of VIX (OHLC), chart is used as shown below. Based on this

information, comment on the VIX daily movements between 2 January 2020 and 31 March 2020 in details.

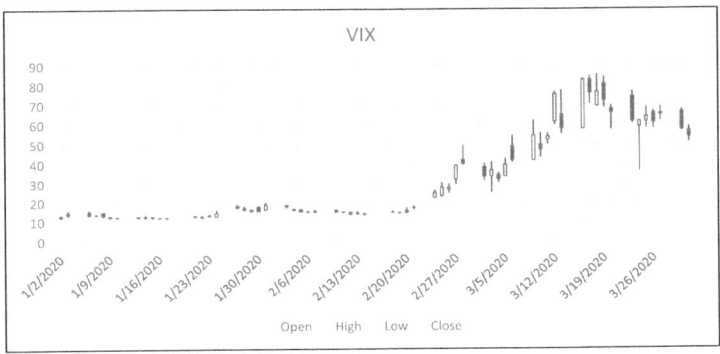

3. An environmentalist want to test the correlation between the macro-climate indicators and COVID-19 pandemic occurrence in the four metropolitan cities of India during 13 July 2020–26 July 2020. Based on his/her analysis environmentalist considers the following eleven macro-climate indicators (variables) are listed below:

Variables
Temperature
Humidity
Pressure
Cloud cover
Sunshine
Wind gust
Wind speed
Wind direction
Soil temperature
Soil moisture
Vapor pressure deficit

To test the correlation between the macro-climate indicators and COVID-19 pandemic occurrence environmentalist used both the Kendall and Spearman Correlation. Obtained correlation estimates are shown below. Based on all of these information prepare a detailed report on whether macro-climate indicators are significant in explaining the occurrence of COVID-19 in four Indian metro cities.

Kendall Correlation Coefficient	Total confirmed case				Mortality			
	Delhi	Kolkata	Mumbai	Chennai	Delhi	Kolkata	Mumbai	Chennai
Humidity	0.428571*	-0.2747	-0.4641*	-0.2210	0.428571*	-0.27473	0.464095*	-0.221
Pressure	0.692308*	0.714286*	0.538462*	0.802198*	0.692308*	0.714286*	0.538462*	0.802198*
Soil moisture	0.2431	-0.0110	-0.1868	-0.2088	0.243098	-0.01099	-0.18681	-0.20879
Soil temperature	-0.38462**	0.0110	0.406593*	0.2747	-0.384615**	0.010989	0.406593*	0.274725
Sunshine	0.0549	0.2308	0.551294*	0.424641*	0.054945	0.230769	0.551294*	0.424641*
Temperature	-0.51648*	0.1209	0.428571*	0.2088	-0.5164848*	0.120879	0.428571*	0.208791
Vapour pressure deficit	-0.45055*	0.2527	0.472527*	0.2088	-0.450549*	0.252747	0.472527*	0.208791
Wind direction	-0.3187	0.2308	0.1648	-0.3407	-0.31868	0.230769	0.164835	-0.34066
Wind gust	-0.2967	-0.0330	-0.3407	-0.2747	-0.2967	-0.03297	-0.34066	-0.27473
Wind speed	0.1648	0.0110	-0.0330	-0.2967	0.164835	0.010989	-0.03297	-0.2967
Cloud cover	-0.1209	-0.2967	-0.52624*	-0.2528	-0.12088	-0.2967	-0.526235*	-0.25275

Spearman Correlation	Total confirmed case				Mortality			
	Delhi	Kolkata	Mumbai	Chennai	Delhi	Kolkata	Mumbai	Chennai
Humidity	0.613187*	-0.35385	-0.70847*	-0.29263	0.613187*	-0.35385	-0.708471*	-0.29263
Pressure	0.81978*	0.881319*	0.705495*	0.920879*	0.81978*	0.881319*	0.705495*	0.920879*
Soil Moisture	0.464247**	0.12967	-0.25275	-0.34945	0.464247**	0.12967	-0.25275	-0.34945
Soil Temperature	-0.59121*	-0.01099	0.626374*	0.41978	-0.591209*	-0.01099	0.626374*	0.41978
Sunshine	-0.02857	0.30989	0.786236*	0.620315*	-0.02857	0.30989	0.786236*	0.620315*
Temperature	-0.74066*	0.16044	0.6*	0.30989	-0.740659*	0.16044	0.6*	0.30989
Vapour pressure deficit	-0.61319*	0.345055	0.70989*	0.27033	-0.613187*	0.345055	0.70989*	0.27033

(continued)

(continued)

Kendall Correlation Coefficient	Total confirmed case				Mortality			
	Delhi	Kolkata	Mumbai	Chennai	Delhi	Kolkata	Mumbai	Chennai
Wind direction	−0.44176	0.30989	0.235165	−0.56044*	−0.44176	0.30989	0.235165	−0.56044*
Wind gust	−0.46374**	−0.08571	−0.38022	−0.41539	−0.463736**	−0.08571	−0.38022	−0.41539
Wind speed	0.323077	0.015385	−0.05495	−0.35385	0.323077	0.015385	−0.05495	−0.35385
Cloud cover	−0.24396	−0.4022	−0.74868*	−0.35385	−0.24396	−0.4022	0.748684*	0.35385

CHAPTER 2

Random Walk Hypothesis

Key Topics Covered

- *Random walk and its implications*
- *Development of a simple mathematical random walk model*
- *Efficient Market Hypothesis*
- *Joint Hypothesis Problem*
- *Dart Throwing Investment Contest*
- *Martingales*
- *Random Walk Hypothesis and Martingales*
- *Illustration of various Random Walk Models*
- *Testing of Random Walk and Martingales using EViews*

2.1 Background

The basic idea is that movement of the stock prices are unpredictable and random. Jules Augustin Frédéric Regnault, a French stock broker's subordinate primarily explained the rationale behind the stock prices stochastic movements using a random walk model. Jules in his book titled "*Calcul des chances et philosophie de la bourse*" states that "*l'écart des cours est en*

© The Author(s), under exclusive license to Springer Nature Singapore Pte Ltd. 2021
M. Maiti, *Applied Financial Econometrics*,
https://doi.org/10.1007/978-981-16-4063-6_2

raison directe de la racine carrée des temps.[1] Which means "*the price difference is a direct result of the square root of the times*" and it clearly indicates that the stock prices movement follows a stochastic process. Later it becomes the foundation of Louis Bachelier PhD thesis titled "Th'eorie de la Sp'eculation".[2] Louis often credited as the first person to introduce advanced mathematics into the field of finance. He established a mathematical model of the stochastic process (known as Brownian motion) for valuing the stock options. For a longer period of time Louis' contribution was overlooked or ignored as his study applied mathematics into the field of finance. Possible reason could be during the nineteenth century the field of interdisciplinary research was not developed or quite accustomed. Then in 1964, Paul H. Cootner, a professor of MIT Sloan School of Management in his book titled "The Random Character of Stock Market Prices" educes the ideas on the stochastic process of stock prices movements. Later on the same ideas are well established by the several known scholars namely Eugene Fama, Burton Malkiel, and others.

2.1.1   What Is Random Walk Hypothesis and Its Implications?

Random walk hypothesis assumes that price movements of individual securities in the stock markets follow a random walk and successive price movements are independent to each other. Therefore, the random walk hypothesis posits that it is impossible to forecast the stock prices movements. Random walk hypothesis also suggests that it is impossible to beat the market by the market participants in the long run. Outperformance of the market by an investor is only possible by taking an extra amount of risk. The Random Walk hypothesis is heavily criticized on several grounds such as market participants differ in terms of the amount of time they spend in the financial market. Then several numbers of the known and unknown factors are responsible for driving the stock prices (Maiti, 2020). It is often not likely to detect the associated trends or patterns that might exist in the stock prices movements due to the presence of several such distinct factors. To test the random walk hypothesis in practice, Wall Street Journal (WSJ) initiated the "Dart Throwing Investment Contest"

---

[1] https://archive.org/details/calculdeschances00regn/page/50/mode/2up,   accessed on 31/03/2021.

[2] Bachelier, L. (1900). Théorie de la spéculation. In *Annales scientifiques de l'École normale supérieure* (Vol. 17, pp. 21–86).

in the year 1988. Two groups were formed: one group belongs to the professional investors whereas other belongs to the dummy. Professional investors group consists of the professionals working with NYSE whereas WSJ staff groups as the dummy. In other words professional investors represent "skill" whereas dummy represents "luck". Professional investors selected stocks based on their skills whereas dummy made their selection of stocks based on the outcome of the dart throwing (luck). After 100 contests the outcomes come as following: professional investors won 61 times or skill wins 61 times versus luck. However, professional investors (skill) are able to beat the market (DJIA) 51 times out of 100. Dart Throwing Investment Contest does not provide any ultimate consensus on "luck versus skills". The current consensus is that the random walk hypothesis is linked to the efficient market hypothesis (EMH). Mathematically a simple random walk model with a drift is represented by following Eq. (2.1):

$$Price_t = Price_{t-1} + \alpha_t \qquad (2.1)$$

// Mean (μ) is zero and standard deviation (σ) is constant

where

Price$_t$ represents current stock price at time (t)
Price$_{t-1}$ represents stock price at time $(t-1)$
α_t represents the drift term

2.1.2   Efficient Market Hypothesis

Efficient market hypothesis assumes that the security prices reflect all available information and follow a random walk. However, the strength of these assumptions depends on the form of EMH as explained by Fama (1970). Thus, the direct implication of EMH is that it is impossible to beat the market steadily merely by ensuing a specific risk adjusted strategy. Fama (1970) labels efficient market hypothesis into three types based on the level of the relevant information as weak, semi-strong and strong forms of EMH, respectively. Weak forms of EMH assume that all historical stock prices information is impounded in the current price of the stock. Then a semi-strong form of EMH assumes that all publicly available information in addition to those historical stock prices information are well impounded in the current price of the stock. Finally, strong forms of EMH assume that all available information both private (insider information) and public is fully impounded in the current price of the stock. The joint hypothesis problem makes it difficult to test the EMH. The argument put forward as the EMH could only be tested with the help of a market equilibrium model (Asset pricing model). The EMH basically tests whether the properties of expected returns suggested by the assumed market equilibrium model (asset pricing model) are noticed in actual returns. If the tests reject, then it is difficult to interpret whether the rejection is made due to the inefficiency of the market or a bad market equilibrium model (asset pricing model). Fama (1970) stressed that the EMH is always tested jointly along with the market equilibrium model and vice versa. Thereafter significant number of studies are done on EMH and asset pricing. All of these studies unanimously emphasized that the EMH is very simple in principle but testing it proved to be difficult. Both the random walk hypothesis and efficient market hypothesis have significant importance in applied financial econometrics study as both of them could provide some relevant information on relative market efficiency. Still distinct views exist on whether markets are really efficient? There are several studies that evidence support for EMH such as on an average mutual funds do not able to outperformed the market. Then "Dart Throwing Investment Contest" results show that the performance of skills versus luck are quite similar in beating the market. On the other hand, there are group of studies that evidence against EMH is as follows: presence of stock market anomalies, presence of excessive volatility in the stock market, behavioural finance theories, and others.

2.1.3   Random Walk Hypothesis and Martingales

Martingale is often used likewise Random Walk Hypothesis in testing the Efficient Market Hypothesis. Let's try to understand: What is martingale and how it is different from a Random walk?

Security price changes with the arrival of relevant new information and the arrival of relevant new information is a random process. Hence by the principle of EMH, security price will follow a random walk on arrival of the relevant new information associated with the security. The below Eq. (2.2) shows the degree of random walk followed by the security on arrival of the relevant new information associated with the security.

$$\text{Price}_{t+1} - \text{Price}_t = \varepsilon_{t+1} \qquad (2.2)$$

In practice individual security's historic prices data is considered in testing the efficient market hypothesis. As a result more generic version of EMH considers "Security prices follow a martingale" as shown below in Eq. (2.3).

$$E(\text{Price}_{t+1} - \text{Price}_t | \Phi_t) = 0 \qquad (2.3)$$

where $\Phi_t = Price_t, Price_{t-1}, \ldots$

Hence, martingales are the random variables and on the basis of martingales' present state information it is impossible to predict the future variations.

2.1.4   Illustrations of Random Walk Models

2.1.4.1   Random Walk Model with a Fixed Drifts

Let define a simple random walk model with a fixed drift as shown below.

$$Price_t = Price_{t-1} \pm \alpha_t$$

where

$Price_t$ represents current stock price at time (t)
$Price_{t-1}$ represents stock price at time (t-1)
α_t represents the drifts.

If current price of the security is 120 € and follows the above random walk model with a fixed drift. The price of the security will move up by 2.4 € on getting a "Head" and move down by 2.4 € on getting a "Tail". The probability of getting a head or tail is equal. The event of spinning a coin repeated after each second up to 18000 seconds. Then what will be the price of security after 18000 seconds.

Possible outcomes for the price of security in each state (after each second up to 18000 seconds) are shown, and it might take any of these random paths as shown below in Fig. 2.1.

To plot the price movements of the above-mentioned security execute the below codes in R console.

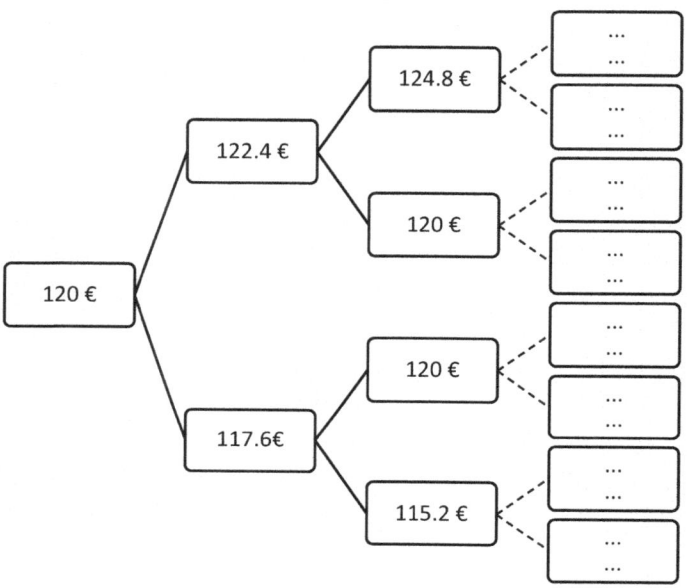

Fig. 2.1   Paths taken by random walk model with a fixed drift

Code:

```
set.seed(200)
n<-18000
Price<-rep(NA,n)
Price[1]<-120
for(time in 2:n)
{
 spin<-sample(c("Head","Tail"),1,replace = TRUE,prob = c(0.5,0.5))
 if(spin=="Head")Price[time]<-Price[time-1]+2.4
 if(spin=="Tail")Price[time]<-Price[time-1]-2.4
}
plot(Price)
abline(h=0,lwd=2,col="blue")
```

On executing the above lines of code following output will be displayed as shown in Fig. 2.2.

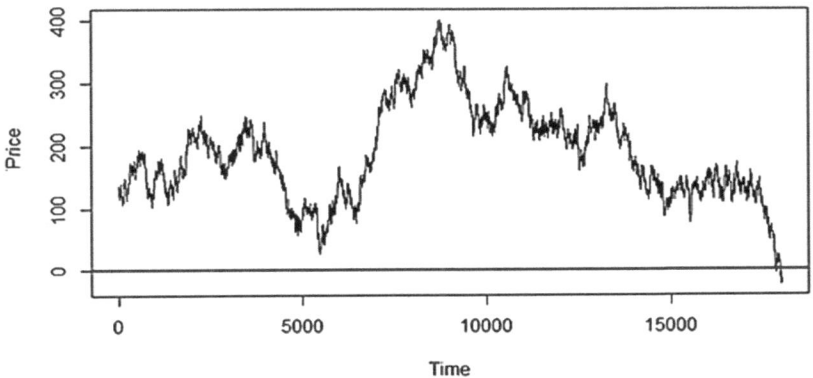

Fig. 2.2 Price movements follow random walk model with a fixed drift

Do you think the above random walk model with a fixed drift is a good applicator to model the security price movements? Developed random walk model with a fixed drift do able to plot the random movements of the security prices but it does not consider the limited liability feature of the security. In other words the security prices never be negative.

2.1.4.2   Random Walk Model with Random Drifts

Let define a simple random walk model with random holding period return drift as shown below.

$$\text{Price}_t = \text{Price}_{t-1}(1 + \text{HPR}_t)$$

where

HPR_t is Holding Period Returns (mean zero and standard deviation 0.01).

If current price of the security is 120 € and follows the random walk model with random holding period return drift. Then what will be the price of security after 18000 seconds. To plot the price movements of the security execute the below codes in R console.

Code:

```
set.seed(200)
n<-18000
Price<-rep(NA,n)
Price[1]<-120
hpr<-rnorm(n,mean=0,sd=0.01)
for(time in 2:n) Price[time]<-Price[time-1]*(1+hpr[time])
par(mfrow=c(1,2))
plot(Price)
abline(h=0,lwd=2,col="blue")
```

On executing the above lines of R codes similar output will be displayed as shown in Fig. 2.3.

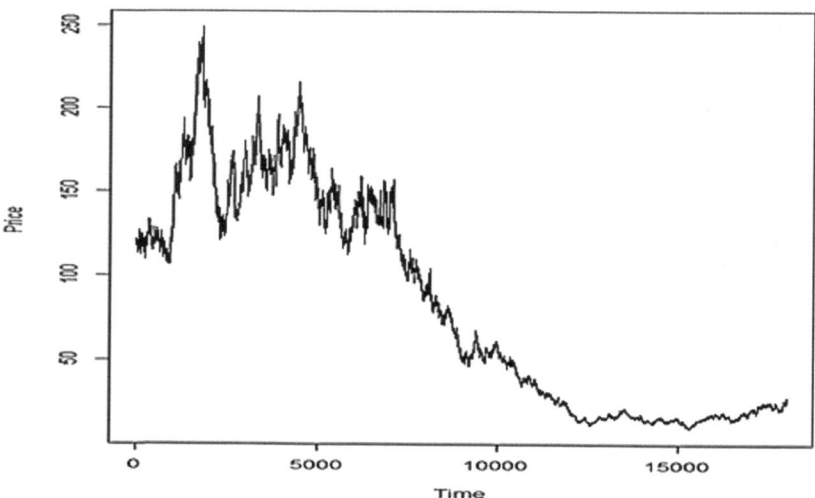

Fig. 2.3 Price movements follow random walk model with random drift (holding period return)

The random walk model with random holding period return drift considers the limited liability feature of the security unlike the random walk model with fixed drifts. The autocorrelation of any time series could easily be estimated in R using the R package "stats" as shown below. Code:

```
library(stats)
Box.test(Series_name,lag=define_the_lag,type = "Ljung-Box")
```

2.2   FINANCE IN ACTION

To check whether Volatility Index or "VIX" daily closing price movements between 01/01/2020 and 31/03/2020 follows random walk? To do so Volatility Index or "VIX" daily movements over the period 02/01/2020 and 31/03/2020 (Data source: Yahoo Finance) is used.

2.2.1   EViews Stepwise Implementations

Step 1:   Import data into the EViews Workfile window.

Step 2:   Double click on the series to test on the Workfile window.

Step 3:   New selected series window will appears showing all datapoints of the series.

Step 4:   Then click on view → Variance Ratio Test → Variance Ratio Test window will appear as shown below in Fig. 2.4.

Step 5:   Select different specification as you want to test as EViews offers several options. Data specification section in the above window provides user with three options: random walk (variance calculated from the differences of data); exponential random walk (variance calculated taking the log difference); and random walk innovations (innovations themselves). The variance ratio test of Lo and MacKinlay (1988) is default under test specification. Test probabilities could be estimated either choosing Asymptotic normal (Lo & MacKinlay, 1988) or Wild bootstrap (Kim, 2006) methods, respectively. The variance ratio test estimates obtained from using the above setting is shown in Fig. 2.5. Both the Chow-Denning maximum $|z|$ (at period 2) and Wald joint tests statistics of variance ratio test estimates reject the null hypothesis of

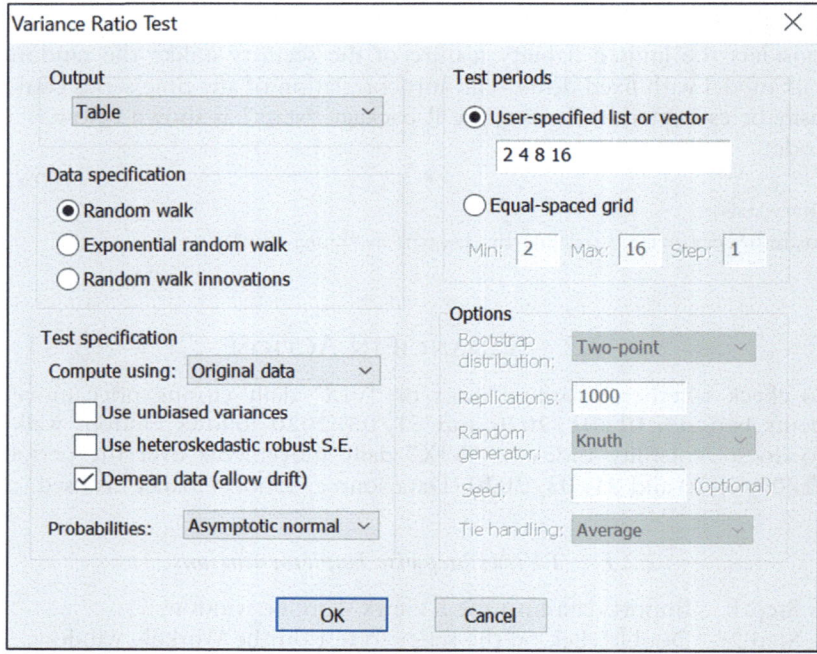

Fig. 2.4 Variance ratio test window

"VIX is a random walk". As the name suggests joint tests give estimates of joint null hypothesis for all periods whereas individual test gives estimates for individual periods. Lower portion of the variance ratio test estimates provides the individual period test estimates in our case example it is for 2, 4, 8, and 16 individual periods.

Then re-execute the variance ratio test with data specification "Exponential Random Walk". The obtained variance ratio test estimates are shown below in Fig. 2.6.

In this case, both the Chow-Denning maximum |z| (at period 2) and Wald joint tests statistics of variance ratio test estimates fail to reject the null hypothesis of "Log VIX is a random walk".

Null Hypothesis: VIX is a random walk
Date: 04/04/21   Time: 09:03
Sample: 1 62
Included observations: 61 (after adjustments)
Standard error estimates assume no heteroskedasticity
Use biased variance estimates
User-specified lags: 2 4 8 16

Joint Tests	Value	df	Probability
Max |z| (at period 2)*	3.466407	61	0.0021
Wald (Chi-Square)	16.81955	4	0.0021

Individual Tests				
Period	Var. Ratio	Std. Error	z-Statistic	Probability
2	0.556172	0.128037	-3.466407	0.0005
4	0.630394	0.239535	-1.543013	0.1228
8	0.629026	0.378738	-0.979500	0.3273
16	0.474595	0.563580	-0.932262	0.3512

*Probability approximation using studentized maximum modulus with
  parameter value 4 and infinite degrees of freedom

Fig. 2.5   Test for random walk assuming no heteroskedasticity

Next test for whether the Volatility Index or "VIX" daily closing price movements between 01/01/2020 and 31/03/2020 follow a martingale? To check whether VIX is a martingale, follow all the steps from 1 to 4 as mentioned in the section "EViews stepwise implementations". In the step 5 check the box "Use heteroskedastic robust S.E." in addition to Demean data (allow drift). Then click OK and following output will be displayed as shown in Fig. 2.7.

The Chow-Denning maximum |z| joint tests statistics of variance ratio test (at period 2) estimates fail to reject the null hypothesis of "VIX is a martingale". Test estimates show that security prices movements do not always follow a random walk. It also shows that a martingale at all times need not to be a random walk.

Summary

This chapter briefly introduced the topic random walk hypothesis and its implications. Why random walk hypothesis is very important in financial studies is discussed in details. Different random walk models are illustrated with examples. Different versions of efficient market hypothesis are

```
Null Hypothesis: Log VIX is a random walk
Date: 04/04/21   Time: 09:06
Sample: 1 62
Included observations: 61 (after adjustments)
Standard error estimates assume no heteroskedasticity
Use biased variance estimates
User-specified lags: 2 4 8 16
```

Joint Tests	Value	df	Probability
Max |z| (at period 2)*	1.814902	61	0.2505
Wald (Chi-Square)	6.033531	4	0.1967

Individual Tests				
Period	Var. Ratio	Std. Error	z-Statistic	Probability
2	0.767626	0.128037	-1.814902	0.0695
4	0.848743	0.239535	-0.631462	0.5277
8	0.907219	0.378738	-0.244974	0.8065
16	0.700885	0.563580	-0.530741	0.5956

*Probability approximation using studentized maximum modulus with parameter value 4 and infinite degrees of freedom

Fig. 2.6   Test for Exponential Random walk assuming no heteroskedasticity

```
Null Hypothesis: VIX is a martingale
Date: 04/04/21   Time: 09:07
Sample: 1 62
Included observations: 61 (after adjustments)
Heteroskedasticity robust standard error estimates
Use biased variance estimates
User-specified lags: 2 4 8 16
```

Joint Tests	Value	df	Probability
Max |z| (at period 2)*	1.565466	61	0.3934

Individual Tests				
Period	Var. Ratio	Std. Error	z-Statistic	Probability
2	0.556172	0.283512	-1.565466	0.1175
4	0.630394	0.505025	-0.731857	0.4643
8	0.629026	0.703264	-0.527504	0.5978
16	0.474595	0.889498	-0.590676	0.5547

*Probability approximation using studentized maximum modulus with parameter value 4 and infinite degrees of freedom

Fig. 2.7   Test for Martingale

discussed along with the role of random walk hypothesis in testing market efficiency is covered in details. Joint hypothesis problem is discussed in details with respect to market efficiency and asset pricing models. Martingale is introduced and discussions are covered on how it is different from a random walk and its importance in finance. EViews stepwise implementations and estimation interpretations of various test for random walk and martingale are discussed Plausibly.

Analysts/Investors Corner

The security price movements do not follow a random or martingale walk at all times. Test of market efficiency seems to be impossible due to joint hypothesis problem. Plausible assessment could be to evaluate: "whether market could be beaten" or "whether the securities are priced correctly" or "whether market bubbles could be sensed"? Martingales are important and martingale at all times need not to be a random walk.

2.3   EXERCISES

2.3.1   Multiple Choice Questions

1. EMH does not assume

    (a) Security prices follow a random walk
    (b) Security prices follow a martingale
    (c) Security prices do not follow a random walk
    (d) None

2. Which of the following statement(s) about martingales is/are false?

    (a) Martingale and random walk are the same
    (b) Martingale is not a stochastic process
    (c) Martingales are the sequences of random variables
    (d) All of the above

3. Which of the following version of EMH does not exists?

(a) Weak form
(b) Semi Weak form
(c) Semi Strong form
(d) Strong form

4. Dart Throwing Investment Contest initiated in which year?

(a) 1987
(b) 1988
(c) 1989
(d) 1991

5. Which of the following test is not associated with testing random walk?

(a) Variance ratio test
(b) Wald (Chi-Square) joint tests
(c) Chow-Denning maximum $|z|$ joint tests
(d) BDS Independence test

6. The random walk hypothesis is mostly related to the

(a) Weak form of EMH
(b) Semi Weak form of EMH
(c) Semi Strong form of EMH
(d) Strong form of EMH

7. An investor notices a particular trend in a security price movements. This is a violation of the

(a) Weak form of EMH
(b) Semi Weak form of EMH
(c) Semi Strong form of EMH
(d) Strong form of EMH

8. Which of the following test is used for testing random walk?

(a) Variance ratio test
(b) Phillips-Perron test
(c) KPSS test
(d) BDS independence test

9. Which among the following test is used for autocorrelation analysis?

   (a) Kendall's tau
   (b) Ljung-Box test
   (c) Pearson correlation
   (d) Shapiro–Wilk test

10. According to Eugene Fama test of the market efficiency is difficult due to

   (a) Joint hypothesis problem
   (b) Forward hypothesis problem
   (c) Backward hypothesis problem
   (d) None of the above

2.3.2   Fill in the Blanks

1. Market efficiency should be tested jointly with the _____ & _____.
2. Test of market efficiency seems to be impossible due to _____ problem.
3. _____ test is used for autocorrelation analysis.
4. Dart Throwing Investment Contest initiated by _____ in the year _____.
5. EMH stands for _____.
6. $E(\text{Price}_{t+1} - \text{Price}_t | \Phi_t) = 0$, represents a _____.
7. In the following random walk model: $\text{Price}_t = \text{Price}_{t-1} \pm \alpha_t$, α_t represents _____.
8. The arrival of relevant new information is a _____ process.
9. Presence of the stock market anomalies evidence against the _____.
10. Martingale follows a _____ process.

2.3.3   Long Answer Questions

1. Define Random walk hypothesis with suitable examples?
2. Define Efficient Market Hypothesis with suitable examples?
3. What are the three versions of EMH and its implications? Explain it in brief.

4. Develop a random walk model with random drifts using Poisson's ratio and execute it with R programming to obtain the estimates?

5. Develop a random walk model with random drifts as the log returns and execute it with R programming to obtain the estimates?

6. Revisit Fig. 2.2 and replot it considering unequal probability of getting a head or tail?

7. Revisit Fig. 2.3 and replot it with the mean value equals to 0.02? Check the difference and comments on its implications.

8. Comment on the statement "Are markets really efficient during COVID-19 pandemic" with suitable examples.

9. Using different R operators define a martingale and execute it in R console?

10. What is your understanding on Joint Hypothesis Problem? Explain it in brief.

11. What are public and private information?

12. Discuss EMH with respect to the technical analysis and fundamental analysis?

13. A researcher wants to conduct a study to understand whether the security prices follow a random walk during the financial crisis 2008 and COVID-19 on the US and UK financial markets? But the researcher does not know from where to begin. So, help him/her to begin with the analysis.

14. A central banker want to examine whether the "USD_EUR" daily exchange rates for the past five years follow a martingale? Put yourself in the place of central banker and finish the task?

15. Define: what is a non-random walk?

2.3.4   Real-World Tasks

1. An instructor ask his/her student to test for the market efficiency during the COVID-19 first and second phase impact on the European stock markets? Assume yourself as the student and perform the task. Then prepare a detailed report of the analysis to be submitted to the instructor.

2. A senior researcher want to analyse whether the top seven cryptocurrencies returns follow a random walk during the noble Coronavirus pandemic. Assume yourself as the researcher: perform the mentioned task in details and develop the analysis report.

3. An investment analyst want to examine whether the world indices before, during, and after the subprime crisis follow a martingale. Help him/her to perform the said analysis and prepare the report.

4. A student need to test the weak form of EMH for the major three currency pairs daily exchange rate for the last three years as his/her project dissertation. Help the student to complete his/her project dissertation successfully and satisfactorily.

5. A senior manager of the Reserve bank of India (RBI) asked an intern working under him/her to conduct semi-strong form of EMH tests for all the technological securities traded in the BSE during the first phase of COVID-19 pandemic. Help the intern in analysing and developing the final report for timely submission to the senior RBI manager.

6. An individual investor is evaluating his/her investing option as the Herzfeld Caribbean Basin Fund (CUBA), a closed ended fund during early 2021. Help the investors to examine the CUBA fund with respect to the EMH and help him/her to make investment decision.

7. Conduct a simple empirical research to show that the security prices do react to the news announcements.

8. Conduct a simple empirical research that evidences against the EMH?

2.3.5   Case Studies

1. A researcher want to conduct a research to test whether stock market reacts to the government policy announcement. During the COVID-19 pandemic Indian government has taken several important policies to tackle the pandemic situation. In that aspect the researcher decided to test the Indian stock market efficiency with respect to the impact of Indian government important policies announcement between the period of January 2021 to September 2021.

Consider yourself in place of the researcher conduct the research and prepare a detail report based on your analysis.

2. Below figures shows the Variance ratio test estimates and descriptive statistics for the GBP_USD currency pair daily exchange rates between the period 01/01/2021 to 31/03/2021. Based on these data comments on the market efficiency and distribution of the data. Then also comment on the relationship between the volatility and market efficiency if any.

Null Hypothesis: GBP_USD is a martingale
Date: 04/04/21   Time: 20:39
Sample: 1 65
Included observations: 64 (after adjustments)
Heteroskedasticity robust standard error estimates
Use biased variance estimates
User-specified lags: 2 4 8 16

Joint Tests	Value	df	Probability
Max |z| (at period 4)*	2.371307	64	0.0690

Individual Tests				
Period	Var. Ratio	Std. Error	z-Statistic	Probability
2	1.369292	0.169949	2.172954	0.0298
4	1.734800	0.309871	2.371307	0.0177
8	1.408492	0.487009	0.838778	0.4016
16	0.582925	0.713661	-0.584416	0.5589

*Probability approximation using studentized maximum modulus with parameter value 4 and infinite degrees of freedom

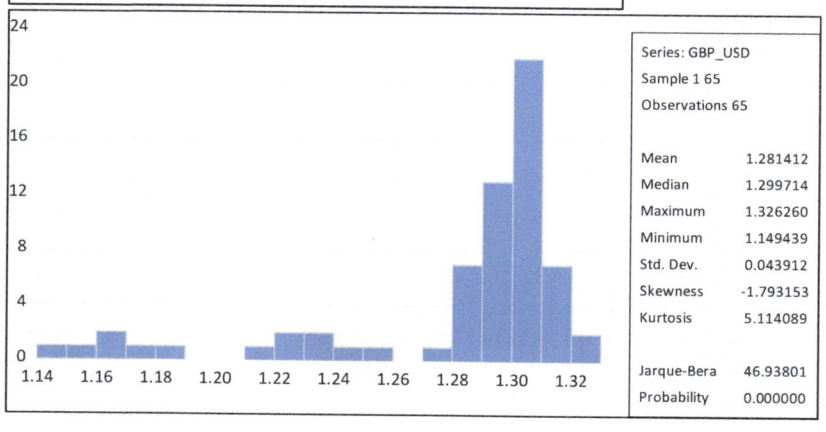

Series: GBP_USD	
Sample 1 65	
Observations 65	
Mean	1.281412
Median	1.299714
Maximum	1.326260
Minimum	1.149439
Std. Dev.	0.043912
Skewness	-1.793153
Kurtosis	5.114089
Jarque-Bera	46.93801
Probability	0.000000

References

Eugene, F. (1991). Efficient capital markets: II. *Journal of Finance, 46*(5), 1575–1617.

Fama, E. F. (1970). Efficient capital markets: A review of theory and empirical work. *The Journal of Finance, 25*(2), 383–417.

Kim, J. H. (2006). Wild bootstrapping variance ratio tests. *Economics Letters, 92*(1), 38–43.

Lo, A. W., & MacKinlay, A. C. (1988). Stock market prices do not follow random walks: Evidence from a simple specification test. *The Review of Financial Studies, 1*(1), 41–66.

Maiti, M. (2020). A critical review on evolution of risk factors and factor models. *Journal of Economic Surveys, 34*(1), 175–184.

CHAPTER 3

Geometric Brownian Motion

Key Topics Covered
- *Brownian Motion*
- *Why Geometric Brownian Motion*
- *Wiener Process*
- *Simulating Stock Prices using Geometric Brownian Motion*
- *Option Valuations*
- *Binomial Option Pricing*
- *Monte Carlo Simulation*
- *Estimating Greeks of the Options*

3.1 BACKGROUND

Robert Brown in the year 1827 first observed that the pollen grains suspended in the water follow a zigzag random motion. The zigzag random motion of these tiny particles suspended in water is known as the Brownian motion. Subsequently Louis Bachelier in his doctoral thesis in the year 1990 established a mathematical model of the stochastic process or Brownian motion or wiener process for valuing the stock options. Louis Bachelier work notably underlined the two fundamental features of Brownian motion namely Markov process and reflection principle as

© The Author(s), under exclusive license to Springer Nature Singapore Pte Ltd. 2021
M. Maiti, *Applied Financial Econometrics*,
https://doi.org/10.1007/978-981-16-4063-6_3

shown below in Eq. 3.1.

$$P\left\{\max_{0\leq b\leq t} W(b) \leq \lambda\right\} = \frac{1}{\sqrt{2\pi t}} \int_0^\lambda e^{-x^2/2t} dx \qquad (3.1)$$

$W(b)$ represents position of Brownian motion at time b whereas the right-hand side of the above equation represents the simple random distribution or probability density function.

Norbert Wiener in the year 1923 formally formulated the mathematical foundation of the Brownian motion. Standardized Brownian motion is often referred to as the Wiener process. Louis Bachelier is often attributed as the first person to introduce advanced mathematics into the field of finance labelled as the random walk model.

Standardized Brownian motion or Wiener process has these following properties:

1. $W(0) = 0$ represents that the Wiener process starts at the origin at time zero.
2. At any given time t > 0 the position of Wiener process follows a normal distribution with mean $(\mu) = 0$ and variance $(\sigma^2) = t$.
3. The random function or Wiener process W() is a continuous function.
4. The displacement from $W(b)$ to $W(t)$ is time homogeneous, independent and non-overlapping random progression.

However, Brownian Motion is not appropriate for modelling stock prices as Brownian Motion can take negative values. A Geometric Brownian Motion is represented by the following Eq. 3.2.

$$db(t) = \mu b(t)dt + \sigma b(t)dW(t) \qquad (3.2)$$

where

$b(t)$ is a random or stochastic process.
μ represents the drift term.
σ volatility term.
$W(t)$ represents the Brownian motion or Wiener process.

Hence, $b(t)$ is said to follow a Geometric Brownian motion if it satisfies the above equation. The expected mean value and variance could be estimated as follows.

$$E[b(t)] = b(0)e^{\mu t}$$

$$Var[b(t)] = b^2(0)e^{2\mu t}(e^{\sigma^2 t} - 1)$$

Commonly distinct types of drifts decide the form of the Brownian motion as explained below.

Zero Drift:	Standard Brownian Motion
Constant Drift:	Brownian Motion with constant drift
Linear Drift:	Geometric Brownian Motion

Illustrations with appropriate examples

Difference between the Brownian motion and Geometric Brownian Motion is illustrated using simple examples.

Brownian Motion

Plot of the approximate sample security prices path that follows a Brownian motion with Mean (μ) = 0 and Standard deviation (σ) = 1 over the time interval [0,T] is shown below. At time t=0 security price is 1 €. Then use the below R codes to plot the movements.
Code:

```
μ=0; σ=1; T=1; n=2^(20); X0=1;
dt=T/n
t=seq(0,T,by=dt)
x=c(X0,α*dt+σ*sqrt(dt)*rnorm(n,mean=0,sd=1))
Price=cumsum(x)
plot(t,Price,type='l',xlab="time")
```

In the above plot shown Fig. 3.1, it is clearly noticed that the security price takes negative values while modelling with the Brownian motion. Hence, Brownian Motion is not appropriate for modelling the security prices.

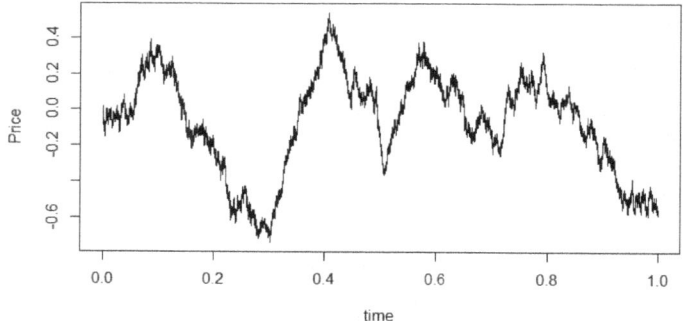

Fig. 3.1 Brownian Motion path plot

Geometric Brownian Motion

Plot the approximate sample security prices path that follows a Geometric Brownian motion with Mean (μ) = 0.2 and Standard deviation (σ) = 0.1 over the time interval [0,T]. At time t = 0 security price is 100 $. Based on this information, run 20 different simulations to plot the different trajectories of the security prices over the time interval [0,T]. Use R package "sde[1]" and run the below R codes to plot the security prices movements.
Codes:

```
library(sde)
μ=0.2; σ=0.1; P0=100; T = 1/252
nt=20; n=2^(12)
dt=T/n; t=seq(0,T,by=dt)
X=matrix(rep(0,length(t)*nt), nrow=nt)
for (i in 1:nt) {X[i,]= GBM(x=P0,r=μ,sigma=σ,T=T,N=n)}
ymax=max(X); ymin=min(X)ymax=max(X); ymin=min(X)
plot(t,X[1,],t='l',ylim=c(ymin, ymax), col=1, ylab="Price",xlab="time")
for(i in 2:nt){lines(t,X[i,], t='l',ylim=c(ymin, ymax),col=i)}
```

[1] https://cran.r-project.org/web/packages/sde/sde.pdf.

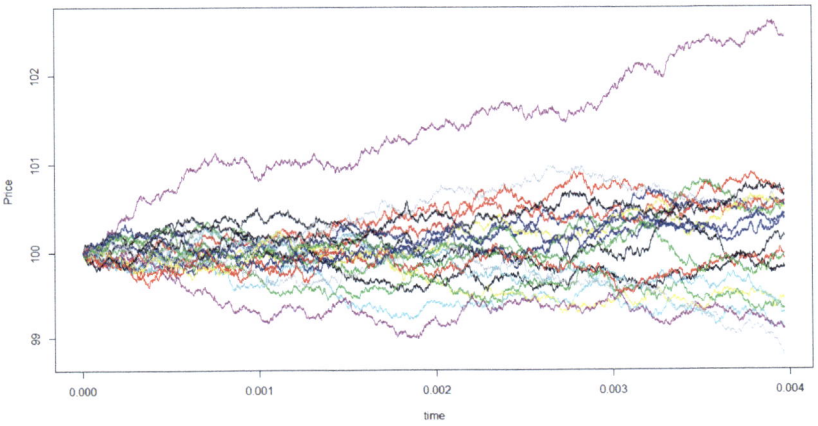

Fig. 3.2 Geometric Brownian Motion paths plots with 20 stimulations

Similarly using the above codes any number of trajectories could be plotted with just varying the different numbers of simulations as shown in Figs. 3.2 and 3.3.

3.2   FINANCE IN ACTION

To compute the value of an option on the security that follows a Geometric Brownian motion.

Binomial Option Pricing

Compute the potential future price of an American call and put options on a security using the Binomial tree option pricing method with these given parameters:

- (**S**) current value of the security: 100 €
- (**X**) exercise price: 100 €
- (**Time**) Time to maturity: 6 months
- (**r**) interest rate: 12% yearly.
- (**sigma**) volatility: 45% yearly.
- (**b**) cost of carry: 10% yearly.
- (**n**) number of steps: 6.

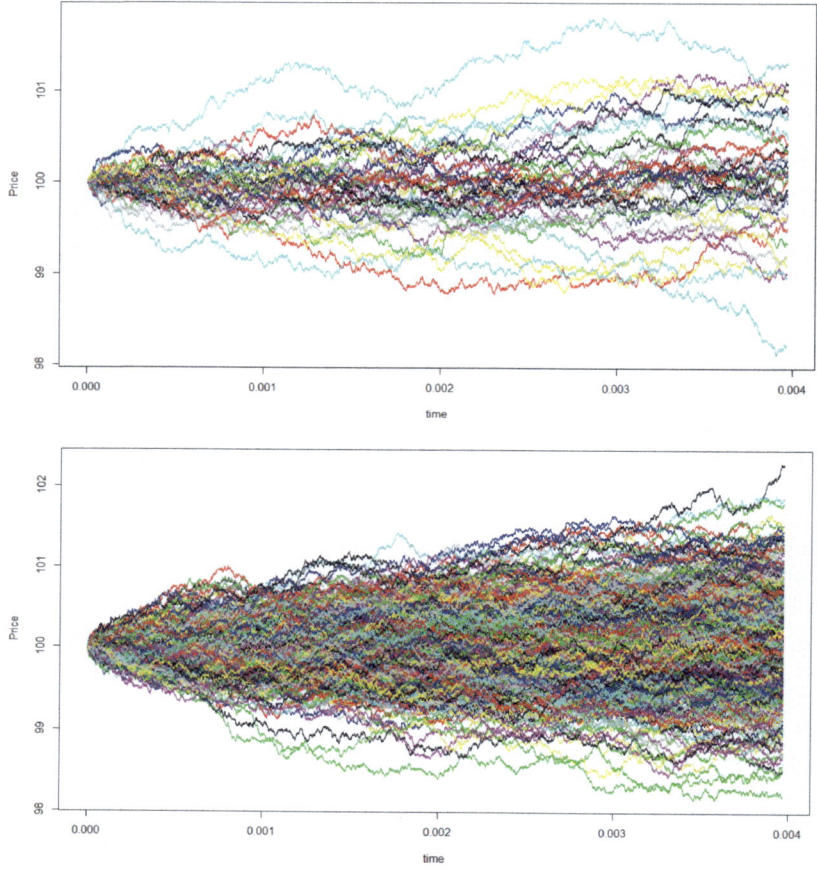

Fig. 3.3   Geometric Brownian Motion paths plots with 40 and 400 stimulations

To estimate the potential future price of an American call and put options on a security using the Binomial tree option pricing method use "fOptions[2]" R package. Use the function CRRBinomialTreeOption() to estimate the price of American call and put options on a security. Whereas

---

[2] https://cran.r-project.org/web/packages/fOptions/fOptions.pdf.

to plot the binomial tree of option valuation call these two functions: BinomialTreeOption() and BinomialTreePlot().
Codes:

```
library("fOptions")
CRRBinomialTreeOption(TypeFlag = "ca", S = 100, X = 100, Time = 6/12, r =
0.12, b = 0.1, sigma = 0.45, n = 6)
CRRTree = BinomialTreeOption(TypeFlag = "ca", S = 100, X = 100, Time =
6/12, r = 0.12, b = 0.1, sigma = 0.45, n = 6)
BinomialTreePlot(CRRTree, dy = 1, cex = 0.8, ylim = c(-7, 7), xlab = "Time
steps", ylab = "Value of the option")
title(main = "Binomial Tree")title(main = "Binomial Tree")
```

Output for American call option price:
The above R estimates (Fig. 3.4A,B) show the estimated call option price and binomial tree plot of the call option valuation. Similarly, to get the estimates for the American put option repeat the above code with TypeFlag = "pa" instead of "ca" as shown below (Fig. 3.5A,B).
Codes:

```
library("fOptions")
CRRBinomialTreeOption(TypeFlag = "pa", S = 100, X = 100, Time = 6/12, r =
0.12, b = 0.1, sigma = 0.45, n = 6)CRRBinomialTreeOption(TypeFlag = "pa", S
= 100, X = 100, Time = 6/12, r = 0.12, b = 0.1, sigma = 0.45, n = 6)
CRRTree = BinomialTreeOption(TypeFlag = "pa", S = 100, X = 100, Time =
6/12, r = 0.12, b = 0.1, sigma = 0.45, n = 6)
BinomialTreePlot(CRRTree, dy = 1, cex = 0.8, ylim = c(-7, 7), xlab = "Time
steps", ylab = "Value of the option")
title(main = "Binomial Tree")
```

Output for American put option price:
The "fOptions" R package provides three options to estimate the price using Binomial Option Pricing of an option as mentioned below:
   CRRBinomialTreeOption(); JRBinomialTreeOption(); and TIANBinomialTreeOption().
   Any of these three binomial tree models (CRR, JR, and TIAN) could be used to estimate the price of an option on a security. Above all examples are shown with American options. To estimate European options run the same codes but replace TypeFlag with either "ce" or "pe" for European call and put options, respectively.

a
```
Title:
 CRR Binomial Tree Option

Call:
 CRRBinomialTreeOption(TypeFlag = "ca", S = 100, X = 100, Time = 6/12,
     r = 0.12, b = 0.1, sigma = 0.45, n = 6)

Parameters:
           Value:
 TypeFlag ca
 S        100
 X        100
 Time     0.5
 r        0.12
 b        0.1
 sigma    0.45
 n        6

Option Price:
 14.2715
```

b

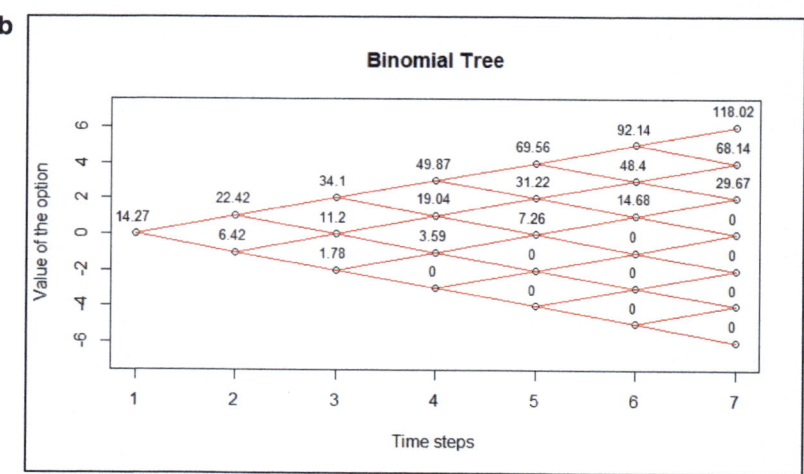

Fig. 3.4 A, B: American call option price estimates using Binomial Option Pricing

a
```
Title:
 CRR Binomial Tree Option

Call:
 CRRBinomialTreeOption(TypeFlag = "pa", S = 100, X = 100, Time = 6/12,
     r = 0.12, b = 0.1, sigma = 0.45, n = 6)

Parameters:
          Value:
 TypeFlag pa
 S        100
 X        100
 Time     0.5
 r        0.12
 b        0.1
 sigma    0.45
 n        6

Option Price:
 10.22345
```

b

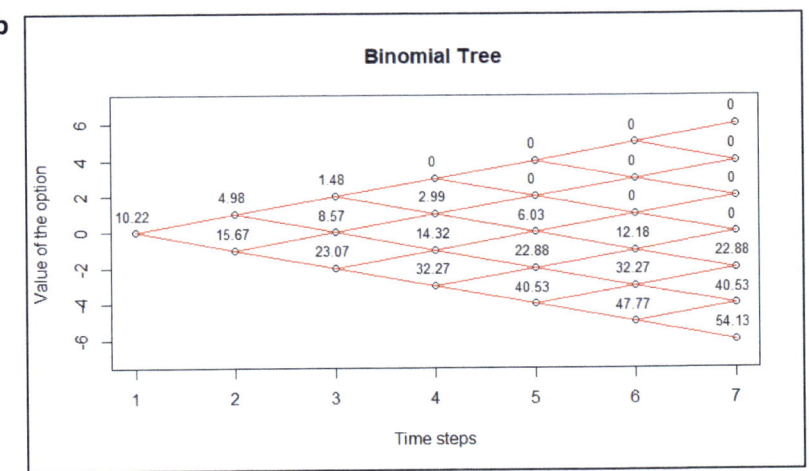

Fig. 3.5 **A, B**: American put option price estimates using Binomial Option Pricing

Monte Carlo Simulation Option Pricing

(a) Compute the potential future price of Plain Vanilla call option on a security using the Monte Carlo Simulation option pricing method with these given parameters:

(**S**) current value of the security: 100 €
(**X**) exercise price: 100 €
(**Time**) Time to maturity: 6 months
(**r**) interest rate: 12% yearly.
(**sigma**) volatility: 45% yearly
(**b**) cost of carry: 10% yearly

To estimate the potential future price of Plain Vanilla call option on a security using the Monte Carlo Simulation option pricing method use "fOptions" R package.

Codes:

#Option innovations with scrambled normal Sobol numbers

```
sobolInnovations <- function(mcSteps, pathLength, init, ...) {
rnorm.sobol(mcSteps, pathLength, init, ...)
}
```

#Wiener process to generate option's price paths

```
wienerPath <- function(eps) {
(b-sigma*sigma/2)*delta.t + sigma*sqrt(delta.t)*eps
}
```

#Plain Vanilla option payoffs

```
plainVanillaPayoff <- function(path) {
ST <- S*exp(sum(path))
if (TypeFlag == "c") payoff <- exp(-r*Time)*max(ST-X, 0)if (TypeFlag == "c")
payoff <- exp(-r*Time)*max(ST-X, 0)
if (TypeFlag == "p") payoff <- exp(-r*Time)*max(0, X-ST)
payoffpayoff
}
```

#Define the parameters

```
TypeFlag <- "c"; S <- 100; X <- 100
Time <- 6/12; sigma <- 0.45; r <- 0.12; b <- 0.1
```

#Monte Carlo Simulations

```
mc <- MonteCarloOption(delta.t = 1/252, pathLength = 20, mcSteps = 5000,
mcLoops = 20, init = TRUE, innovations.gen = sobolInnovations, path.gen =
wienerPath, payoff.calc = plainVanillaPayoff, antithetic = TRUE, standardization =
FALSE, trace = TRUE, scrambling = 2, seed = 2500)
```

#Monte Carlo simulations Iteration path plot

```
par(mfrow = c(1, 1))
mcPrice <- cumsum(mc)/(1:length(mc))
plot(mcPrice, type = "l", main = "Plain Vanila Option", xlab = "Monte Carlo
Loops", ylab = "Option Price")
```

Output for Plain Vanilla call option price using Monte Carlo Simulation: The above R estimates (Fig. 3.6A,B) show the Plain Vanilla call option price using Monte Carlo Simulation call option price.

(b) Compute the potential future price of Asian Arithmetic put option on a security using the Monte Carlo Simulation option pricing method with these given parameters:

(**S**) current value of the security: 100 €
(**X**) exercise price: 100 €
(**Time**) Time to maturity: 6 months.
(**r**) interest rate: 12% yearly.
(**sigma**) volatility: 45% yearly.
(**b**) cost of carry: 10% yearly.

To estimate the potential future price of Asian Arithmetic put option on a security using the Monte Carlo Simulation option pricing method use "fOptions" R package.
Codes:

#Option innovations with scrambled normal Sobol numbers

```
sobolInnovations <- function(mcSteps, pathLength, init, ...) {
rnorm.sobol(mcSteps, pathLength, init, ...)
}
```

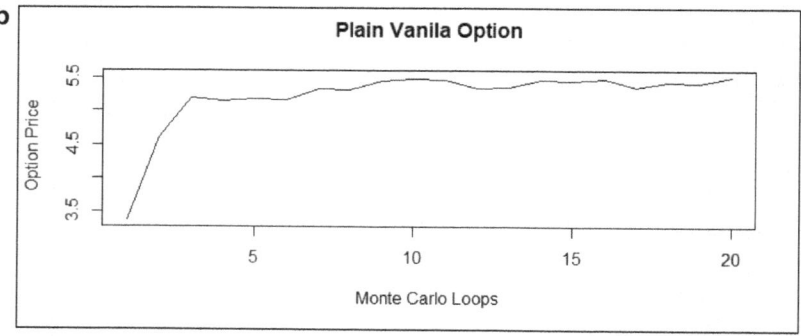

a Monte Carlo Simulation Path:

```
Loop:    No
Loop:    1     :  4.95443 4.95443
Loop:    2     :  7.080987 6.017709
Loop:    3     :  3.66219 5.232536
Loop:    4     :  6.588252 5.571465
Loop:    5     :  4.837238 5.424619
Loop:    6     :  6.738656 5.643625
Loop:    7     :  6.220604 5.726051
Loop:    8     :  3.994752 5.509638
Loop:    9     :  3.289514 5.262958
Loop:    10    :  4.919516 5.228614
Loop:    11    :  4.606873 5.172092
Loop:    12    :  7.092379 5.332116
Loop:    13    :  6.192896 5.39833
Loop:    14    :  4.665064 5.345954
Loop:    15    :  4.126388 5.264649
Loop:    16    :  6.367618 5.333585
Loop:    17    :  7.142509 5.439992
Loop:    18    :  5.182462 5.425685
Loop:    19    :  5.445863 5.426747
Loop:    20    :  6.870388 5.498929
```

Fig. 3.6   A, B: Plain Vanilla call option price estimates using Monte Carlo Simulation

#Wiener process to generate option's price paths

```
wienerPath <- function(eps) {
(b-sigma*sigma/2)*delta.t + sigma*sqrt(delta.t)*eps
}
```

Asian Arithmetic option payoffs

```
arithmeticAsianPayoff <- function(path) {
SM <- mean(S*exp(cumsum(path)))
```

```
if (TypeFlag == "c") payoff <- exp(-r*Time)*max(SM-X, 0)
if (TypeFlag == "p") payoff <- exp(-r*Time)*max(0, X-SM)
payoff }payoff }
```

#Define the parameters

```
TypeFlag <- "p"; S <- 100; X <- 100
Time <- 6/12; sigma <- 0.45; r <- 0.12; b <- 0.1
```

#Monte Carlo Simulations

```
mc <- MonteCarloOption(delta.t = 1/252, pathLength = 20, mcSteps = 5000,
mcLoops = 20, init = TRUE, innovations.gen = sobolInnovations, path.gen =
wienerPath, payoff.calc = arithmeticAsianPayoff, antithetic = TRUE, standardization
= FALSE, trace = TRUE, scrambling = 2, seed = 2500)
```

#Monte Carlo simulations Iteration path plot

```
par(mfrow = c(1, 1))par(mfrow = c(1, 1))
mcPrice <- cumsum(mc)/(1:length(mc))
plot(mcPrice, type = "l", main = "Asian Arithmetic option", xlab = "Monte Carlo
Loops", ylab = "Option Price")
```

Output for Asian Arithmetic option put option price using Monte Carlo Simulation:

The above R estimates (Fig. 3.7A,B) show the Asian Arithmetic put option price using Monte Carlo Simulation call option price.

Estimating Greeks of an Option

Compute the potential future price of Plain Vanilla call option with below-mentioned parameters. Then estimate the Greeks of the said option?

(**S**) current value of the security: 100 €
(**X**) exercise price: 100 €
(**Time**) Time to maturity: 6 months
(**r**) interest rate: 12% yearly.
(**sigma**) volatility: 45% yearly

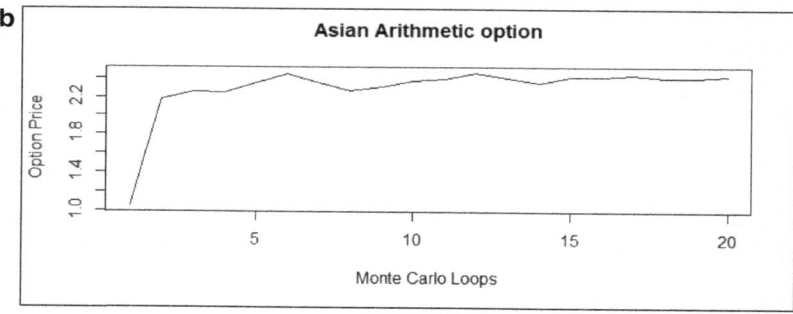

a

```
Monte Carlo Simulation Path:

Loop:     No
Loop:     1        : 1.050062 1.050062
Loop:     2        : 3.293184 2.171623
Loop:     3        : 2.423551 2.255599
Loop:     4        : 2.211374 2.244543
Loop:     5        : 2.736333 2.342901
Loop:     6        : 2.89578 2.435047
Loop:     7        : 1.840977 2.35018
Loop:     8        : 1.673238 2.265562
Loop:     9        : 2.609564 2.303785
Loop:     10       : 2.929296 2.366336
Loop:     11       : 2.551558 2.383174
Loop:     12       : 3.16896 2.448656
Loop:     13       : 1.736754 2.393895
Loop:     14       : 1.708538 2.344941
Loop:     15       : 3.192258 2.401429
Loop:     16       : 2.455926 2.404835
Loop:     17       : 2.821231 2.429329
Loop:     18       : 1.792744 2.393963
Loop:     19       : 2.432199 2.395975
Loop:     20       : 2.857063 2.41903
```

b

Fig. 3.7 A, B: Asian Arithmetic put option price estimates using Monte Carlo Simulation

(**b**) cost of carry: 10% yearly

R codes with outputs to the above problem are shown below:

Plain Vanilla call option price

GBSOption(TypeFlag = "c", S = 100, X = 100, Time = 6/12, r = 0.12, b = 0.10, sigma = 0.45)

Option Price: **14.77334**

Greeks of the option

GBSGreeks(Selection = "delta",TypeFlag = "c", S = 100, X = 100, Time = 6/12, r = 0.12, b = 0.10, sigma = 0.45)

Delta: **0.6178777**

GBSGreeks(Selection = "gamma",TypeFlag = "c", S = 100, X = 100, Time = 6/12, r = 0.12, b = 0.10, sigma = 0.45)

Gamma: **0.01180739**

GBSGreeks(Selection = "vega",TypeFlag = "c", S = 100, X = 100, Time = 6/12, r = 0.12, b = 0.10, sigma = 0.45)

Vega: **26.56664**

GBSGreeks(Selection = "theta",TypeFlag = "c", S = 100, X = 100, Time = 6/12, r = 0.12, b = 0.10, sigma = 0.45)

Theta: **−16.36096**

GBSGreeks(Selection = "rho",TypeFlag = "c", S = 100, X = 100, Time = 6/12, r = 0.12, b = 0.10, sigma = 0.45)

Rho: **23.50721**

The Greeks' measures of the options are important as they provide useful information about the different factors that could affect the price of an option. Delta measures the likely change in the option price for a unit price change of the underlying asset. A delta value of 0.6178777 tentatively signifies that the option price will change 0.6178777 € for every €uro change in the price of the underlying asset (S). Gamma measures the possible change in the option delta value for a unit price change of the underlying asset. Likewise Vega measures the probable change in the option price for a percentage implied volatility change of the underlying asset. Theta measures the time decay value of an option. Similarly Rho measures the impact of variation in the prevailing interest rates on the option price. Hence, the Greeks' measures of the options provide significant information to the traders in making investment decisions.

Summary

This chapter briefly introduced the topic Geometric Brownian Motion and its implications. Why Geometric Brownian Motion is preferred over Brownian motion in financial studies is discussed in details. What is the Wiener process and its important properties are discussed in detail. Different stock prices simulation exercises using Geometric Brownian Motion are illustrated with examples. Option valuations using the Binomial Option Pricing and Monte Carlo Simulation methods are discussed with appropriate examples. In the end different Greeks' measures of the options and its implications are covered in details.

Analysts/Investors Corner

Brownian Motion is not appropriate for modelling stock prices as Brownian Motion can take negative values. Any number of the simulated security prices trajectories could be plotted using a Geometric Brownian Motion model. If security prices follow a Geometric Brownian Motion then the value of an option on that security could easily be assessed using the Binomial Option Pricing methods and Monte Carlo Simulation techniques. The Greeks' measures of an option are very useful in deciding which option to invest and when to invest.

3.3   EXERCISES

3.3.1   Multiple Choice Questions

1. Which of the following is not appropriate for modelling stock prices?

    (a) Geometric Brownian Motion
    (b) Brownian Motion

(c) Both

(d) None of the above

2. Which of the following is not belongs to the Greeks' measures of an option?

   (a) Delta
   (b) Sigma
   (c) Theta
   (d) Rho

3. Wiener process is also known as the

   (a) Simple Brownian motion
   (b) Standardized Brownian motion
   (c) Structured Brownian motion
   (d) Second order Brownian motion

4. The "fOptions" R package does not include which of the following binomial tree models for valuation of an option?

   (a) CRR binomial tree model
   (b) JR binomial tree model
   (c) TIAN binomial tree model
   (d) TRR binomial tree model

5. Which of the following Greeks' value of an option measures the probable change in the option price for a percentage implied volatility change of the underlying asset?

   (a) Delta
   (b) Gamma
   (c) Vega
   (d) Theta

6. Which among the following measures the time decay value of an option?

   (a) Delta
   (b) Theta
   (c) Vega
   (d) Gamma

7. Which of the following measures the impact of variation in the prevailing interest rates on the option price?

   (a) Delta
   (b) Vega
   (c) Rho
   (d) Theta

8. Price of an option cannot be estimated by the following technique?

   (a) Monte Carlo Stimulation
   (b) Black Scholes model
   (c) Gravity model
   (d) Binomial tree model

9. Which of the following is not an example of an option?

   (a) British Geometric option
   (b) Put and Call option
   (c) Plain Vanilla option
   (d) Asian Arithmetic option

10. Geometric Brownian Motion can take

   (a) Positive values
   (b) Negative values
   (c) Alpha Numeric values
   (d) Both Positive and negative values

3.3.2   Fill in the Blanks

1. _____ is not appropriate for modelling stock prices.

2. _____ measures the time decay value of an option.

3. _____ measures the impact of variation in the prevailing interest rates on the option price.

4. _____ measures the likely change in the option price for a unit price change of the underlying asset.

5. Standardized Brownian motion is often referred to as the _____.

6. $db(t) = \mu b(t)dt + \sigma b(t)dW(t)$, represents a _____.

7. In the following equation: $db(t) = \mu b(t)dt + \sigma b(t)dW(t)$, $b(t)$ represents _____.

8. Geometric Brownian Motion has the property of _____ process.

9. Wiener process follows a _____ distribution.

10. Brownian motion with a linear drift is known as the _____.

3.3.3 Long Answer Questions

1. Define Geometric Brownian Motion with suitable examples?

2. Define the difference between Brownian Motion and Geometric Brownian Motion with suitable examples?

3. What are the key properties of the Wiener process?

4. Explain any three key properties of the Geometric Brownian Motion?

5. Develop a simple Geometric Brownian Motion model with random drifts using Poisson's ratio and execute it with R programming to obtain the estimates?

6. A Geometric Brownian Motion is represented by the following equation:

$$db(t) = \mu b(t)dt + \sigma b(t)dW(t)$$

Briefly explain the above equation.

7. Plot the approximate sample security prices path that follows a Geometric Brownian motion with Mean $(\mu) = 0.23$ and Standard deviation $(\sigma) = 0.2$ over the time interval [0,T]. At time t = 0 security price is 25 $. Run 200 different simulations to plot the different trajectories of the security prices over the time interval [0,T].

8. Plot the approximate sample security prices path that follow a Brownian motion with Mean $(\mu) = 0$ and Standard deviation $(\sigma) = 1.01$ over the time interval [0,T]. At time $t=0$ security price is 1.2 €.

9. Compute the probable future price of an American call and put options on a security using the Binomial tree option pricing method with these given parameters:

(S) current value of the security: 70 €
(X) exercise price: 72 €
(Time) Time to maturity: 8 months
(r) interest rate: 7.49 % annual
(sigma) volatility: 51% annual
(b) cost of carry: 8.77 % annual
(n) number of steps: 5

10. Compute the likely future price of an European call and put options on a security using the three Binomial tree option pricing methods available with the "fOptions" R package.

(S) current value of the security: 170 €
(X) exercise price: 172 €
(Time) Time to maturity: 8 months
(r) interest rate: 9.49 % annual
(sigma) volatility: 31% annual
(b) cost of carry: 7.73 % annual
(n) number of steps: 6

11. Compute the potential future price of Plain Vanilla call option on a security using the Monte Carlo Simulation option pricing method with these given parameters:

(S) current value of the security: 65 €
(X) exercise price: 65 €
(Time) Time to maturity: 6 months
(r) interest rate: 10% yearly
(sigma) volatility: 30% yearly
(b) cost of carry: 10% yearly

12. Compute the probable future price of Asian Arithmetic put option on a security using the Monte Carlo Simulation option pricing method with these given parameters:

(S) current value of the security: 80 ₹
(X) exercise price: 80 ₹
(Time) Time to maturity: 10 months
(r) interest rate: 8.5% yearly
(sigma) volatility: 35% yearly
(b) cost of carry: 9% yearly

13. Compute the likely future price of Plain Vanilla call option with below mentioned parameters. Then estimate the Greeks of the said option?

(S) current value of the security: 60 €
(X) exercise price: 63 €
(Time) Time to maturity: 7 months
(r) interest rate: 7% yearly
(sigma) volatility: 37% yearly
(b) cost of carry: 7.5% yearly

14. Describe Brownian Motion as the Limit of a Random Walk?
15. Show that the Geometric Brownian Motion is a Markov process?
16. Elucidate Binomial model as an approximation to the Geometric Brownian Motion?
17. Black–Scholes–Merton (BSM) develops the famous option pricing model under the following assumption on the stock price dynamics:

$$db(t) = \mu b(t)dt + \sigma b(t)dW(t)$$

Elaborate the above statement.

3.3.4   Real-World Tasks

1. A professor ask his/her student to simulate and plot the NYSE daily log returns from normal distribution with a simulation size of 600. Assume yourself as the student and perform the task. Then prepare a detailed report of the analysis to be submitted to the professor.
2. A junior researcher want to analyse the SENSEX options between 3–6 months maturity Greeks' values to make the investment decision. Assume yourself as the researcher: perform the mentioned task in details and develop the analysis report.
3. A stock analyst (risk taking nature) wants to invest in the available technology stocks options with less than 6 months maturity traded in the FTSE. Help the analyst to pick the right option for investment based on the risk preference.

4. A scholar need to test the efficiency of the Black Scholes option pricing models in Asian major markets for his/her project dissertation. Help the scholar to complete his/her project dissertation successfully and satisfactorily.

5. A Deputy Manager of the Reserve bank of India (RBI) asked an intern working under him/her to test the impact of variation in the prevailing interest rates on the option prices on pharmaceutical stocks traded in the BSE. Help the intern in analysing and developing the final report for timely submission to the RBI's Deputy manager.

3.3.5   Case Studies

1. A research estimates following Greeks' measures of a Plain Vanilla call option (S = 90, X = 90, Time = 4/12, r = 0.11, b = 0.9, sigma = 0.25) as shown below.

   Comment on the obtained estimates with respect to the investment decision making.

   Delta: 1.280762
   Gamma: 0.003956409
   Vega: 2.670576
   Theta: −101.3933
   Rho: 28.27176

2. An analyst while evaluating an investment decision on a Plain Vanilla put option (S = 85, X = 85, Time = 5/12, r = 0.95, b = 0.79, sigma = 0.37) referred the below estimates. Based on these information suggest your view on the investment.

   Delta: −0.06278499
   Gamma: 0.005989581
   Vega: 6.67152
   Theta: 1.839546
   Rho: −2.480516

CHAPTER 4

Efficient Frontier and Portfolio Optimization

Key Topics Covered

- *Risk: Systematic and Unsystematic*
- *Return and Risk estimations*
- *Portfolio diversification*
- *Variance and Covariance*
- *Mean–Variance & Multifactor Mean Variance Efficient Frontiers*
- *Portfolio Optimization*
- *Capital Market Line & Security Market Line*
- *Illustration on plotting the Mean–Variance efficient frontier*
- *Illustration on Portfolio Optimization*

4.1 BACKGROUND

Markowitz (1952) formally provides the theoretical framework for analyzing the risk and return relationship. He pioneered the concept of modern portfolio theory that considers risk and return as the investors primary consideration while making investment decisions. Modern portfolio theory puts forward three important arguments as follows:

    I. Portfolio's aggregate risk and return profiles matter over each individual assets risk and return profiles

© The Author(s), under exclusive license to Springer Nature Singapore Pte Ltd. 2021
M. Maiti, *Applied Financial Econometrics*,
https://doi.org/10.1007/978-981-16-4063-6_4

II. Through the process of diversification, overall portfolio risk could be reduced

III. Mean-Variance efficient frontier represents the set of optimal portfolios

These three arguments are made under the following assumptions:

1. Investors are rational and risk adverse
2. Market is efficient
3. Investors prefer higher returns over lower returns for a given level of risk
4. Investors make decision based on risk and returns
5. There is no taxes and cost of trading
6. Borrowing and lending takes place at risk-free rate
7. Investors have constant investment time horizon

It is important to understand each of these three arguments of the modern portfolio theory in detail and thereby its implications. Risk and uncertainty are the two buzz words that are often used in the finance study. The basic difference is that risk could be quantified, whereas the latter is not.

Risk can be divided into two groups, namely systematic and unsystematic risk. Systematic risk cannot be diversified unlike unsystematic risk. It is important to understand how these two types of risk matters in portfolio selection. Figure 4.1 illustrates the effect of systematic and unsystematic risks on portfolio selection. The Y-axis represents risk, whereas the X-axis represents the number of securities in the diagram. Likewise, the curved line represents unsystematic risk or specific risk or idiosyncratic risk, whereas the horizontal line parallel to the X-axis represents systematic risk or market risk. The systematic component of the risk remains constant throughout as it is not diversifiable. Now, carefully analyse the curved line. First security added to the portfolio has a standard deviation of 35%. Then the second security added to the portfolio and the overall standard deviation of the portfolio declined from 35 to 27%. Similarly, addition of the securities (from security number 3 to 15) into the portfolio further declined the overall portfolio standard deviations from 27 to 9%. In this particular instance, further addition of the securities (16,

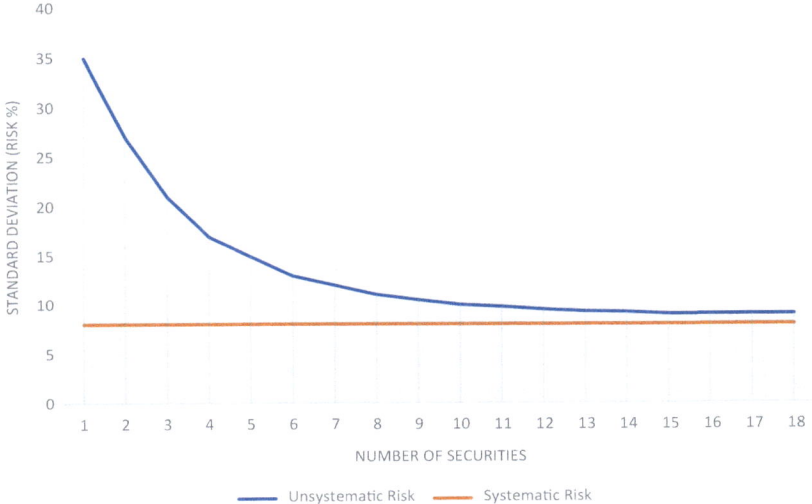

Fig. 4.1 Portfolio diversification

17, and 18) to the portfolio does not reduce the overall portfolio standard deviation. After addition of the fifteenth security into the portfolio, it reached the optimal level of portfolio diversification often referred as the fully diversified portfolio. Beyond it, further portfolio diversification is not possible. The vital question here is why so?

Consider this following example:

Suppose that 60% of your portfolio is invested in Security A and the rest is invested in Security B. You expect that over the coming year, Security 1 will give a return of 5% and Security 2, 9%. Also, in the past, the standard deviation of returns was 17% for Security 1 and 21% for Security 2. Based on these above information calculate the expected (a) portfolio return and (b) portfolio standard deviation (risk)?

For the foremost part of the task, it is easy to calculate the expected portfolio returns by taking the weighted average of the expected returns on the individual stocks as shown below:

$$E(R_p) = W_1 * R_1 + W_2 * R_2 + \ldots + W_n * R_n \tag{4.1}$$

where

W (1 to n) represents the individual security weights in the portfolio
R (1 to n) represents the individual security expected returns

Using the above notation (4.1) expected portfolio return $E(R_p)$ is

$$E(R_p) = 0.6 * 5 + 0.4 * 9 = 6.6\%$$

For the next part of the task, do you think that the expected portfolio standard deviation (risk) could be estimated by taking the weighted average of the expected standard deviation (risk) on the individual stocks as shown in Eq. 4.2?

$$E(\sigma_p) = W_1 * \sigma_1 + W_2 * \sigma_2 + \ldots + W_n * \sigma_n \qquad (4.2)$$

where

W (1 to n) represents the individual security weights in the portfolio
σ R (1 to n) represent individual security expected standard deviation (risk)

Using the above notation (4.2) expected portfolio standard deviation $E(\sigma_p)$ is

$$E(\sigma_p) = 0.6 * 17 + 0.4 * 21 = 18.6\%$$

The above representation (4.2) will yield correct estimates only if the two securities moved in perfect lockstep. The reason is that the resultant portfolio variance is due to combined effect of both the individual security variances and covariance between the securities. In general, below Eq. (4.3) shows the portfolio variance $E(\sigma_{1,2}^2)$ for the two securities:

$$E(\sigma_{1,2}^2) = W_1^2 * \sigma_1^2 + W_2^2 * \sigma_2^2 + 2 * \rho_{1,2} * W_1 * W_2 * \sigma_1 * \sigma_2 \quad (4.3)$$

where

W_i represents the weight of individual securities in portfolio
σ_i represents the standard deviation of individual securities.

σ_i^2 represents the variance of individual securities.

$\rho_{1,2}$ represents the correlation between security 1 and 2

$$\rho_{1,2} = \frac{Cov_{1,2}}{\sigma_1 \sigma_2}$$

The expected portfolio standard deviation $E(\sigma_p)$ could then easily be calculated by taking the square root of the portfolio variance $E(\sigma_{1,2}^2)$.

Recall the above example:

60% of your portfolio is invested in Security 1 and the rest is invested in Security 2. The past standard deviation of returns was 17% for Security 1 and 21% for Security 2.

Consider three scenario now as follows:

(a) If the two securities are perfectly positively correlated ($\rho_{1,2} = 1$)
(b) If the two securities do not move in perfect lockstep ($\rho_{1,2} = 0.23$)
(c) If the two securities are perfectly negatively correlated ($\rho_{1,2} = -0.1$)

Apply the variance formula (4.3) for the two securities and then estimate the expected portfolio standard deviation $E(\sigma_p)$ values.

Solutions:

(a) If the two securities are perfectly positively correlated ($\rho_{1,2} = 1$)

$$E(\sigma_{1,2}^2) = (0.6)^2 * (17)^2 + (0.4)^2 * (21)^2 + 2 * 1 * 0.6 * 0.4 * 17 * 21$$
$$E(\sigma_{1,2}^2) = 345.96$$
$$E(\sigma_p) = 18.6\%$$

(b) If the two securities do not move in perfect lockstep ($\rho_{1,2} = 0.23$)

$$E(\sigma_{1,2}^2) = (0.6)^2 * (17)^2 + (0.4)^2 * (21)^2 + 2 * 0.23 * 0.6 * 0.4 * 17 * 21$$
$$E(\sigma_{1,2}^2) = 214.01$$
$$E(\sigma_p) = 14.63\%$$

(c) If the two securities are perfectly negatively correlated ($\rho_{1,2} = -1$)

$$E(\sigma_{1,2}^2) = (0.6)^2 * (17)^2 + (0.4)^2 * (21)^2 + 2 * (-1) * 0.6 * 0.4 * 17 * 21$$
$$E(\sigma_{1,2}^2) = 3.24$$
$$E(\sigma_p) = 1.8\%$$

From the above estimates, it is clearly noticed that if the two stocks are perfectly positively correlated than Eqs. 4.2 and 4.3 will yield same estimates for the expected portfolio standard deviation $E(\sigma_p)$. Estimation of the expected portfolio return $E(R_p)$ is simple, and it could be easily valued by taking the weighted average of the expected returns on the individual stocks as shown in Eq. 4.1. Whereas estimation of the expected portfolio standard deviation $E(\sigma_p)$ is the challenging task. Covariance values between the securities play an important role in estimating the expected portfolio standard deviation $E(\sigma_p)$. Above estimates show that if the two stocks are perfectly correlated then the expected portfolio standard deviation $E(\sigma_p)$ is higher. While if the two securities are perfectly negatively correlated then the expected portfolio standard deviation $E(\sigma_p)$ is minimum.

How much more important the covariances become as we add more securities to the portfolio? Portfolio variance $E(\sigma_{1,2}{}^2)$ for the three securities can be estimated using the following equation:

$$E\left(\sigma_{1,2,3}{}^2\right) = W_1{}^2 * \sigma_1{}^2 + W_2{}^2 * \sigma_2{}^2 + W_3{}^2 * \sigma_3{}^2$$
$$+ 2 * \rho_{1,2} * W_1 * W_2 * \sigma_1 * \sigma_2 + 2 * \rho_{1,3} * W_1 * W_3 * \sigma_1 * \sigma_3$$
$$+ 2 * \rho_{2,3} * W_2 * W_3 * \sigma_2 * \sigma_3 \tag{4.4}$$

Similarly, portfolio variance $E(\sigma_{1,2,\ldots,n}{}^2)$ for the n securities can easily be estimated using this equation:

$$E\left(\sigma_{1,2,\ldots,n}{}^2\right) = W_1{}^2 * \sigma_1{}^2 + \ldots + W_n{}^2 * \sigma_n{}^2 + 2 * \rho_{1,2} * W_1 * W_2 * \sigma_1 * \sigma_2$$
$$+ \ldots + 2 * \rho_{n-1,n} * W_{n-1} * W_n * \sigma_{n-1} * \sigma_n \tag{4.5}$$

Above Eq. (4.5) represented with the help of a "n X n" matrix as shown in Table 4.1. Where n represents the n number of securities in the portfolio. In this n X n matrix, all the diagonal elements (dark cells) represent individual securities variances. Whereas white empty boxes represent all the covariances terms.

When there are just only two securities, there are equal numbers of variance and covariance terms. Addition of the third security into the portfolio increased the numbers of variance terms from 2 to 3, while the numbers of covariance terms increased from 2 to 6. Further accumulation of the number of securities into the portfolio increases the

Table 4.1 Variances and covariances matrix

	Security 1	Security 2	Security 3	...	...	...	Security n
Security 1	$W_1^2 * \sigma_1^2$						
Security 2		$W_2^2 * \sigma_2^2$					
Security 3			$W_3^2 * \sigma_3^2$				
...				...			
...					...		
...						...	
Security n							$W_n^2 * \sigma_n^2$

number of covariances terms much larger than the number of variances terms. Accordingly, the well-diversified portfolio standard deviation $E(\sigma_p)$ echoes primarily the covariances.

4.1.1 Mean-Variance Efficient Frontier

Mean-Variance efficient frontier provides mechanism for weighting the associated risk against the expected returns. Investors make their decisions based on the mean variance efficient frontier. Each point lying on the mean variance efficient frontier represents optimal expected investment return for the given level of risks.

Figure 4.2 represents mean variance efficient frontier. A, B, and C represents the three portfolios. Rank these three portfolios with respect to the mean variance efficient frontier definition.

From the above Fig. 4.2 it is observed that

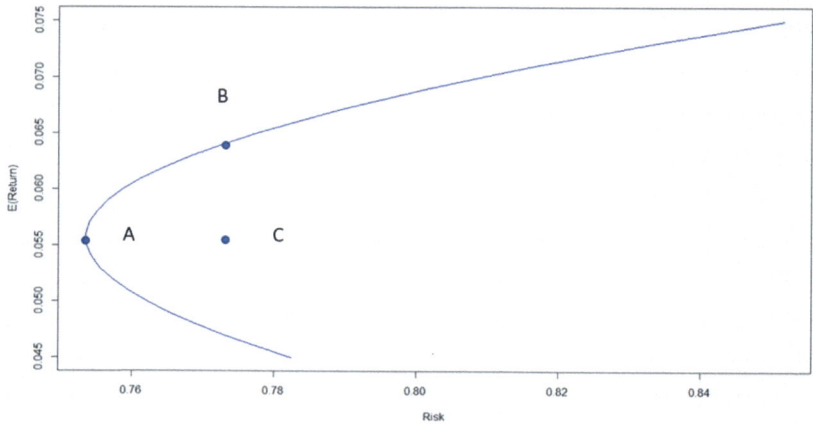

Fig. 4.2   Mean variance efficient frontier

Portfolio A:

- Lies in the mean variance efficient frontier
- Risk associated with portfolio A is lesser than Both Portfolio B and C
- Expected returns of Portfolio A is equal to Portfolio C but lower than Portfolio B

Portfolio B:

- Lies in the mean variance efficient frontier
- Risk associated with Portfolio B is equal to Portfolio C but higher than Portfolio A
- Expected returns of Portfolio B is higher than both Portfolio A and C

Portfolio C:

- Does not lie in the mean variance efficient frontier
- Risk associated with Portfolio C is higher than Portfolio A
- Expected returns of Portfolio C is equal to Portfolio A

Based on these above option, definitely Portfolio C is the worst with respect to the mean variance efficient frontier definition. For a given amount of risk, Portfolio C has expected returns much lower than the Portfolio B. Both the Portfolios A and B lie on the efficient frontier. Risk adverse investors would prefer Portfolio A over Portfolio B.

Multifactor Mean Variance Efficient Frontier
In case of the mean variance efficient frontier, investors care about the mean and variance. However, in the multifactor world, the investors care about the state variables innovation in addition to the mean and variance. The multifactor portfolio efficiency is often described with the Multifactor Mean Variance (MMV) efficient frontier (see Fama, 1996). The diagrammatic version of the Multifactor Mean Variance (MMV) efficient frontier is shown in Fig. 4.3 (see Cochrane, 1999). Now, the movement is not only limited to just up and down (as in case of the Mean–variance frontier). Rather, the movement is now all over the Multifactor Mean

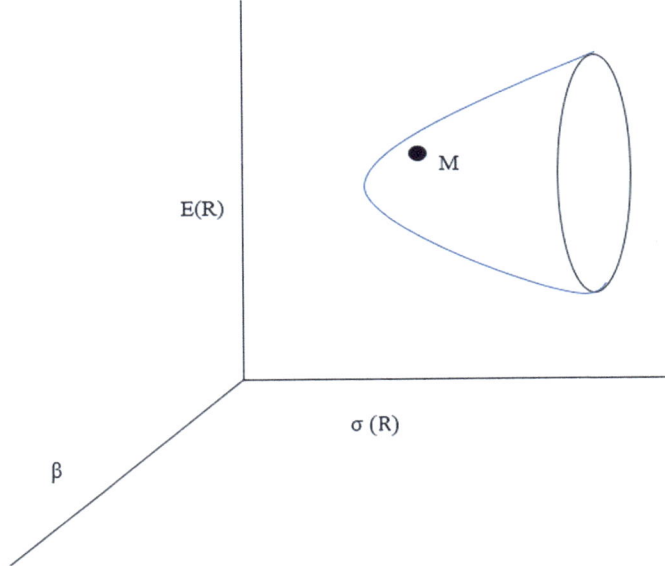

Fig. 4.3 Multifactor Mean Variance (MMV) efficient frontier

Variance (MMV) efficient frontier (Nose cone) as shown in Fig. 4.3. The market portfolio (M) will now remain anywhere in the MMV (nose cone as shown in Fig. 4.3) but not on the mean variance efficient frontier.

4.1.2   Portfolio Optimization

Portfolio Optimization is the process of selecting the best portfolio out of the set of all portfolios. Once the optimized portfolio is estimated. Next compute the selected optimized portfolio's expected return and risk. Finally, plot the mean variance efficient frontier.

Markowitz's modern portfolio theory becomes the basis for developing Sharpe (1964) theory of price formation for financial assets, well known as the capital asset pricing theory (CAPM).

4.1.3   Capital Market Line and Mean Variance Efficient Frontier

Likewise Mean Variance Efficient Frontier, the Capital Market Line (CML) is a graphical representation of all the portfolios that optimally combine risk and return. The basic different lies between the Mean Variance Efficient Frontier and Capital Market Line is that the Capital Market Line combines the risky assets with the non-risky assets.

In Fig. 4.4, the thin solid line represents the Capital Market Line. The Capital Market Line is the straight line drawn from the risk-free return rate (Y-axis) that cuts the Mean Variance Efficient Frontier (combinations of the risky assets) at the point M (represents optimal portfolio) as shown in Fig. 4.4. Hence, slope of the Capital Market Line represents Sharpe ratio of the market portfolio. Risk of the portfolio increases on moving up along the CML while portfolio risk decreases on moving down along the CML. The Capital Market Line is represented by the following equation.

$$E(P_r) = r_f + \left[\frac{r_m - r_f}{\sigma_m} \right] * \sigma_p \qquad (4.6)$$

where

$E(P_r)$ represents the expected portfolio returns
r_f is risk-free rate of return
r_m is market return
σ_m is the measure of standard deviation for market

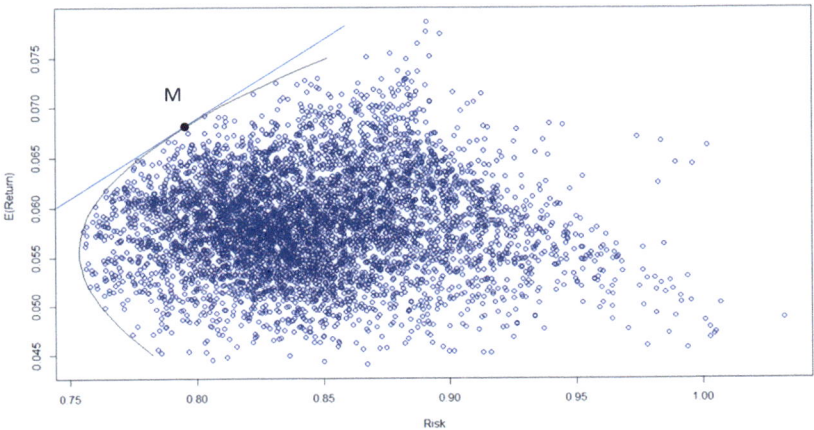

Fig. 4.4 Capital market line and mean variance efficient frontier

σ_p is the measure of standard deviation for portfolio

$\left[\frac{r_m - r_f}{\sigma_m}\right]$ is Sharpe ratio of the market portfolio

Likewise, there is Security Market Line (SML) that visually represents the Capital Asset Pricing Model (CAPM). The Security Market Line is represented by the following Eq. (4.7).

$$SML = r_f + [\beta * (r_m - r_f)] \tag{4.7}$$

The Security Market Line (SML) represents all the securities present in the market along with their corresponding β values as shown in Fig. 4.5.

The Security Market Line is often refereed by the market participants to decide whether an asset is priced correctly or not? According to the principle of Security Market Line, price of the asset labelled as A is overpriced while asset B is underpriced as shown in Fig. 4.5.

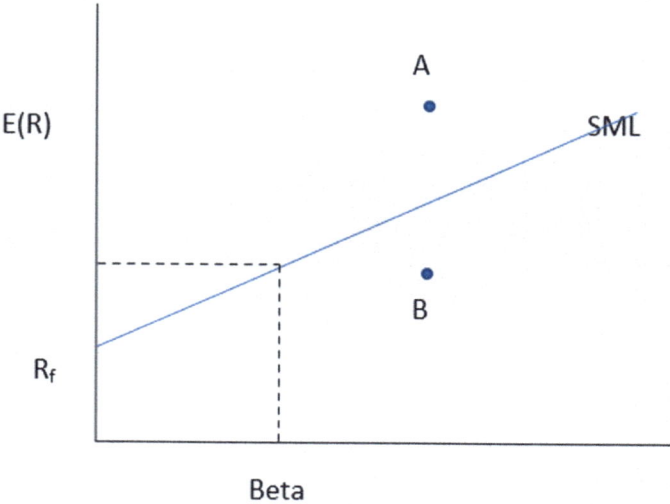

Fig. 4.5   Security market line

4.2   FINANCE IN ACTION

Illustration 1: *Illustration on Plotting an efficient frontier*
An investor follows the passive investment strategy and wants to invest in the following assets: FTSE, DAX, SMI, and CAC [Use: EuStockMarkets dataset].

(a) Stimulate and estimate the E(return) and risk for 5000 portfolios that could be constructed with varying the portfolio weights of the assets under consideration.
(b) Then plot the mean variance efficient frontier.

The above task can be easily implemented by executing the below codes with "tseries[1]" R package as shown below.

---

[1] https://cran.r-project.org/web/packages/tseries/tseries.

Code:
Codes for calculating returns (μ) and risk (σ).

```
library(tseries)
Data<-as.matrix(EuStockMarkets)
return<-diff(log(Data))*100
nportfolio<-5000
set.seed(10)
σ<-μ<-rep(NA,nportfolio)
for(k in 1:nportfolio){
weight <- sample(1:1200,4,replace=T)
weight <- weight/sum(weight)
rpreturn <- return%*%weight
μ[k] <- mean(rpreturn)
σ[k] <- sd(rpreturn)
}
plot(σ,μ,xlab = "Risk",ylab="E(Return)",col="blue")
```

#Codes for plotting the Mean Variance Efficient Frontier.

```
σ1<-cov(return)
expected_return<-seq(0.045,0.075,0.001)
efficient_frontier<-matrix(NA,nrow=length(expected_return),ncol=2)
for(j in 1:length(expected_return)){
   portfolio_optimization<-portfolio.optim(return,pm=expected_return[j],covmat=σ1)
   efficient_frontier[j,]<-c(portfolio_optimization$ps,portfolio_optimization$pm)
}
lines(efficient_frontier,col="black")
```

Output:

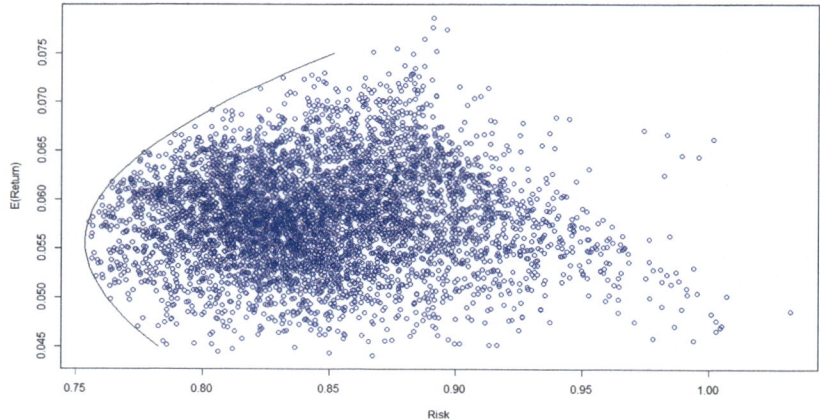

Fig. 4.6   Mean Variance Efficient Frontier and 5000 portfolios plot

Figure 4.6 shows estimates obtained from the R interface. The curve line represents the mean variance efficient frontier. Dots represent 5000 portfolios constructed by varying the portfolio weights of FTSE, DAX, SMI and CAC respectively.

Illustration 2: *Illustration on Portfolio Optimization*

Consider the same example: An investor follows the passive investment strategy and wants to invest in the following assets: FTSE, DAX, SMI and CAC [Use: EuStockMarkets dataset]. Investor's annualized expected return is 12.75% and current risk-free rate as 3.01%. Based on these information optimized the portfolio and then plots the efficient frontier.

The above task can be easily implemented by executing the below R codes as shown in Fig. 4.7:

Code:
#Codes *for Estimating the Optimized Portfolio Weights*

```
library(tseries)
Data<-as.matrix(EuStockMarkets)
return<-diff(log(Data))*100
er <- 12.75/252er <- 12.75/252
σ<-cov(return)
portfolio_optimization<-portfolio.optim(return,pm=er,covmat=σ,risk_free=3.01/252)
w<-portfolio_optimization$pw*100
names(w)<-colnames(EuStockMarkets)
w
```

```
      DAX       SMI       CAC      FTSE
 0.000000 19.143226  1.791415 79.065359
```

#Codes for estimating the optimized portfolio returns and risk.

portfolio_optimization$pm

Return: 0.05059524

portfolio_optimization$ps

Risk: 0.7604976

#Codes for Plotting the Mean Variance Efficient Frontier

```
expected_return<-seq(0.045,0.075,0.001)
efficient_frontier<-matrix(NA,nrow=length(expected_return),ncol=2)
for(j in 1:length(expected_return))
{portfolio_optimization<-portfolio.optim(return,pm=expected_return[j],covmat=σ,
risk_free =3.01/252)
efficient_frontier[j,]<-c(portfolio_optimization$ps,portfolio_optimization$pm)
}
plot(efficient_frontier,col="blue",type = "l",xlab="Risk",ylab = "E(Return)")
```

Output:

The above estimates show the details of portfolio optimizations and mean variance frontier.

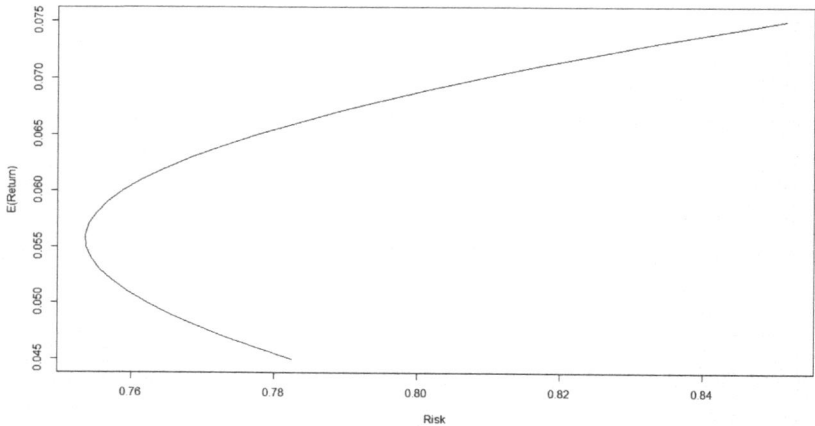

Fig. 4.7   Mean Variance Frontier

Summary

This chapter briefly introduced the topic efficient frontier and its implications. Discussion initiated with the three key arguments of Markowitz's modern portfolio theory. Basic assumptions of the Markowitz modern portfolio theory is discoursed. What is risk and uncertainty is discussed. Subsequently, detailed discussion is made on systematic and unsystematic risk with respect to the portfolio diversification. Next, expected return and risk calculations are illustrated with the suitable examples. How much more important the covariances terms become as we add more securities to the portfolio are covered in details. Mean variance efficient frontier is discussed in details with different investment option. The Central Market Line and Security Market Line are discussed in details. Stepwise implementations and estimation interpretations on plotting the mean variance efficient frontier and portfolio optimization are covered in details.

Analysts/Investors Corner

Risk can be divided into two parts, namely systematic risk and unsystematic risk. In case of an individual security, specific risk matters the more. Whereas for a reasonably well-diversified portfolio only market risk matters. The covariances terms become much more weighty as more number of the securities are added to the portfolio. Efficient frontiers are important for making investment decisions and portfolio optimization. The Security Market Line can be used to determine whether an asset is priced correctly?

4.3   EXERCISES

4.3.1   Multiple Choice Questions

1. Harry Markowitz introduced

    (a) Random walk
    (b) Modern Portfolio Theory
    (c) Two fund theorem
    (d) Advanced Portfolio Theory

2. Mean variance efficient frontier is associated with

    (a) Henry Markowitz
    (b) Harry Markowitz
    (c) William F. Sharpe
    (d) Eugene Fama

3. Market risk is an example of?

    (a) Specific risk
    (b) Systematic risk
    (c) Unsystematic risk
    (d) Idiosyncratic risk

4. For a well-diversified portfolio which of the following risk matters the most?

    (a) Specific risk

   (b) Unsystematic risk
   (c) Systematic risk
   (d) Idiosyncratic risk

5. Two securities are said to be perfectly correlated when

   (a) $\rho_{1,2} = 0$
   (b) $\rho_{1,2} = 1$
   (c) $\rho_{1,2} = -2$
   (d) $\rho_{1,2} = 2$

6. Portfolio overall risk is least when

   (a) Securities are perfectly positively correlated
   (b) Securities are perfectly negatively correlated
   (c) Securities are positively correlated
   (d) Securities are negatively correlated

7. Modern Portfolio Theory is based on

   (a) Mean and Variance
   (b) Mean and Covariance
   (c) Variance and Covariance
   (d) Skewness and Kurtosis

8. Risk can be measured by

   (a) Standard Deviation
   (b) Variance
   (c) Both a and b
   (d) None of these

9. Which of the following statement(s) is/are false with regard to the suboptimal portfolio?

   (a) Suboptimal portfolio lies below the efficient frontier
   (b) Suboptimal portfolio don't provide enough returns for their risk levels
   (c) Suboptimal portfolio provides much higher returns for their risk levels
   (d) Suboptimal portfolios and optimal portfolios are different

10. If a security added to the portfolio then market risk of the portfolio will

(a) Increase
(b) Decrease
(c) remains the same
(d) either increase or decrease

11. If a security added to the poorly diversified portfolio then specific risk of the portfolio will

(a) Increase
(b) Decrease
(c) remains the same
(d) either increase or decrease

12. If a security added to the well-diversified portfolio then specific risk of the portfolio will

(a) Increase
(b) Decrease
(c) remains the same
(d) ither increase or decrease

13. Through portfolio diversification one cannot reduce

(a) Market risk
(b) Specific risk
(c) Idiosyncratic risk
(d) Portfolio risk

14. Which of the following risk is not included in the Security Market Line

(a) Market risk
(b) Beta
(c) Idiosyncratic risk
(d) Systematic risk

15. If an asset price lies above the Security Market Line then

(a) asset is under priced
(b) asset is over priced
(c) asset is correctly priced
(d) asset is risk free

16. Which of the following is not a component of CML?

(a) Risk-free rate
(b) Market return
(c) Beta
(d) Standard Deviation

4.3.2   Fill in the Blanks

1. Risk can be categorized as the _____ & _____.
2. Standard deviation and variance are the measures for the _____.
3. _____ risk cannot be diversified.
4. Through portfolio diversification one cannot reduce _____ risk.
5. Through portfolio diversification _____ risk can be reduced.
6. Forex exchange risk is an example of the _____ risk.
7. Announce of stock split is an example of the _____ risk.
8. Mean–Variance efficient frontier represents the set of _____.
9. The _____ become much more significant as more number of the securities are added to the portfolio.
10. If a security added to the poorly diversified portfolio then specific risk of the portfolio will _____.
11. SML stands for _____.
12. If an asset price lies below the Security Market Line then asset is said to be _____ priced.
13. Security Market Line visually represents the _____.
14. $\left[\frac{r_m - r_f}{\sigma_m}\right]$ represents Sharpe ratio of the _____.

4.3.3   Long Answer Questions

1. Define modern portfolio theory with suitable examples?
2. Define mean variance efficient frontier with suitable examples?
3. What are the basic assumptions of modern portfolio theory and its implications?
4. How efficient frontier and the process of portfolio optimization is related. Explain it by taking suitable examples.

5. What is risk, randomness and uncertainty? How they are different explain it with suitable examples.
6. Elaborate the following statement: "Through the process of diversification overall portfolio risk could be reduced".
7. Explain the process of portfolio diversification with suitable example?
8. Explain the multifactor portfolio efficiency with respect to the MMV?
9. Comment on the statement "Are markets really efficient during COVID 19 pandemic" with suitable examples.
10. Can portfolio weights be negative? What does it implies?
11. Derive the expression for estimating the variance of a three securities portfolio.
12. Why Mean Variance Efficient Frontier shape is a curved line?
13. Why CML is not a curved line?
14. Explain the key differences between the CML and SML?
15. If a stock does not lie on the Security Market Line then what is its implications?

4.3.4 Real-World Tasks

1. A senior lecturer asked his/her student to plot the mean variance efficient frontier using any two funds that are traded in FTSE during 2010 and 2019. Assume yourself as the student and perform the task. Then prepare a detailed report of the analysis to be submitted to the senior lecturer.
2. A researcher wants to create a portfolio with the top seven cryptocurrencies that consider option for the short selling and expected return of 22.75% annually. He is interested in estimating the optimized portfolio weights for the assets under consideration. Assume yourself as the researcher: perform the mentioned task in details and develop the analysis report.
3. An investment analyst is currently evaluating an investment option to invest in the currency basket of the top six currencies that are traded globally. He/she wants to stimulate and estimate the expected return and risk for 10,000 portfolios that could be constructed with varying the portfolio weights of the six currencies.

Finally to plot the mean variance efficient frontier. Help him/her to perform the said analysis and prepare the report.

4. A scholar needs to test the modern portfolio theory's key arguments taking reference from the precious metals that are traded in the BSE index. Help the scholar to complete his/her project dissertation successfully and satisfactorily.

5. An Assistant manager of the Reserve bank of India (RBI) asked an intern working under him/her to prepare a detailed report on "why modern portfolio theory is still relevant in wealth management"? Help the intern in developing the final report for timely submission to the Assistant manager of RBI.

4.3.5   Case Studies

1. An investor banker wants to rank three credit portfolios based on the risk-reward trade-off. The information of these three portfolios are listed below. Based on the provided information rank these credit portfolios in ascending order.

Portfolio	Expected Return (%)	Standard Deviation (%)
X	11	8
Y	12	11
Z	14	10

2. 45% of your portfolio is invested in Security X and the rest is invested in Security Y. The past standard deviation of returns was 27% for Security X and 16% for Security Y.

Consider three scenario as follows:

(a) If the two securities are perfectly positively correlated ($\rho_{1,2} = 1$)
(b) If the two securities do not move in perfect lockstep ($\rho_{1,2} = 0.34$)
(c) If the two securities are perfectly negatively correlated ($\rho_{1,2} = -0.1$)

Calculate the portfolio standard deviation in each case and also comment on its implications with respect to the portfolio diversification.

3. 3. 70% of your portfolio is invested in Security A and the rest is invested in Security B. You expect that over the coming year, Security A will give a return of 6% and Security B, 10%. The past standard deviation of returns was 14% for Security X and 23% for Security Y. Calculate the portfolio expected return and standard deviation.
4. Comment on the quoted statement validity with supportive data analysis. *"Modern Portfolio Theory and Efficient Market Hypothesis does not contradict to each other."*
5. An investment banker is currently evaluating an investment option to invest in the portfolio consisting of the following: crude oil, gold, and silver. He/she wants to stimulate and estimate the expected return and risk for 20000 portfolios that could be constructed with varying the portfolio weights of the crude oil, gold, and silver. Then to plot the mean variance efficient frontier and CML to obtain the optimal portfolio. Assume the current risk-free rate of return as 2.5%. Help him/her to perform the said analysis and prepare the report.

REFERENCES

Cochrane, J. H. (1999). *Portfolio advice for a multifactor world* (No. w7170). National Bureau of Economic Research.

Fama, E. F. (1996). Multifactor portfolio efficiency and multifactor asset pricing. *The Journal of Financial and Quantitative Analysis, 31*(4), 441. https://doi.org/10.2307/2331355

Markowitz, H. M. (1952, March). Portfolio selection. *Journal of Finance, 7*, 77–91.

Sharpe, W. F. (1964). Capital asset prices: A theory of market equilibrium under conditions of risk. *The Journal of Finance, 19*(3), 425–442.

CHAPTER 5

Introduction to Asset Pricing Factor Models

Key Topics Covered

- *What is asset pricing*
- *CAPM and its implications*
- *Rising of multifactor asset pricing model*
- *ICAPM and APT*
- *Fama and French risk mimicking portfolio construction*
- *Notable multifactor asset pricing models*
- *Illustration on the implementation and testing of various asset pricing models*
- *Illustration on the panel regressions*

5.1 BACKGROUND

Asset pricing studies deal with the pricing of assets where assets can be debts, equity, bonds, derivatives, and others. In general, asset prices follow the law of demand and supply. The asset pricing studies have basically two schools of thought, namely theoretical and empirical. The former deals with the theoretical aspects of asset prices, whereas empirical asset pricing deals more with the quantitative characteristics. Empirical asset pricing deals with the real market data resulting more preferred by

M. Maiti, *Applied Financial Econometrics*,
https://doi.org/10.1007/978-981-16-4063-6_5

the market participants. Pricing of the debt instruments is considered to be much easier as compared to the equity pricing. Presence of various risk factors and uncertainty make asset pricing quite a challenging task. Markowitz (1952) modern portfolio theory laid the theoretical foundation for analysing the risk and return relationship. Thereafter Sharpe (1964) developed a single factor asset pricing model often referred as the capital asset pricing model (CAPM). According to the CAPM, cross section of the asset returns depends only on the cross section of the asset βs. Since then over 300 different risk factors have been identified by the various studies, resulting in several multifactor asset pricing models developing since the development of CAPM. Maiti (2020a) highlighted that the evolution process of risk factors and factor models seems to be an endless development. Several risk factors that drive the asset prices are continuously changing and evolving over time. In addition to that still numerous risk factors are yet to be identified. All of these safe bets jointly make asset pricing a topic of somewhat more than that of the class room coaching.

The capital asset pricing model (CAPM) is the primary successful formal model of market equilibrium. CAPM fundamentally describes the relationship between the expected returns and systematic risk for financial assets. Similarly, the consumption-based capital asset pricing model (CCAPM) uses consumption beta instead of the market beta. The capital asset pricing model (CAPM) is represented by the below Eq. 5.1:

$$E(r_i) = r_f + \beta * (r_m - r_f) \tag{5.1}$$

where

$E(r_i)$ represent expected return of the assets
r_f is risk free rate of return
r_m is market return
β measures return volatility

The capital asset pricing model (CAPM) has the following assumptions:

1. Investors are rational and risk adverse
2. Market is efficient
3. Investors prefer higher returns over lower returns for a given level of risk

4. Investors make decision based on risk and returns
5. There is no taxes and cost of trading
6. Borrowing and lending take place at risk free rate
7. Investors have constant investment time horizon and homogeneous expectation

CAPM was quite a successful asset pricing model for a longer period of time, though it is heavily criticized on several grounds as listed below.

- Condition of high volatility of market returns
- Taxation effects
- Rise of several security market labelled anomalies
- Cross correlational issues
- Data snooping bias

Strong disagreement against the CAPM is that a single factor model does not fit the data well. Hence, there arises demand for the CAPM substitutes with increasing power of the model in predicting risk and return variations. Merton (1973) introduced the extension of the CAPM well known as the Intertemporal Capital Asset Pricing Model (ICAPM). The ICAPM offers additional precision over the previous models by considering the time horizons. "Intertemporal" in the ICAPM signifies investment time horizons. The Intertemporal Capital Asset Pricing Model (ICAPM) is an extension of the CAPM with additional factor as a portfolio to hedge the state variable as shown in Eq. 5.2.

$$E(r_i) = r_f + \beta_{im} * (r_m - r_f) + \beta_{ih} * (r_h - r_f) \qquad (5.2)$$

where

$E(r_i)$ represent expected return of the assets
r_f is risk free rate of return
r_m is market return
r_h is hedge portfolio return
β_i measures return volatility of each factors

The ICAPM has several important practical applications. Let's take an example to understand the ICAPM in detail. An Asian-based company purchases machine parts from a German company, and in the meantime,

EURO weakens relative to the Asian currency. Due to the appreciation of the Asian currency, the costs of purchases reduced and had a direct impact into the company's overall profitability. The ICAPM gives market participants to consider foreign currency risk premium (portfolio to hedge the state variable) as an additional factor while estimating the investments expected returns.

Then notably Ross (1976) Arbitrage Pricing Theory (APT) multifactor asset pricing model progressed as the another CAPM substitutes. Macroeconomic variables represent multifactor in the Arbitrage Pricing Theory (APT) multifactor asset pricing model. The Arbitrage Pricing Theory (APT) multifactor asset pricing model is much flexible and complex as compared to the CAPM. The APT model of asset pricing measures the expected returns of assets as a linear function of different macroeconomic factors.

Mathematically, the Arbitrage Pricing Theory (APT) multifactor asset pricing model is represented by following Eq. 5.3.

$$E(r_i) = r_f + \beta_1 Rp_1 + \beta_2 Rp_2 + \cdots + \beta_n Rp_n \tag{5.3}$$

where

$E(r_i)$ represent expected return of the assets

r_f is risk free rate of return

Rp_i represents risk premiums associated with the each macroeconomic variables

β_i measures return volatility of each macroeconomic variables

The Arbitrage Pricing Theory (APT) multifactor asset pricing model is often referred to in the literature of asset pricing studies. Due to its innovative idea of estimating the assets expected returns as a linear function of different factors. Even though the Arbitrage Pricing Theory (APT) multifactor asset pricing model is more flexible than the CAPM yet it failed to clear many empirical assessments. Since 1980 different stock market anomalies have begun to emerge that further challenges asset pricing. Both of these ICAPM and APT multifactor models allow the researchers to choose different risk factors from a wide range of possibilities. However, Fama (1991) warns against using them just as a "fishing license". Largely three techniques are used, namely statistical methods, macroeconomic variables, and firm specific fundamental variables for selecting different risk factors from a wide range of possibilities.

Fama and French (1993) developed three factor asset pricing model expanding the Merton's ICAPM equation as shown in Eq. 5.4.

$$E(r_i) = r_f + \beta_{irm} * (r_m - r_f) + \beta_{ismb} * (\text{SMB}) + \beta_{ihml} * (\text{HML}) + \varepsilon_i$$
(5.4)

where

$E(r_i)$ represent expected return of the assets
r_f is risk free rate of return
β_i represents different factors coefficients
SMB represents size premium
HML represents value premium
ε_i error terms.

5.1.1   What Is So Special About Fama and French (1993) Three Factor Asset Pricing Model?

Fama and French estimated risk factors using the mimicking portfolio approach. The risk factors are estimated directly from the cross-sectional asset returns sorted by the firm characteristics. Fama and French constructed their mimicking portfolios by using the single and double sorting techniques as shown in Table 5.1. Fama and French ranked the sample stocks every year in the month of June based on their market capitalization (MC) and formed two portfolios, namely Big(B) and Small(S) using the NYSE median market cap breakpoint. Similarly,

Table 5.1 Fama and French portfolio construction techniques

Single sorting		Double sorting
MC (2 Portfolios)	BE/ME (3 Portfolios)	6 Portfolios (2 MC & 3 BE/ME portfolios)
Big(B) Small(S)	High(H) Neutral(M)	S/L; S/M; S/H; B/L; B/M; and B/H
	Low(L)	

three BE/ME weighted portfolios, namely High(H), Neutral(M), and Low(L), are constructed using the 30:40:30 breakpoint. Then using the double sorting technique six portfolios are formed, namely S/L, S/M, S/H, B/L, B/M, and B/H. Portfolio (S/L) consists of the small MC stocks and low value BE/ME stocks, whereas (B/H) consists of the big MC stocks and high value BE/ME stocks. The revision of portfolio formation is done every next year, and this process of portfolio revision continues till the end year.

SMB stands for the "small minus big" and represents risk mimicking portfolio for the size factor. Similarly, HML represents risk mimicking portfolio for the value factor. SMB and HML risk mimicking portfolios are estimated using the Eqs. 5.5 and 5.6.

$$SMB = (S/L + S/M + S/H)/3 - (B/L + B/M + B/H)/3 \qquad (5.5)$$

$$HML = (S/H + B/H)/2 - (S/L + B/L)/2 \qquad (5.6)$$

Subsequently, other notable multifactor asset pricing models that developed are shown below in equation numbers from 5.7 to 5.9:

Carhart (1997) *four factor model (additional factor added is Momentum)*

$$E(r_i) = r_f + \beta_{im} * (r_m - r_f) + \beta_{ismb} * (\text{SMB})$$
$$+ \beta_{ihml} * (\text{HML}) + \beta_{iwml} * (\text{WML}) + \varepsilon_i \qquad (5.7)$$

where WML is the Momentum factor

Fama and French (2015) *five factor model (additional factor added are investment and profitability)*

$$E(r_i) = r_f + \beta_{im} * (r_m - r_f) + \beta_{ismb} * (\text{SMB}) + \beta_{ihml} * (\text{HML})$$
$$+ \beta_{icma} * (\text{CMA}) + \beta_{irmw} * (\text{RMW}) + \varepsilon_i \qquad (5.8)$$

where CMA and RMW are the investment and profitability factors

$$CMA = (S/C + B/C)/2 - (S/A + B/A)/2 \qquad (5.8a)$$

$$RMW = (S/R + B/R)/2 - (S/W + B/W)/2 \qquad (5.8b)$$

Maiti and Balakrishnan (2018) *six factor model (additional factor added is Human Capital)*

$$E(r_i) = r_f + \beta_{im} * (r_m - r_f) + \beta_{ismb} * (\text{SMB}) + \beta_{ihml} * (\text{HML})$$
$$+ \beta_{icma} * (\text{CMA}) + \beta_{irmw} * (\text{RMW}) + \beta_{hc} * (HC) + \varepsilon_i \quad (5.9)$$

where HC is the Human Capital factor

Recall Maiti (2020a) detailed that the evolution process of risk factors and factor models seems to be an endless development. These multifactor models mentioned above ultimately do not put an end to the asset pricing study discussion.

Thus, upcoming era will witness more advanced multifactor asset pricing models.

5.1.2   Econometrics of Linear Factor Pricing Models

All of the above asset pricing models that are discussed can be easily implemented by linear regressions.

Any linear asset pricing model is defined by below Eq. 5.10 looks like as shown below.

$$E(r_i) = \alpha_i + \beta_{i,a}\lambda_a + \beta_{i,b}\lambda_b + \cdots + \beta_{i,n}\lambda_n \quad (5.10)$$

The above equation specifies that the expected returns should be high when (β) betas are high, where λ represents the slope and α represents the modelling error. Graphically above model can be represented as shown in Fig. 5.1.

Econometrics tasks are to estimate the free parameters $(\lambda, \beta, \text{and } \alpha)$, standard errors, and finally to test whether the joint alphas values are equal to zero. But in practice all sorts of other informal assessments also looked into while examining the asset pricing models. The informal assessments list includes the following:

- Is Security Market Line (SML) too flat?
- Beta versus characteristics: Small firms yield higher expected returns due to their characteristics or betas are high?
- How one model performs relative to another asset pricing model?
- Others

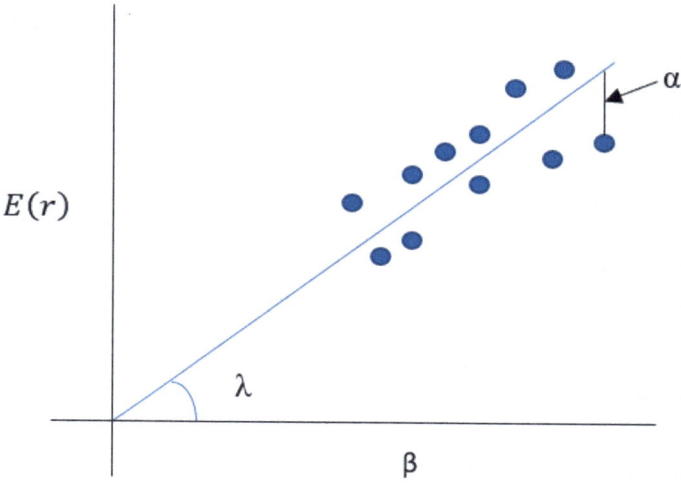

Fig. 5.1 Graphical representation of the linear asset pricing model

The above Eq. 5.10 can be represented in terms of the linear regressions arrangement as shown in the Eq. 5.11.

$$R_{i,t} = \alpha_i + \beta_{i,a}\lambda_{a,t} + \beta_{i,b}\lambda_{b,t} + \cdots + \beta_{i,n}\lambda_{n,t} + \varepsilon_{i,t} \qquad (5.11)$$

Thus, the Fama and French (1993) three factor regression equation can be represented as Eq. 5.12.

$$R_{i,t} = \alpha_i + \beta_{i,rm}\lambda_{rm,t} + \beta_{i,smb}\lambda_{smb,t} + \beta_{i,hml}\lambda_{hml,t} + \varepsilon_{i,t} \qquad (5.12)$$

The risk factors (rm, smb, and hml) here are the excess returns. As a consequence, the price of the risk (λ) is the mean of the factor. The important point here to understand is that the implied cross-sectional relationship of how the expected returns $E(r)$ line up with the βetas as shown in Fig. 5.2. The slope of this line is estimated by making it run through the risk free rate of return and factor expected returns $\lambda = E_t(\widehat{\text{Factor}})$ identically. Accordingly, the intercept of the time series regression becomes the implied errors of the cross-sectional relationship.

From the econometrics point of view next is to estimate the free parameters (λ, β, and α), standard errors (ε), and finally to test whether the joint alphas values are equal to zero. Fama and French used the GRS test (see

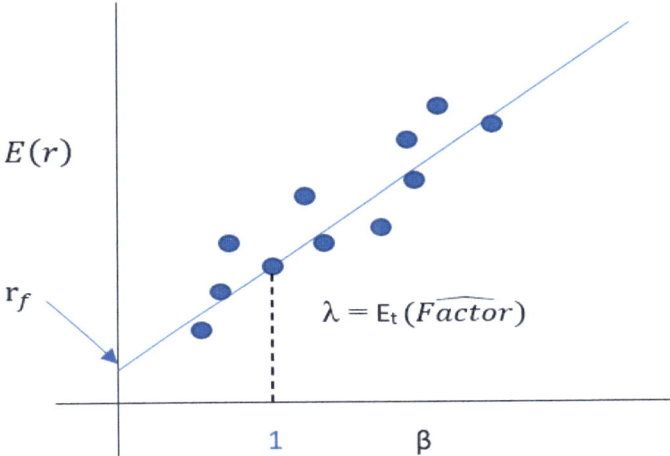

Fig. 5.2 Graphical representation of the implied cross-sectional relationship

Gibbons et al., 1989) to test whether the joint alphas values are equal to zero. GRS or the joint alphas equal to zero test is a bit tricky. So, it is important to understand how the GRS test works.

GRS Test

The GRS test (see Gibbons et al., 1989) is often used to check the performance of the asset pricing models (See Balakrishnan & Maiti, 2017; Fama and & French, 1993, 2015; Maiti, 2018, 2019, 2020b; Maiti & Balakrishnan, 2018, 2020; Maiti & Vuković 2020& others). The multifactor ICAPM model can be represented by the following Eq. 5.13.

$$R_{i,t} = \alpha_i + \sum_{f=1}^{K} \beta_{i,f} (\text{Factor})_{f,t} + \varepsilon_{i,t} \qquad (5.13)$$

where

$$I = 1,2,3,\ldots,N \text{ and } t = 1,2,3,\ldots,T$$

Then the empirical implications of the ICAPM are as follows. $K-1$ represents the number of the priced state variables. In a system with S state variables if each factor portfolio is multifactor minimal variance, then $\alpha_i = 0 \, for \, all \, i$, and the minimal variance boundary is crossed by a linear combination of factor portfolios. The above statements can be tested statistically using the GRS test. The GRS examines whether the joint alphas value equal to zero that is $\alpha_i = 0 \, for \, all \, i$.

Empirically GRS test F statistics can be calculated by using the following Eq. 5.14.

$$\left(\frac{T}{N}\right)\left(\frac{T-N-K}{T-K-1}\right)\left[\frac{\alpha' \sum^{-1} \alpha}{1 + \mu'\Omega^{-1}\mu}\right] \sim F(N, T-N-K) \qquad (5.14)$$

where

T sample size
N number of assets/portfolios returns
K number of risk factors
α is a $N \times 1$ vector of the estimated intercepts
Σ is residual covariance matrix
μ is a $K \times 1$ vector of the factor portfolios' sample means
Ω is the factor portfolios covariance matrix
$\alpha' \sum^{-1} \alpha$ and $\mu'\Omega^{-1}\mu$ are scalar terms.

Thus if calculated value of the GRS F statistics is zero then $\alpha_i = 0 \, for \, all \, i$. Likewise if calculated value of the GRS F statistics is more, then the alpha values are greater than zero.

5.1.3   How to Test One Model Versus the Other

Testing one model versus the other model is vital in asset pricing studies. All of the available notable asset pricing models are not absolutely accurate. It is also true that if there is not enough data then any asset pricing model can be easily rejected by the standard tests. Every so often it is tacit that in the data which model is the better model than some other model? To do so numerous statistical inferences are used.

Let's consider the Fama and French five factor model as shown in Eq. 5.8.

$$E(r_i) = r_f + \beta_{im} * (r_m - r_f) + \beta_{ismb} * (\text{SMB}) + \beta_{ihml} * (\text{HML})$$
$$+ \beta_{icma} * (\text{CMA}) + \beta_{irmw} * (\text{RMW}) + \varepsilon_i$$

Can a factor be dropped from the above model?

For instance, consider the HML factor dropped from the above model. How to respond to such critical problems? Very often such critical problems are responded to or approached wrongly as conversed below.

Can a factor (HML) be dropped from the above model just by looking into the obtained time series regressions t-statistics or p-values of the factor coefficients?

The answer is no as the statistical inference certainly provides measure on whether the coefficients (βetas) are significant or not. In general, it does not provide any measures on whether the factor (HML) should be dropped or deleted from the model or not. Thus, the valid question here is whether dropping or deletion of the factor (HML) from the model significantly changes the (α) alpha values or not.

Can R-squared values provide adequate measure on whether a factor (HML) can be dropped from the model?

Similarly R-squared values provide measures on whether the model is a good model of variance. But it does not provide measures on whether dropping or deletion of the factor (HML) from the model noticeably reduced R-squared values as the model of mean.

Compare the model with the factor (HML) and without the factor (HML). Then check for if the combined (α) alpha values is equal to zero $(\alpha' \sum^{-1} \alpha)$.

This statistical test only tests if the model is true or not. But it does not test if one model is better than the other model. To examine it appropriately if one model is better than the other model, proper comparison of the Chi-square tests must be done. Accordingly check if the Chi-square value increases on dropping or deletion of the factor (HML) using the same residual covariance (Σ) matrix.

5.1.4   Panel Regression

In this section, panel regression is covered in detail. The panel regressions use longitudinal data. Thus the panel data consists of both the cross section and time series characteristics. As a result of which panel data has certain advantages over the time series and cross-sectional data as mentioned below.

- Panel data can deal with the heterogeneity issues related to the cross-sectional units.
- Panel data are enhanced quality data.
- Panel data allow to examine more complex models

For instance, panel data can be used to examine the reason behind the country-wise variations in banks net profits (NP) due to non-interest (NI) and interest incomes (INTI) of the banks. The above problem can be mathematically represented as shown in the Eq. 5.15.

$$NP_{i,t} = \alpha + \beta_1 NI_{i,t} + \beta_2 INTI_{n,t} + \varepsilon_{i,t} \tag{5.15}$$

where

$$I = 1,2,3,...,N \text{ and} t = 1,2,3,...,T$$

In the above Eq. 5.15, the subscript i captures the cross-sectional aspects whereas t captures the time series aspects of the data. Next task is to choose the correct panel data model.

Panel Data Models

There are three different types of the panel data models namely:

- Constant coefficients model (CCM)
- Fixed effects model
- Random effects model

The above three models differ in terms of the assumptions made for the intercept, slope coefficients, and error terms of the panel data model. All of these three different types of the panel data models are discussed below in detail.

Constant Coefficients Model (CCM)

The constant coefficients model is the basic and simple among all the panel data models. The constant coefficients model assumes that all the coefficients (intercepts and slopes) are constant across all the cross-sectional units over time. The CCM assumes homogeneity or pooling and applies ordinary least square (OLS) methods to the panel data in estimating the unknown parameters of the model. Thus the CCM is very straightforward in terms of application. However, the assumption of homogeneity or pooling is itself a limitation of the constant coefficients model. Because in real world different cross-sectional units do have varying coefficients for the intercepts and slopes over time. Referring to the above model as shown in Eq. 5.15, apart from the non-interest (NI) and interest incomes (INTI) factors, banks net profits (NP) may be affected due to the several other factors. Then each country has separate banking rules and regulations. Also the bank's net profit function may change over a time due to government policies. Thus ignoring the cross-sectional (country) differences and estimating a single net profits equation with pooled or panel data is likely to provide incorrect estimates. One may argue that the error terms ($\varepsilon_{i,t}$) of the model capture the effect of such omitted variables. But again some of those error terms are likely to be correlated with the explanatory variables of the model. And such condition results in inconsistent and biased estimates for the unknown parameters of the model. However, such problem can be avoided by picking the fixed effects or random effects panel models.

To understand the basic mechanism of the CCM, consider the Eq. 5.16. Let us assume that the relationship between the banks net profits (NP) and non-interest (NI) is same for all banks. The CCM model assumes that the (α) alpha and (β) beta values are constant for all banks. Usually (α) alpha values are different for the different banks.

$$NP_{i,t} = \alpha + \beta NI_{i,t} + \varepsilon_{i,t} \tag{5.16}$$

For instance, consider the two scenarios that could arise as shown in Figs. 5.3 and 5.4.

Scenario 1:

Running different regressions yields different scatter plots diagram for all banks as shown in Fig. 5.3. The diagram shows that the intercepts values are different for different banks. Thus ignoring this element and estimating a single net profit function using pooled data will yield incorrect estimates.

Scenario 2:

In the above "Scenario 1", the estimated regression slope coefficients (βetas) are positive and indicate that there exists a positive relationship

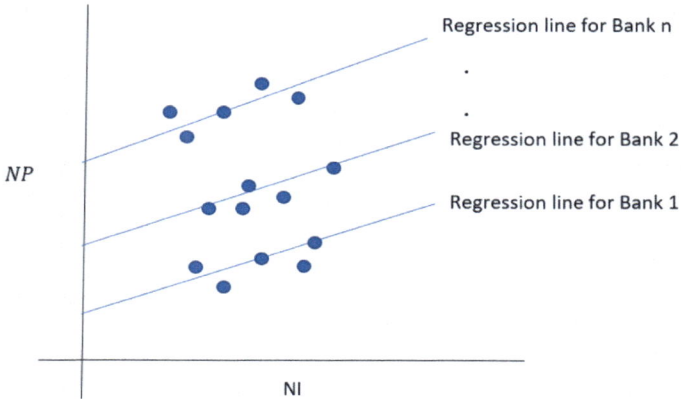

Fig. 5.3 Scenario 1 scatter plots of the data

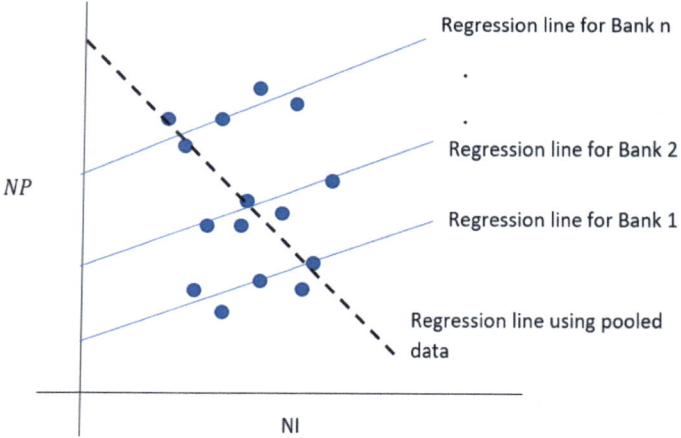

Fig. 5.4 Scenario 2 scatter plots of the data

between the banks net profits (NP) and non-interest (NI). Running a regression with the pooled data yields a dotted line as shown in Fig. 5.4. The regression line using the pooled data not only displays a different intercept but the slope coefficient (βeta) also changes to negative. Similar condition like "Scenario 2" would lead into more serious problems as compared to the "Scenario 1".

The above two scenarios clearly indicate that ignoring the cross-sectional variances and estimating a single equation with the pooled or panel data is likely to provide incorrect estimates. Thus the heterogeneity characteristics of the cross-sectional units should not be ignored while dealing with the panel or pooled data. Next sections discuss on how the fixed effects and random effects model deal with the problem of heterogeneity in detail.

Fixed Effects Model

To understand the basic mechanism of the fixed effects model, rewrite the Eq. 5.16 in terms of the fixed effects model as shown in Eq. 5.17.

$$\text{NP}_{i,t} = \alpha_i + \beta \text{NI}_{i,t} + \varepsilon_{i,t} \tag{5.17}$$

The fixed effects model accommodates the issue of heterogeneity by considering the intercept as a variable as shown in Eq. 5.17. For n number of the cross sections include n number of the dummy variables in the fixed effects model as shown in Eq. 5.18.

$$\begin{aligned} \text{NP}_{i,t} = {} & \alpha_1 \text{Dummy}_{1,t} + \alpha_2 \text{Dummy}_{2,t} + \cdots + \alpha_n \text{Dummy}_{n,t} \\ & + \beta \text{NI}_{i,t} + \varepsilon_{i,t} \end{aligned} \tag{5.18}$$

For the first cross-sectional unit the value of the *Dummy*$_{1,t}$ is one and zero for all other dummies. Similarly for the nth cross-sectional unit the value of the *Dummy*$_{n,t}$ is one and zero for all other dummies. α_1 is the intercept of the first cross-sectional unit while α_n represents coefficient for the nth cross-sectional unit. Both the above Eqs. (5.17 & 5.18) represent the fixed effects model and consider the heterogeneity features of the cross-sectional units. The fixed effects model can be implemented using the ordinary least squares (OLS) method. There could be one-way and two-way fixed effects models. The one-way fixed effects model allows only the intercept to change among the cross-sectional units while two-way fixed effects model considers both the cross section and period effects specification. There are few limitations associated with the fixed effects model as listed below.

- Working with the multiple dummy variables may cause the multicollinearity problem.
- The error terms $\varepsilon_{i,t}$ likely to have issues related to the autocorrelation and heteroscedastic.

Random Effects Model
The random effects model accommodates the issue of heterogeneity by considering the intercept as a stochastic variable with a mean value of α_1. The intercept value of the ith cross-sectional unit is represented by the following.

$$\alpha_i = \alpha_1 + u_i$$

Thus the random effects model can be represented mathematically by the following Eq. 5.19.

$$NP_{i,t} = (\alpha_1 + u_i) + \beta NI_{i,t} + \varepsilon_{i,t} \tag{5.19}$$

Hausman Test
Selection between the fixed effects and random effects panel models is grounded on the Hausman test estimates. The null hypothesis of the Hausman test assumes that the random effects are consistent and efficient. Based on the Hausen test *Chi*-square statistics and p value estimates decisions are made.

5.2   Finance in Action

5.2.1   *Illustration on Implementation of the Asset Pricing Models*

To examine the CAPM and Fama–French three factor models in Indian context. Based on the obtained regression estimates comment on these two models.

Data Description:
BSE 500 companies are used to construct the study portfolios based on the size and value factors by means of the Fama–French (1993) technique. For risk free rate 91 days T-bills returns are used. BSE-200 index mean excess returns used as proxy for the market. The study period is between July 2000 and June 2014. All data points are in monthly frequency.
    Regression models used are as follows:

CAPM & Fama–French Three Factor Model

$$E(r_i) - r_f = \alpha_i + \beta_{im} * \left(r_m - r_f\right) + \varepsilon_i$$

$$E(r_i) - r_f = \alpha_i + \beta_{im} * \left(r_m - r_f\right) + \beta_{is} * (\text{Size}) + \beta_{iv} * (\text{Value}) + \varepsilon_i$$

EViews stepwise implementations

Above regression models can be executed easily in EViews by following the below steps.

Step 1: Import data into the EViews Workfile window.
Step 2: Then click on Quick → Estimate Equation → The Equation Estimation window will appear as shown in Fig. 5.5.

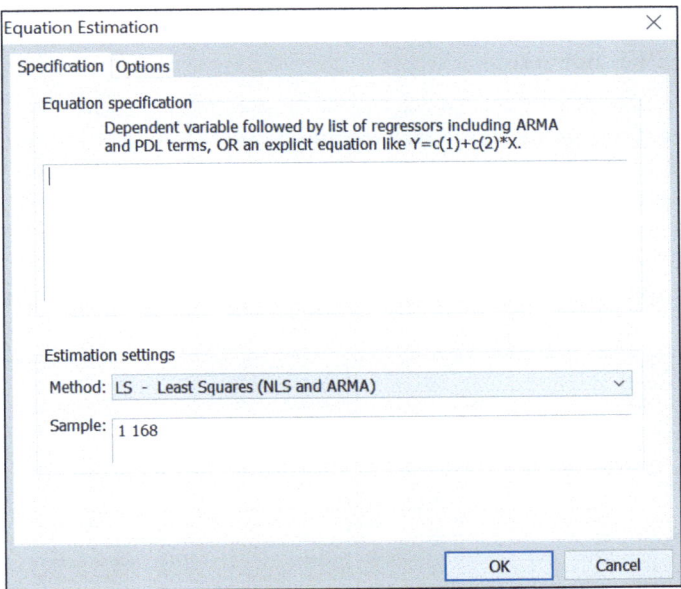

Fig. 5.5 Regression Equation Estimation window

Step 3: Under the equation specification space write dependable variable followed by list of regressors as shown below. Hence, dependable variables are portfolios P1 to P25. Whereas regressors are the risk factors (market, size, and value) and c is the regression intercept.

CAPM: P1 c Rm.

Fama–French three factor model: P1 c Rm Size Value.
    Choose Methods as Least Square (from the drop down list).
    Then click OK button. Regression estimates will appear as shown in Figs. 5.6 and 5.7.
    P1 labelled portfolio consists of all the stocks that have small size and low values. Whereas P25 consists of all the stocks that have big size and high values. CAPM regression estimates show that market factor is statistically significant at 5% level for both the portfolios P1 and P25. R-squared values for P1 and P25 are 0.30 and 0.87, respectively. Intercept or alpha value of P1 is not zero.

Fama–French three factor model regression estimates show that all risk factors coefficients are statistically significant at 5% level for both the portfolios P1 and P25. R-squared values for P1 and P25 are 0.711 and 0.899, respectively. Intercept or alpha values of both P1 and P25 are zero. Above all estimates confirmed superiority of the Fama–French three factor model over CAPM. However, in practice more robust test such as GRS test is essential to check the model performance. GRS test will check whether all

Dependent Variable: P1				
Method: Least Squares				
Date: 04/18/21 Time: 21:41				
Sample: 1 168				
Included observations: 168				
Variable	Coefficient	Std. Error	t-Statistic	Prob.
C	0.056924	0.011162	5.099625	0.0000
RM	1.201742	0.142217	8.450089	0.0000
R-squared	0.300770	Mean dependent var		0.066953
Adjusted R-squared	0.296558	S.D. dependent var		0.171525
S.E. of regression	0.143861	Akaike info criterion		-1.028109
Sum squared resid	3.435521	Schwarz criterion		-0.990919
Log likelihood	88.36115	Hannan-Quinn criter.		-1.013015
F-statistic	71.40400	Durbin-Watson stat		1.992644
Prob(F-statistic)	0.000000			

Dependent Variable: P25				
Method: Least Squares				
Date: 04/18/21 Time: 21:42				
Sample: 1 168				
Included observations: 168				
Variable	Coefficient	Std. Error	t-Statistic	Prob.
C	-0.002611	0.002204	-1.184254	0.2380
RM	0.951889	0.028085	33.89271	0.0000
R-squared	0.873737	Mean dependent var		0.005333
Adjusted R-squared	0.872976	S.D. dependent var		0.079713
S.E. of regression	0.028410	Akaike info criterion		-4.272313
Sum squared resid	0.133984	Schwarz criterion		-4.235123
Log likelihood	360.8743	Hannan-Quinn criter.		-4.257220
F-statistic	1148.716	Durbin-Watson stat		2.017432
Prob(F-statistic)	0.000000			

Fig. 5.6   CAPM estimates for Portfolio 1 and Portfolio 25

Dependent Variable: P1				
Method: Least Squares				
Date: 04/18/21 Time: 21:44				
Sample: 1 168				
Included observations: 168				

Variable	Coefficient	Std. Error	t-Statistic	Prob.
C	0.007402	0.007908	0.936008	0.3506
RM	1.008077	0.098808	10.20239	0.0000
SIZE	2.245479	0.221148	10.15374	0.0000
VALUE	1.254280	0.152632	8.217682	0.0000

R-squared	0.711899	Mean dependent var	0.066953
Adjusted R-squared	0.706629	S.D. dependent var	0.171525
S.E. of regression	0.092904	Akaike info criterion	-1.890969
Sum squared resid	1.415523	Schwarz criterion	-1.816589
Log likelihood	162.8414	Hannan-Quinn criter.	-1.860782
F-statistic	135.0817	Durbin-Watson stat	1.913764
Prob(F-statistic)	0.000000		

Dependent Variable: P25				
Method: Least Squares				
Date: 04/18/21 Time: 21:45				
Sample: 1 168				
Included observations: 168				

Variable	Coefficient	Std. Error	t-Statistic	Prob.
C	-0.000611	0.002179	-0.280657	0.7793
RM	1.015497	0.027221	37.30519	0.0000
SIZE	0.148553	0.060926	2.438264	0.0158
VALUE	-0.265910	0.042050	-6.323715	0.0000

R-squared	0.898755	Mean dependent var	0.005333
Adjusted R-squared	0.896902	S.D. dependent var	0.079713
S.E. of regression	0.025595	Akaike info criterion	-4.469323
Sum squared resid	0.107436	Schwarz criterion	-4.394943
Log likelihood	379.4232	Hannan-Quinn criter.	-4.439136
F-statistic	485.2753	Durbin-Watson stat	2.095334
Prob(F-statistic)	0.000000		

Fig. 5.7 Fama–French three factor model estimates for Portfolio 1 and Portfolio 25

alphas are jointly equal to zero. 25 Regressions (P1 to P25) will yield 25 different values for alphas or intercepts. But GRS test will check whether these 25 intercepts are jointly zero.

Test for Multicollinearity

To test the multicollinearity in EViews do the following:

Regression estimates output window → View → Coefficient Diagnostics → Variance Inflation Factors → VIF estimates will appear as shown below in Fig. 5.8.

VIF estimates (Fig. 5.8) show that there is no multicollinearity in the regression.

5.2.2   *Illustration on Testing the Asset Pricing Models Performance*

GRS test Estimation

Above section discussed how to implement multifactor asset pricing models using regressions in EViews. Each Regressions (P1 to P25) will yield 25 different values for alphas or intercepts. But to test the asset pricing models performance it is important to check whether these 25 alphas or intercepts are jointly zero? GRS test is often used to check the performance of the asset pricing models.

Variance Inflation Factors Date: 04/18/21 Time: 22:19 Sample: 1 168 Included observations: 168			
Variable	Coefficient Variance	Uncentered VIF	Centered VIF
C	4.75E-06	1.217202	NA
RM	0.000741	1.170665	1.157431
SIZE	0.003712	1.257525	1.088965
VALUE	0.001768	1.344164	1.213915

Fig. 5.8   VIF estimates of Fama–French three factor model for Portfolio 25

Now let's obtain GRS test estimates of the CAPM and Fama–French three factor models for the same task. And based on the obtained GRS estimates comment on the performance of these two asset pricing models in Indian context. GRS test could be performed with the support of R package "GRS.test[1]".

Code:

```
library(GRS.test)
data(File_name)
factor.mat = File_name[Column_range,Column_numbers] #Risk Factors
ret.mat  = File_name[Column_range,Column_numbers] # 25 Size-value portfolio returns
GRS.MLtest(ret.mat,factor.mat)
```

Output:
The lower GRS P-values indicate that both the CAPM and Fama–French three factor model are rejected by the GRS test (Fig. 5.9). However, lower value of GRS F-statistics for the Fama–French three factor model (2.635631) than the CAPM (3.86319) indicates superiority of Fama–French three factor model.

---

[1] https://cran.r-project.org/web/packages/GRS.test/GRS.test.pdf.

```
$`GRS.stat`                        $`GRS.stat`
              GRS                                GRS
[1,] 3.86319                       [1,] 2.635631

$GRS.pval                          $GRS.pval
              GRS                                GRS
[1,] 1.466961e-07                  [1,] 0.0001827492

$thetas                            $thetas
              [,1]                               [,1]
[1,] 0.8320016                     [1,] 0.8778972

$theta                             $theta
              [,1]                               [,1]
[1,] 0.1098716                     [1,] 0.4618159

$ratio                             $ratio
              [,1]                               [,1]
[1,] 0.1320569                     [1,] 0.5260478
```

Fig. 5.9   GRS test estimates for CAPM and Fama–French three factor model

5.2.3   Illustration on Panel Regression Model

To examine the reason behind the country-wise variations in banks net profits due to non-interest and interest incomes of the banks.

Countries: Albania; Bulgaria; Croatia; Romania; and Slovenia (5 cross section).

Years: 2005 to 2015 (11 time series).

EViews stepwise implementations

Above task can be easily implemented by using the panel regressions in EViews by following the below steps.

Step 1: Import data into the EViews Workfile window.

Step 2: Then click on Quick → Estimate Equation → Equation Estimation window will appear as shown in Fig. 5.10.

Step 3: Under the equation specification space write dependable variable followed by list of regressors as shown below. Hence, dependable variables are the net profit. Whereas regressors are the non-interest and interest incomes, and c is the regression intercept.

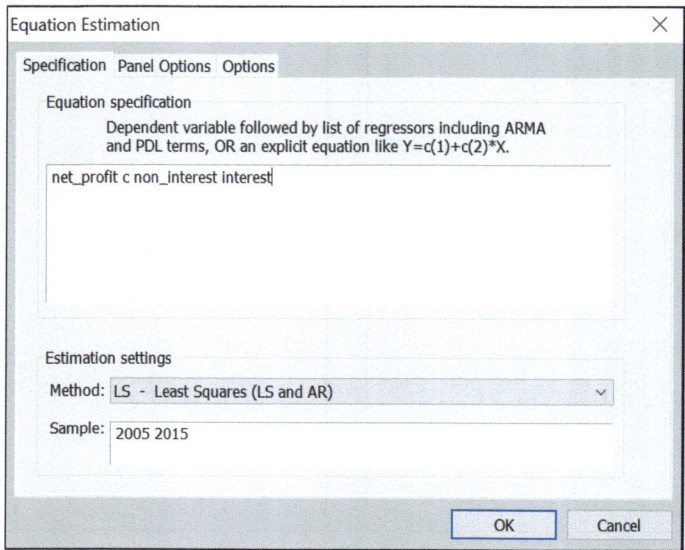

Fig. 5.10   Panel Regression Equation Estimation window

net_profit c non_interest interest

Choose Methods as Least Square (from the drop down list).
Then click OK button. Regression estimates will appear as shown in Fig. 5.11.

The constant coefficients model(CCM) regression estimates are shown in Fig. 5.11. The CCM works on the principle of homogeneity or pooling assumption that coefficients of all the intercepts and slope will remain same across the cross sections over time. The CCM basically applies linear regression on the panel (pooled) data for estimating the unknown parameters of the model. The CCM estimates show that none of the variables is statistically significant at 5% level.

Step 4: Then fixed effect model is estimated. To run the fixed effect model make cross section fixed as shown in Fig. 5.12 and click OK.

Figure 5.13 shows the fixed effects panel regression estimates. The fixed effects panel regression estimates show that non-interest

Dependent Variable: NET_PROFIT Method: Panel Least Squares Date: 04/19/21 Time: 15:22 Sample: 2005 2015 Periods included: 11 Cross-sections included: 5 Total panel (balanced) observations: 55				
Variable	Coefficient	Std. Error	t-Statistic	Prob.
C	-29.72039	27.80704	-1.068808	0.2901
NON_INTEREST	0.720498	0.495431	1.454286	0.1519
INTEREST	0.069334	0.272928	0.254037	0.8005
Root MSE	98.72350	R-squared		0.124474
Mean dependent var	28.24840	Adjusted R-squared		0.090800
S.D. dependent var	106.4806	S.E. of regression		101.5314
Akaike info criterion	12.13161	Sum squared resid		536048.2
Schwarz criterion	12.24110	Log likelihood		-330.6194
Hannan-Quinn criter.	12.17396	F-statistic		3.696423
Durbin-Watson stat	1.181964	Prob(F-statistic)		0.031550

Fig. 5.11   Constant coefficients model estimates

income is positively related to the bank's net profit and statistically significant at 5% level. R-squared value also increased in case of fixed effects model over the CCM. Durbin–Watson statistics value also improved and much closer to 2.

Now check for the cross section fixed effects values. To do so go to the fixed effects model estimation window → View estimated. To run the fixed Fixed/Random effects → Cross Section effects → Cross section fixed effects window will appear as shown in Fig. 5.14.

Above estimates (Fig. 5.14) show that the values of all cross section fixed effects are not zero. Hence, it confirms the presence of cross section effects and the fixed effects model appears to be more appropriate than the CCM.

Step 5: For further confirmations run the random effect model. To run the random effect model make cross section random as shown in Fig. 5.15 and click OK.

Figure 5.16 shows the random effects panel regression estimates.

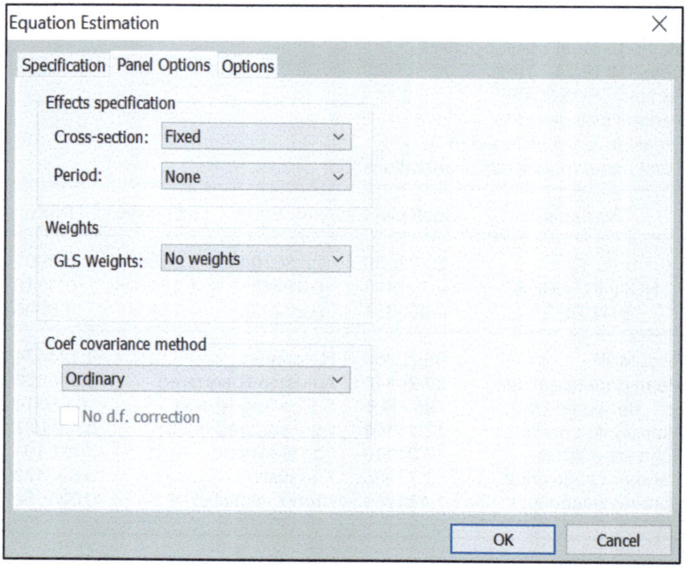

Fig. 5.12 Fixed effects Panel Regression Equation Estimation window

The random effects panel regression estimates also show that non-interest income is positively related to the bank's net profit and statistically significant at 5% level. R-squared value does not increase in case of random effects model over the fixed effects model. Durbin–Watson statistics value also not improved and the problem of autocorrelation is not absent in case of the random effects model. All of these estimates confirm that the random effects model is not better than the fixed effects model.

Now check for the cross section random effects values. To do so go to the random effects model estimation window → View → Fixed/Random effects → Cross Section effects → Cross section random effects window will appear as shown in Fig. 5.17.

Above estimates (Fig. 5.17) show that the values of all cross section random effects are not zero. Hence, it confirms the presence of cross section effects.

Step 6: To clear the ambiguity on the selection of the appropriate panel models run Hausman Test.

Dependent Variable: NET_PROFIT
Method: Panel Least Squares
Date: 04/19/21   Time: 15:47
Sample: 2005 2015
Periods included: 11
Cross-sections included: 5
Total panel (balanced) observations: 55

Variable	Coefficient	Std. Error	t-Statistic	Prob.
C	-139.1273	50.07133	-2.778582	0.0078
NON_INTEREST	2.729062	0.522640	5.221685	0.0000
INTEREST	-0.098193	0.354262	-0.277177	0.7828

Effects Specification

Cross-section fixed (dummy variables)

Root MSE	71.91829	R-squared	0.535371
Mean dependent var	28.24840	Adjusted R-squared	0.477292
S.D. dependent var	106.4806	S.E. of regression	76.98393
Akaike info criterion	11.64348	Sum squared resid	284473.2
Schwarz criterion	11.89896	Log likelihood	-313.1958
Hannan-Quinn criter.	11.74228	F-statistic	9.218022
Durbin-Watson stat	1.483393	Prob(F-statistic)	0.000001

Fig. 5.13 Fixed effects model estimates

Fig. 5.14 Cross section fixed effects estimates

	COUNTRY	Effect
1	Albania	147.1785
2	Bulgaria	95.73213
3	Croatia	-68.14807
4	Romania	-40.47911
5	Slovenia	-134.2835

Hausman test could be estimated in EViews as mentioned below. To do so go to the random effects model estimation window → View → Fixed/Random Effects Testing → Correlated Random Effects-Hausman Test → Correlated Random Effects-Hausman Test window will appear as shown in Fig. 5.18. Correlated Random Effects-Hausman test estimates prefer the fixed effects model over the random effects model as the computed Chi-square value is statistically significant at 5% level.

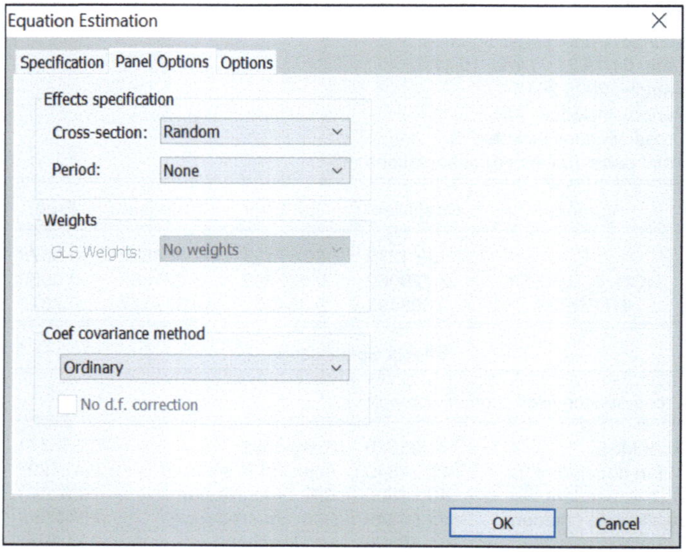

Fig. 5.15   Random effects Panel Regression Equation Estimation window

Summary

This chapter briefly introduced the topic asset pricing models. Discussion initiated with the definition of the asset pricing and different schools of thoughts. Presence of the different risk factors and uncertainty in the financial markets make asset pricing difficult. The CAPM, its implications and assumptions are discussed in detail. What are the issues that lead to the fallacy of CAPM are covered in details? Significance of different multifactor asset pricing models such as ICAPM and APT is enclosed in detail. Different approaches for selecting the risk factors are discussed. Fama–French (1993) mimicking portfolios construction mechanism is discussed in detail. Other notable multifactor models such as the five factor and six factor models are discussed in detail. Many illustrations such as implementation of the various asset pricing models and related testing are discussed in detail with stepwise EViews or R implementations. At the end, panel regression is also covered with suitable illustration.

```
Dependent Variable: NET_PROFIT
Method: Panel EGLS (Cross-section random effects)
Date: 04/19/21   Time: 16:18
Sample: 2005 2015
Periods included: 11
Cross-sections included: 5
Total panel (balanced) observations: 55
Swamy and Arora estimator of component variances
```

Variable	Coefficient	Std. Error	t-Statistic	Prob.
C	-71.59491	42.64387	-1.678902	0.0992
NON_INTEREST	2.059836	0.479072	4.299638	0.0001
INTEREST	-0.257220	0.291590	-0.882130	0.3818

Effects Specification		S.D.	Rho
Cross-section random		51.59763	0.3100
Idiosyncratic random		76.98393	0.6900

Weighted Statistics			
Root MSE	80.58637	R-squared	0.276493
Mean dependent var	11.58907	Adjusted R-squared	0.248666
S.D. dependent var	95.61471	S.E. of regression	82.87838
Sum squared resid	357178.9	F-statistic	9.936082
Durbin-Watson stat	1.311191	Prob(F-statistic)	0.000222

Unweighted Statistics			
R-squared	-0.038588	Mean dependent var	28.24840
Sum squared resid	635883.8	Durbin-Watson stat	0.736502

Fig. 5.16 Random effects model estimates

Fig. 5.17 Cross section random effects estimates

	COUNTRY	Effect
1	Albania	74.51141
2	Bulgaria	58.08317
3	Croatia	-32.42172
4	Romania	5.042050
5	Slovenia	-105.2149

Correlated Random Effects - Hausman Test			
Equation: Untitled			
Test cross-section random effects			
Test Summary	**Chi-Sq. Statistic**	**Chi-Sq. d.f.**	**Prob.**
Cross-section random	10.267856	2	0.0059

Cross-section random effects test comparisons:

Variable	Fixed	Random	Var(Diff.)	Prob.
NON_INTEREST	2.729062	2.059836	0.043643	0.0014
INTEREST	-0.098193	-0.257220	0.040477	0.4293

Cross-section random effects test equation:
Dependent Variable: NET_PROFIT
Method: Panel Least Squares
Date: 04/19/21   Time: 17:00
Sample: 2005 2015
Periods included: 11
Cross-sections included: 5
Total panel (balanced) observations: 55

Variable	Coefficient	Std. Error	t-Statistic	Prob.
C	-139.1273	50.07133	-2.778582	0.0078
NON_INTEREST	2.729062	0.522640	5.221685	0.0000
INTEREST	-0.098193	0.354262	-0.277177	0.7828

Effects Specification			
Cross-section fixed (dummy variables)			

Root MSE	71.91829	R-squared	0.535371
Mean dependent var	28.24840	Adjusted R-squared	0.477292
S.D. dependent var	106.4806	S.E. of regression	76.98393
Akaike info criterion	11.64348	Sum squared resid	284473.2
Schwarz criterion	11.89896	Log likelihood	-313.1958
Hannan-Quinn criter.	11.74228	F-statistic	9.218022
Durbin-Watson stat	1.483393	Prob(F-statistic)	0.000001

Fig. 5.18 Correlated Random Effects-Hausman Test estimates

Analysts/Investors Corner

Equity pricing is relatively more difficult than the debt pricing due to the presence of several risk factors and uncertainty in the financial markets. Fama and French mimicking portfolio approach for the construction of various risk factors is still valuable. Risk factors should be chosen very wisely and license for fishing of the various risk factors must be held carefully. Alpha values are very important component of the asset pricing models as it carries information of the pricing errors. Test for the joint alpha values should be implemented to check the performance of the asset pricing models. Hence, an asset pricing model is said to be a good model if it is able to allocate the expected returns on the efficient frontier. To examine the interstate variations, panel regressions are useful. The panel regression models should be executed carefully. To clear the ambiguity on the selection of the appropriate panel models run Hausman Test.

5.3   EXERCISES

5.3.1   *Multiple Choice Questions*

1. Sharpe introduced

   a. Random walk
   b. Modern Portfolio Theory
   c. CAPM
   d. Advanced Portfolio Theory

2. APT model is associated with the

   a. Henry Markowitz
   b. Stephen Ross
   c. William F. Sharpe
   d. Eugene Fama

3. CAPM considers

   a. Specific risk

b. Systematic risk
c. Unsystematic risk
d. Idiosyncratic risk

4. Which of the following risk factor does not belong to the Fama–French three factor model?

   a. Market
   b. SMB
   c. HML
   d. Momentum

5. Which of the following test is used for testing the joint alpha values?

   a. CAPM test
   b. GRS test
   c. Hausman test
   d. Gauss test

6. Which of the following test belongs to the selection of appropriate panel models?

   a. Gauss test
   b. Hausman test
   c. ARCH test
   d. GARCH test

7. Which of the following does not belong to the panel models?

   a. Constant coefficients model
   b. Fixed effects model
   c. Random effects model
   d. Exponential effects model

8. Which of the following technique is not used for selecting different risk factors from a wide range of possibilities?

   a. Statistical methods
   b. Macroeconomic variables
   c. Firm specific fundamental variables
   d. Control variables

9. Durbin–Watson statistics is used to check?

a. Multicollinearity
b. Autocorrelation
c. Covariances
d. Correlations

10. Variance Inflation Factor test is used to identify the degree of

a. Autocorrelation
b. Multicollinearity
c. Normality
d. Correlations

11. Which of the following risk factor does not belong to the Fama–French five factor model?

a. SMB
b. HML
c. CMA
d. WML

12. Which of the following is not a multifactor model?

a. CAPM
b. ICAPM
c. APT
d. a and b

13. The consumption-based CAPM uses

a. Market beta
b. Consumption beta
c. Wealth beta
d. Income beta

5.3.2   *Fill in the Blanks*

1. In the ICAPM "I" represents _____.
2. In the CAPM beta represents _____.
3. The APT model of asset pricing measures the expected returns of assets as a linear function of different _____ factors.

4. The three risk factors of Fama–French three factor model are
   _____, _____, and _____.
5. These two risk factors namely _____ and _____
   are extra addition to the Fama–French five factor model.
6. _____ and _____ make asset pricing a challenging task.
7. To clear the ambiguity on the selection of the appropriate panel
   models run the _____ Test.
8. _____ test is often used to check the performance of the
   asset pricing models.
9. _____ studies deal with the pricing of assets.
10. In the fixed effects model _____ are fixed.

5.3.3   Long Answer Questions

1. What is CAPM? Also comment on its basic assumptions.
2. How these three asset pricing models are different? CAPM;
   CCAPM; and ICAPM
3. If an asset price turns negative will it still be an asset? Defend this
   statement with suitable example and explanation?
4. Fama and French has defined SMB and HML as the risk proxies for
   size and value factors. Likewise is it possible to derive the COVID-
   19 pandemic risk proxy?
5. Explain the term "fishing license" with respect to the asset pricing.
6. How to construct the Fama and French factors? Explain it in detail.
7. Discuss and compare all the techniques that are used for selecting
   different risk factors from a wide range of possibilities?
8. In 2020 "oil futures went negative" appeared as the important
   news headlines. Explain this event with relation to the asset pricing
   theory?
9. What are the state variables in ICAPM and its implications?
10. What is so special about Fama and French (1993) three factor asset
    pricing model?
11. Broadly discuss on the three forms of panel models with appro-
    priate examples.
12. What is Arbitrage Pricing Theory and its implications?
13. Why asset pricing models are generally implemented by the regres-
    sions?

14. What are alpha values in a regression? Why alpha values are vital with respect to the asset pricing models?
15. How anomalies are different from the risk factors? Explain it with suitable examples.
16. The table below shows the Fama and French risk factors coefficients of four securities. The current interest rate is 1.5%, expected market premium is 6.5%, expected size premium is 4.7%, and expected value premium is 3.57%. Based on this data estimate the expected return on each security.

Risk factorscoefficients	Security A	Security B	Security C	Security D
β_{rm}	0.73	1.15	0.87	0.56
β_{smb}	0.65	−0.77	0.34	0.75
β_{hml}	−0.47	0.43	0.58	0.22

17. The table below shows the Fama and French risk factors coefficients of four securities. The current interest rate is 1.25%, expected market premium is 6.35%, expected size premium is 4.17%, expected value premium is 3.7%, expected profitability premium is 2.32%, and expected investment premium is 1.53%. Based on this data estimate the expected return on each security.

Risk factors coefficients	Security I	Security II	Security III	Security IV
β_{rm}	0.83	1.25	0.77	0.54
β_{smb}	1.05	−0.57	0.41	0.72
β_{hml}	−0.47	0.33	0.59	0.20
β_{rmw}	0.71	−0.37	0.34	0.59
β_{cma}	−0.55	0.14	0.58	−0.38

5.3.4   Real-World Tasks

1. A professor asks his/her student to test CAPM in Australian context. Assume yourself as the student and perform the task. Then prepare a detailed report of the analysis to be submitted to the professor.

2. A researcher want to test the performance of the CAPM and APT models in crypto markets. Assume yourself as the researcher: perform the mentioned task in detail and develop the analysis report.
3. An analyst is currently evaluating an investment option to invest in the major global currencies. To do so he/she want to test the APT model for making the investment decision. Help him/her to perform the said analysis and prepare the report.
4. A student needs to identify whether there exists size and value patterns in the BSE 500 securities mean excess returns. Help the student to complete his/her project dissertation successfully and satisfactorily.
5. An assistant manager of the Reserve Bank of New Zealand asked a junior working under him/her to prepare a detailed report on "How efficient is Fama and French multifactor models in Australia and New Zealand"? Help the junior in developing the final report for timely submission to the assistant manager of Reserve Bank of New Zealand.
6. There is a disagreement between two market participants that "the CCAPM isn't Perfect". So they approach to an expert to clarify it? Assume yourself as that expert and advise them on it with appropriate examples.
7. A researcher want to examine whether financial leverage is an important firm specific factor specially in the emerging markets? The researcher is also interested to check whether financial leverage alone or financial leverage along with other firm specific factors can capture risk-return relationship better. Help the researcher to conduct and complete the analysis satisfactorily.

5.3.5 Case Studies

1. To examine the performance of CAPM and Fama–French three factor models in Sri Lankan context. The regressions and GRS test are implemented to examine the asset pricing models performance. The obtained regressions and GRS test estimates are shown below. Based on these obtained estimates comment on the performance of these two asset pricing models.

Data Description:
Colombo Stock Exchange traded securities are used to construct the study portfolios based on the size (market capitalization) and value (P/B ratio) factors by means of the Fama–French (1993) technique. For risk free rate Sri Lankan government 10 years bond are used. S&P 20 index mean excess returns used as proxy for the market. The study period is between July 2008 and May 2016. All data points are in monthly frequency.

Regression models used are as follows:

CAPM & Fama–French Three Factor Model

$$E(r_i) - r_f = \alpha_i + \beta_{im} * (r_m - r_f) + \varepsilon_i$$

$$E(r_i) - r_f = \alpha_i + \beta_{im} * (r_m - r_f) + \beta_{is} * (\text{Size}) + \beta_{iv} * (\text{Value}) + \varepsilon_i$$

Estimates:
CAPM regression estimates for 25 portfolios based on size and value factors.

a						ta				
	Low	2	3	4	High	Low	2	3	4	High
Small	0.012	0.019	0.023	0.011	0.010	0.926	1.281	2.098	1.142	1.069
2	0.003	0.013	0.007	0.005	0.008	0.392	1.367	0.896	0.721	1.055
3	0.017	0.016	0.008	0.004	0.015	2.490	1.813	1.211	0.775	1.691
4	0.012	0.003	0.008	0.004	0.010	1.820	0.465	1.282	0.599	1.196
Big	0.008	0.006	0.000	0.003	0.000	2.319	1.584	0.107	0.643	0.045

b						ta				
	Low	2	3	4	High	Low	2	3	4	High
Small	0.838	0.914	0.715	0.739	0.731	7.226	6.924	7.195	8.644	8.816
2	0.835	0.874	0.825	0.607	0.84	12.541	10.167	11.745	8.884	12.172
3	0.967	1.047	0.934	0.91	0.849	15.552	13.208	15.568	17.530	10.610
4	0.881	0.861	0.822	0.904	0.786	14.827	14.871	15.135	13.885	9.888
Big	0.975	1.004	0.892	0.867	0.76	29.191	28.837	23.756	24.323	14.452

R^2

	Low	2	3	4	High
Small	0.362	0.345	0.358	0.446	0.455
2	0.631	0.526	0.597	0.459	0.614
3	0.724	0.652	0.723	0.768	0.548
4	0.707	0.704	0.711	0.679	0.513
Big	0.902	0.899	0.859	0.864	0.692

Fama–French three factor model regression estimates for 25 portfolios based on size and value factors.

a						ta				
	Low	2	3	4	High	Low	2	3	4	High
Small	0.002	0.008	0.023	0.009	0.011	0.172	0.626	2.418	1.315	1.518
2	0.001	0.008	0.004	0.006	0.009	0.073	0.904	0.631	0.784	1.422
3	0.013	0.010	0.008	0.002	0.017	2.032	0.245	1.193	0.330	1.944
4	0.009	0.002	0.007	0.004	0.013	1.396	0.286	1.117	0.604	1.446
Big	0.007	0.005	0.000	0.002	0.001	1.896	1.308	0.025	0.556	0.198

b						tb				
	Low	2	3	4	High	Low	2	3	4	High
Small	0.823	0.886	0.885	0.895	0.921	8.896	6.889	9.244	12.622	12.637
2	0.853	0.876	0.872	0.684	0.980	11.939	10.352	12.371	9.321	14.702
3	0.938	0.942	0.938	0.997	0.878	14.169	11.186	13.787	18.040	9.824
4	0.826	0.850	0.835	0.904	0.859	12.592	13.025	13.838	12.156	9.713
Big	0.948	1.000	0.884	0.884	0.799	25.825	25.915	20.801	22.389	14.269

s						ts				
	Low	2	3	4	High	Low	2	3	4	High
Small	1.917	1.475	1.570	1.745	1.544	7.500	4.111	5.902	8.854	7.269
2	0.591	1.028	0.921	0.658	1.045	2.989	4.371	4.700	3.230	5.643
3	0.387	0.028	0.016	0.325	− 0.193	2.107	0.118	0.086	2.121	− 0.779

(continued)

(continued)

s					ts				
Low	2	3	4	High	Low	2	3	4	High
4	−0.051	0.101	0.300	−0.036	0.255	−0.277	0.559	1.789	−0.160	1.036
Big	0.043	0.159	−0.007	0.224	0.531	0.423	1.484	−0.060	2.042	3.411

l					tl				
	Low	2	3	4	High	Low	2	3	4	High
Small	−1.111	−1.044	0.620	0.415	0.804	−3.779	−2.547	2.037	1.842	3.473
2	−0.156	−0.518	−0.077	0.302	0.643	−0.674	1.925	−0.343	1.297	3.035
3	−0.440	−0.908	0.023	0.569	0.344	2.083	3.394	0.104	3.238	1.213
4	−0.449	−0.150	−0.048	0.023	0.490	2.144	0.723	−0.252	0.096	1.741
Big	−0.255	−0.117	−0.061	0.028	0.057	2.186	0.952	−0.450	0.221	0.318

R^2	Low	2	3	4	High
Small	0.686	0.515	0.536	0.703	0.672
2	0.672	0.643	0.684	0.516	0.720
3	0.757	0.695	0.723	0.795	0.561
4	0.722	0.708	0.723	0.680	0.530
Big	0.908	0.904	0.859	0.870	0.728

GRS test estimates

Factor model	GRS F-Statistics	P-Value	Average absolute alpha value	Average R^2
CAPM	1.01	0.530	0.009	63
EFTF	0.967	0.519	0.007	70

2. Below tables show the mean excess returns and T-statistics for the twenty-five portfolios constructed from the BSE 500 securities based on the size (market capitalization) and value (P/B ratio) factors. Based on these estimates comment on the size and value patterns if any exists in the portfolios mean excess returns.

| | | Mean excess return | | | |
	Low	2	3	4	High
Small	0.067	0.042	0.038	0.032	0.026
2	0.037	0.027	0.022	0.021	0.014
3	0.031	0.018	0.015	0.013	0.013
4	0.022	0.019	0.021	0.012	0.011
Big	0.023	0.020	0.020	0.012	0.005

| | | T-Statistics | | | |
	Low	2	3	4	High
Small	5.059	4.693	4.840	4.062	3.144
2	3.819	3.297	2.885	2.935	2.147
3	3.267	2.155	1.924	1.751	1.953
4	2.400	2.135	2.512	1.602	1.782
Big	2.488	2.456	2.728	1.705	0.867

References

Balakrishnan, A., & Maiti, M. (2017). Dynamics of size and value factors in stock returns: Evidence from India. *Indian Journal of Finance, 11*(6), 21–35.

Carhart, M. M. (1997). On persistence in mutual fund performance. *The Journal of Finance, 52*(1), 57–82.

Fama, E. F. (1991). Efficient capital markets: II. *The Journal of Finance, 46*(5), 1575–1617.

Fama, E. F., & French, K. R. (1993). Common risk factors in the returns on stocks and bonds. *Journal of Financial Economics, 33*, 3–56.

Fama, E. F., & French, K. R. (2015). A five-factor asset pricing model. *Journal of Financial Economics, 116*(1), 1–22.

Gibbons, M. R., Ross, S. A., & Shanken, J. (1989). A test of the efficiency of a given portfolio. *Econometrica: Journal of the Econometric Society*, 1121–1152.

Markowitz, H. M. (1952, March). Portfolio selection. *Journal of Finance, 7*, 77–91.

Maiti, M. (2018). *A six factor asset pricing model* (Doctoral dissertation).

Maiti, M. (2019). Is idiosyncratic risk ignored in asset pricing: Sri Lankan evidence? *Future Business Journal, 5*(1), 1–12.

Maiti, M. (2020). A critical review on evolution of risk factors and factor models. *Journal of Economic Surveys, 34*(1), 175–184. https://doi.org/10.1111/joes.12344

Maiti, M. (2020b). Is ESG the succeeding risk factor? *Journal of Sustainable Finance & Investment*, 1–15.

Maiti, M., & Balakrishnan, A. (2018). Is human capital the sixth factor? *Journal of Economic Studies, 45*(4), 710–737.

Maiti, M., & Balakrishnan, A. (2020). Can leverage effect coexist with value effect? *IIMB Management Review, 32*(1), 7–23.

Maiti, M., & Vuković, D. (2020). Role of human assets in measuring firm performance and its implication for firm valuation. *Journal of Economic Structures, 9*(1), 1–27.

Merton, R. C. (1973, September). An intertemporal capital asset pricing model. *Econometrica, 41*(5), 867–887.

Ross, S. A. (1976). The arbitrage theory of capital asset pricing. *Journal of Economic Theory, 13*(3), 341–360.

Sharpe, W. F. (1964). Capital asset prices: A theory of market equilibrium under conditions of risk. *The Journal of Finance, 19*(3), 425–442.

CHAPTER 6

Risk Analysis

Key Topics Covered

- *STL*
- *ARIMA Models*
- *ARCH and GARCH Models*
- *VAR Model*
- *Illustration on STL using EViews*
- *Illustration on ARIMA models using EViews*
- *Illustration on ARCH and GARCH Models using EViews*
- *Illustrations on VAR Models, Impulse response analysis and Variance decomposition using EViews*

6.1   BACKGROUND

Risk analysis is the heart of any financial decision-making process. Time series of a variable consists of the data points over time. Time series data of a variable comprises several important information about the variable over time. Original time series data can be decomposed into various components, namely seasonal, trend, and remainder components. Time series can be easily decomposed into its various components by using the STL (Seasonal and Trend decomposition using LOESS) decomposition technique as suggested by Cleveland et al. (1990). The LOESS is a robust technique and its abbreviation stands for the "*locally estimated scatter-plot smoothing*". The LOESS is a non-parametric technique used for the smooth curve fitting. The STL decomposes the time series into different components using an additive function as shown below in Eq. 6.1.

$$Timeseries = Trend + Seasonal + Remainder \qquad (6.1)$$

The STL technique has certain limitations such as it is not efficient enough in handling the trading day or calendar variation automatically. This above limitation can be overcome by using a multiplicative decomposition function as defined in Eq. 6.2.

$$Timeseries = Trend * Seasonal * Remainder \qquad (6.2)$$

Thus to analyse the time series, a good knowledge of the essential time series econometrics methods are necessary. The time series econometrics deal with the measurement of the random variables over time. The time series analysis is useful for determining how a variable changes over time. It is also equally important in assessing the impact of the other factors on the study variable over the same time frame. The paragraphs below covered all such essential time series econometrics techniques to deal with the time series data.

6.1.1   ARIMA

An important aspect of the time series is that time series data is often used for the forecasting. Based on the information of the past and present states of the variable, the future states of the variable are forecasted. The ARIMA models are introduced by the Box-Jenkins in the year 1976. The ARIMA stands for the "*Auto Regressive Integrated Moving Average*". Thereafter, ARIMA models are widely used in finance for forecasting the stationary time series. The ARIMA models are useful for modelling both the univariate and multivariate time series. Commonly, time series is generated using the following: AR (Autoregressive) or MA (Moving average) or both (ARMA) or ARIMA processes.

AR (Autoregressive) Process

The AR (Autoregressive) process considers the past values of the time series for modelling. The first order AR (Autoregressive) model is represented by following Eq. 6.3.

$$R_t = \Phi_t R_{t-1} + u_t \tag{6.3}$$

Where

R_t represents the present value of the variable at time t
R_{t-1} represents the past value of the variable at time $t - 1$
Φ_t represents the proportion at time t
u_t represents the white noise error term

The above Eq. (6.3) represents that the present value of the variable (R) at time (t) is equal to the some proportion (Φ_t) of the past value of the variable (R) at time $(t - 1)$ plus the white noise error term (u_t). Likewise, nth order AR (Autoregressive) process or AR(n) can be represented as Eq. (6.4). The AR(n) model as shown in (6.4) includes only the current and previous values of the variable R.

$$R_t = \Phi_1 R_{t-1} + \Phi_2 R_{t-2} + \ldots + \Phi_n R_{t-n} + u_t \tag{6.4}$$

Basic properties of the AR (Autoregressive) process are as follows:

- Mean of the R_t for AR(1) model is zero
- Variance of R_t for AR(1) model is represented by the Eq. (6.5)

$$\frac{\sigma_u^2}{(1 - \Phi_1^2)} \tag{6.5}$$

- Covariance between R_t and R_{t-1} is represented by the Eq. (6.6)

$$\frac{\Phi_1 \sigma_u^2}{(1 - \Phi_1^2)} \tag{6.6}$$

Similarly for lag (n) the expression is shown below

$$\frac{\Phi_1^n \sigma_u^2}{(1 - \Phi_1^2)}$$

- Autocorrelation function of R_t at lag 1 is represented by the Eq. (6.7)

$$\frac{\Phi_1 \sigma_u^2}{(1 - \Phi_1^2)} \frac{\sigma_u^2}{\left(1 - \Phi_1^2\right)} \tag{6.7}$$

Similarly for lag (n) the expression is shown below

$$\frac{\Phi_1^n \sigma_u^2}{(1 - \Phi_1^2)} \Big/ \frac{\sigma_u^2}{(1 - \Phi_1^2)}$$

MA (Moving Average) Process

The MA (Moving Average) process considers the past values of the white noise error term for modelling. The first order MA (Moving Average) model is represented by following Eq. 6.8.

$$R_t = u_t + \theta_t u_{t-1} \tag{6.8}$$

Where

R_t represents the present value of the variable at time t
u_t represents the present value of the white noise error term
u_{t-1} represents the past value of the white noise error term
θ_t represents the proportion at time t

The above Eq. (6.8) represents that the present value of the variable (R) at time (t) is equal to the present and some proportion (Φ_t) of the past value of the white noise error term (u_t). Likewise, the mth order MA (Moving Average) process or MA(m) can be represented as Eq. (6.9). The MA(m) model as shown in (6.9) includes only the current and previous values of the white noise error term (u_t).

$$R_t = u_t + \theta_1 u_{t-1} + \theta_2 u_{t-2} + \ldots + \theta_m u_{t-m} \tag{6.9}$$

Basic properties of the MA (Moving Average) process are as follows:

- Mean of the R_t is zero
- Variance of R_t for MA(1) model is represented by the Eq. (6.10)

$$(1 + \theta^2)\sigma_u^2 \tag{6.10}$$

- Covariance between R_t and R_{t-1} is $\theta \, \sigma_u^2$, whereas other covariance terms are zero.
- Autocorrelation function of R_t at lag 1 is

$$\frac{\theta}{(1 + \theta^2)}$$

Whereas zero for the higher lags.

ARMA Model

The ARMA model considers both the AR (Autoregressive) and MA (Moving Average) processes for modelling. The first order ARMA model AR (Autoregressive) model is represented by following Eq. 6.11.

$$R_t = \Phi_1 R_{t-1} + u_t + \theta_1 u_{t-1} \tag{6.11}$$

Likewise, the ARMA (n, m) model is represented in Eq. (6.12).

$$R_t = \Phi_1 R_{t-1} + \Phi_2 R_{t-2} + \ldots + \Phi_n R_{t-n} + u_t + \theta_1 u_{t-1}$$
$$+ \theta_2 u_{t-2} + \ldots + \theta_m u_{t-m} \tag{6.12}$$

The ARIMA (n, 0, m) model is same as the ARMA (n, m) model, if the original time series is stationary. Likewise, if the time series is not stationary, then first transform the time series into a stationary series. Thereafter, choose the appropriate model based on the autocorrelation function (ACF) and partial autocorrelation function (PACF).

6.1.2   ARCH & GARCH

The ARMA models are good in explaining the serial correlation but not efficient in capturing the conditional heteroskedasticity or volatility clustering. Thus, for forecasting the time series accurately, there is need for more sophisticated techniques. The ARCH (see Engle, 1982, 1983) and GARCH (see Bollerslev, 1986) techniques are used widely for modelling the volatility or volatility clustering of the time series. An ARCH model can be estimated from the best fitting autoregressive (AR) model using the OLS. Then perform the ARCH test to check whether ARCH effect is present in the residuals obtained from the autoregressive (AR) regression. The best fitting autoregressive (AR) model can be represented by the Eq. (6.13).

$$Y_t = \alpha_0 + \alpha_1 Y_{t-1} + \alpha_2 Y_{t-2} + \ldots + \alpha_n Y_{t-n} + u_t \qquad (6.13)$$

Next, estimate the squares of the error term $(\hat{u}_t^2)\hat{e}^2$ by running a regression on the lagged value of the squares of the error term $(\hat{u}_t^2)\hat{e}^2$.

$$\hat{u}_t^2 = \alpha_0 + \sum_{i=1}^{p} \alpha_i \hat{u}_{t-i}^2 u \qquad (6.14)$$

In the above Eq. (6.14), p represents the length of The ARCH lags. The null hypothesis of the ARCH test assumes that there is no ARCH effect present in the time series. The GARCH model considers the lagged conditional variance term in addition to the lagged value of the squares of the error term $\hat{e}^2$. The generalized GARCH (p, q) model can be represented mathematically as shown in the Eq. (6.15).

$$\hat{u}_t^2 = \alpha_0 + \sum_{i=1}^{p} \alpha_i \hat{u}_{t-i}^2 + \sum_{i=1}^{q} \beta_i \sigma_{t-i}^2 \qquad (6.15)$$

Where

P represents the lags length of the lagged value of the squares of the error term $\hat{e}^2$

Q represents the lags length of the lagged conditional variance terms.

6.1.3   VAR

The VAR stands for the "Vector Autoregressive". The VAR models are introduced by Christopher A. Sim in the year 1960. VAR models are useful specially on dealing with the multivariate time series over time. The VAR model structure of a variable includes linear function of the lagged values of the variable and all other variables included in the VAR model. Let's characterize a VAR model for examining the variations in the X and Y variables. Mathematically, the above VAR model can be represented as Eq. (6.16 and 6.17).

$$X_t = \alpha_1 + \sum_{i=1}^{p} \beta_i X_{t-i} + \sum_{i=1}^{p} \gamma_i Y_{t-i} + u_{1t} \qquad (6.16)$$

$$Y_t = \alpha_2 + \sum_{i=1}^{p} \theta_i X_{t-i} + \sum_{i=1}^{p} \lambda_i Y_{t-i} + u_{2t} \qquad (6.17)$$

The above two Eqs. (6.16 and 6.17) represent the VAR(p) model. Where, p represents the length of the lags. The VAR models assume that the variables are stationary. However, if the variables are not stationary but cointegrated, then VECM (Vector Error Correction Model) may be useful. The regression analysis expresses the dependency of one variable on the other. But it does not express the causality among the variables. The Granger Causality Test estimates provide detailed information on the causality among the variables. The VAR models are likewise useful to estimate the impulse response analysis and variance decomposition.

6.2   FINANCE IN ACTION

Illustration 1: Decompose the crude oil time series daily mean returns between 2 January 2020 and 18 June 2020 into different components.

EViews Stepwise Implementations

Step 1: Import data into the EViews Workfile window.
Step 2: Double click on the series to test on the Workfile window.
Step 3: New selected series window will appear showing all data-points of the series.
Step 4: Then click on Proc → Seasonal Adjustment → STL Decomposition Window will appear as shown below in Fig. 6.1.
Step 5: Select different specification as you want to decompose the time series as EViews offers several options. The STL decomposition estimates obtained from using the above setting is shown in Fig. 6.2. The STL decomposition window shows that original crude oil time series daily mean returns decomposition into different components, namely: Trend, Season, Remainder, and finally season adjusted data.

Illustration 2: To forecast the S&P 500 daily mean returns for the next three days using ARIMA model.

EViews Stepwise Implementations

Step 1: Import data into the EViews Workfile window.
Step 2: Double click on the series to test on the Workfile window and check if the series is stationary. Open the variable Workfile window → View → Unit Root Tests → Standard Unit Root Test → Unit

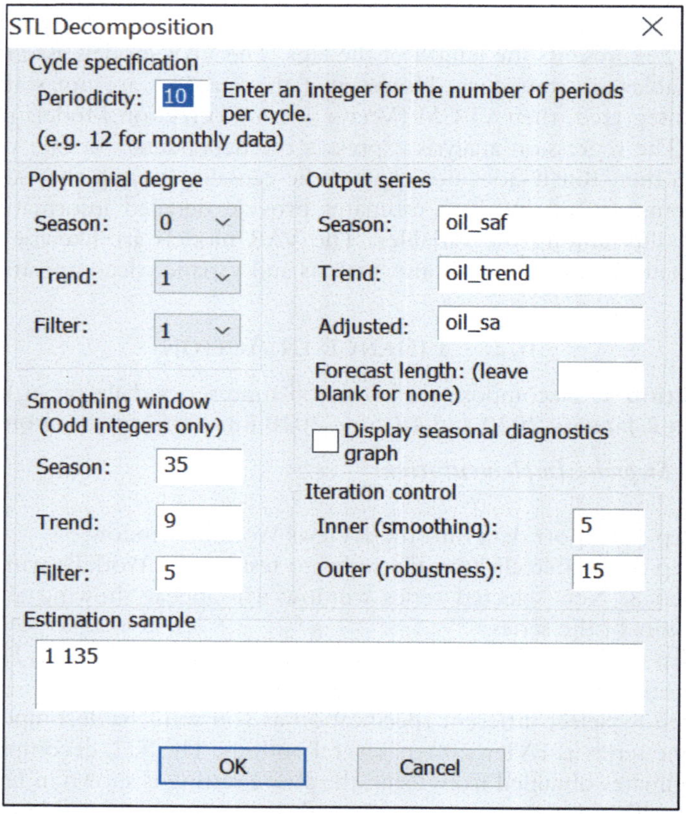

Fig. 6.1   STL decomposition Window

Root Test window will appear and select test for the level → Click OK → Unit root test estimates will appear as shown in Fig. 6.3.

The unit root estimates show that the original time series is stationary.

Step 3: To check the ACF and PACF values using the Correlogram diagram. View → Correlogram → Correlogram window will appear as shown in Fig. 6.4 → Select level and click OK → Correlogram Window will appear as shown in Fig. 6.5.

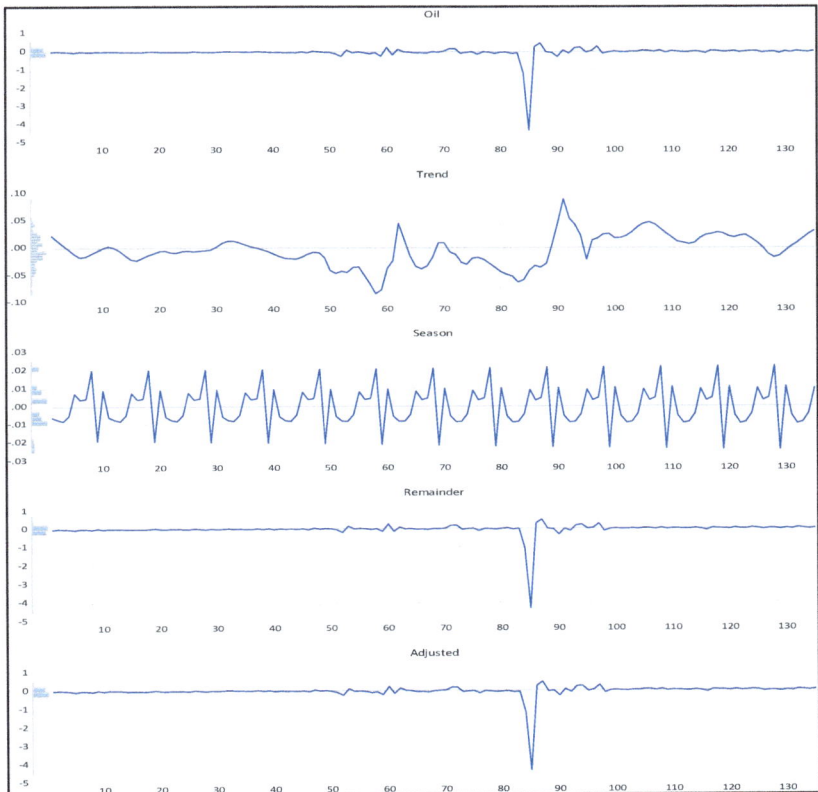

Fig. 6.2 STL decomposition of S&P 500 daily returns

The above diagram shows that the ACF has significant spikes at the lag (8) and lag (11). The ACF has significant highest spike at the lag (11) and thereafter no clear pattern is observed. Likewise, in case of PACF, only significant highest spike observed at the lag (8). Based on these information model selected is ARMA (11, 8).

Step 4: Workfile Window → Double click on the range → Increase the range to 84 from 81 to accommodate the forecasting data.

Step 5: Estimate the ARMA (11, 8) model → View → Estimate Equation → Type "s_p500 c ar(11) ma(8)" in the equation specification → In the options tab select method as CLS as shown in

	t-Statistic	Prob.*
Null Hypothesis: S_P500 has a unit root Exogenous: Constant Lag Length: 0 (Automatic - based on SIC, maxlag=11)		
Augmented Dickey-Fuller test statistic	-9.828770	0.0000
Test critical values: 1% level	-3.514426	
5% level	-2.898145	
10% level	-2.586351	
*MacKinnon (1996) one-sided p-values.		

Fig. 6.3   Unit root test estimates

Fig. 6.4   Correlogram Specification

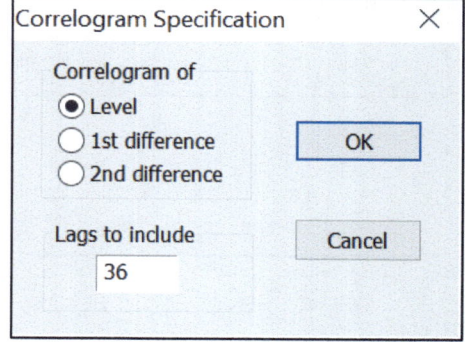

Fig. 6.6 → Click Ok → Estimated output of the model will be displayed as shown in the Fig. 6.7.

The ARMA conditional least square estimates show that both the coefficients of AR(11) and MA(8) are statistically significant.

Step 5: To check the Inverted AR and MA roots plot: View → ARIMA structure → Select a diagnostics as Roots and Display as graph → Click Ok → Following Window will appear as shown in Fig. 6.8. However, same estimates are also shown in the lower part of the Fig. 6.7.

Figure 6.8 shows that all the inverse roots of the AR and MA lies within the range of 1.

Date: 04/27/21   Time: 11:07
Sample: 1 81
Included observations: 81

Autocorrelation	Partial Correlation		AC	PAC	Q-Stat	Prob
		1	-0.108	-0.108	0.9722	0.324
		2	0.054	0.043	1.2191	0.544
		3	-0.186	-0.179	4.2128	0.239
		4	0.065	0.028	4.5786	0.333
		5	-0.139	-0.121	6.2774	0.280
		6	-0.160	-0.232	8.5721	0.199
		7	0.079	0.069	9.1443	0.242
		8	-0.335	-0.411	19.492	0.012
		9	0.161	0.048	21.925	0.009
		10	-0.060	-0.046	22.268	0.014
		11	0.376	0.199	35.872	0.000
		12	-0.068	0.050	36.321	0.000
		13	0.241	0.194	42.053	0.000
		14	-0.138	-0.121	43.973	0.000
		15	-0.054	-0.008	44.267	0.000
		16	0.075	0.107	44.852	0.000
		17	-0.125	-0.032	46.497	0.000
		18	-0.077	-0.104	47.126	0.000
		19	-0.203	0.056	51.584	0.000
		20	0.148	-0.069	53.996	0.000
		21	-0.208	-0.112	58.836	0.000
		22	0.108	-0.142	60.156	0.000
		23	0.085	0.048	60.997	0.000
		24	0.124	-0.051	62.809	0.000
		25	-0.006	0.054	62.813	0.000
		26	0.013	-0.045	62.832	0.000
		27	0.081	0.018	63.649	0.000
		28	-0.073	0.071	64.325	0.000
		29	0.015	-0.026	64.353	0.000
		30	-0.088	0.065	65.382	0.000
		31	-0.026	0.041	65.473	0.000
		32	-0.031	0.101	65.601	0.000
		33	0.012	-0.000	65.621	0.001
		34	-0.006	0.014	65.626	0.001
		35	-0.008	-0.056	65.636	0.001
		36	0.024	-0.136	65.720	0.002

Fig. 6.5 Correlogram Estimates

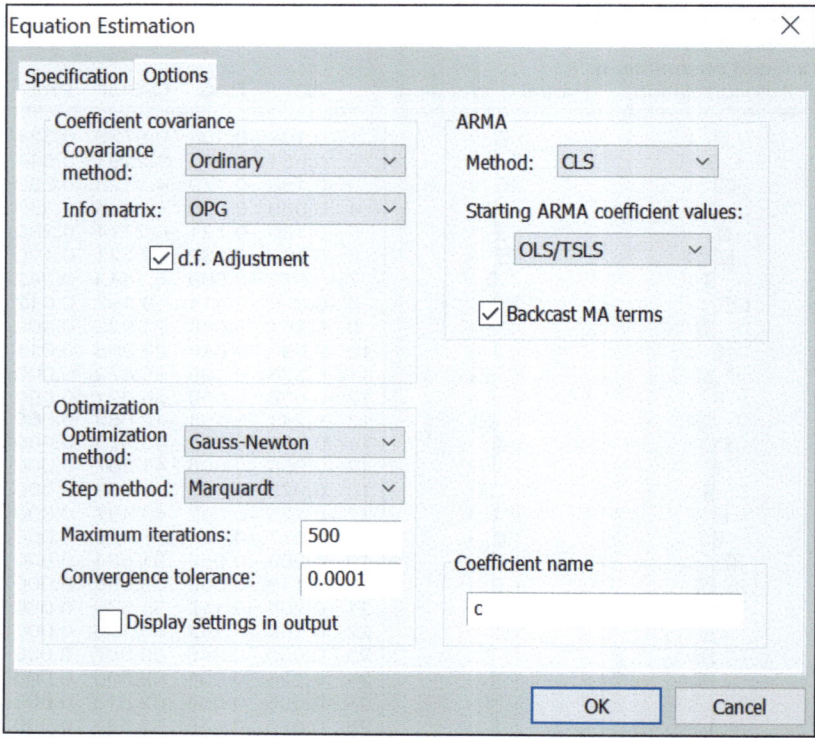

Fig. 6.6 Equation Estimation Window

Step 6: Estimate Q statistics for ARMA. View → Residual Diagnostics → Correlogram Q Statistics → Correlogram of the Residuals will appear as shown in Fig. 6.9. Q statistics estimates for the ARMA show that no serial correlation is left in the residuals as shown in the Fig. 6.9. Thus, it indicates that the specified ARMA (11, 8) model is correct.

Step 7: For forecasting: Estimated output Window → Click Forecast → The Forecast Window will appear as shown in the Fig. 6.10 → Select the forecast specifications as required → Click OK → Forecasted series will be displayed as shown in Fig. 6.11 (a) and (b).

Dependent Variable: S_P500
Method: ARMA Conditional Least Squares (Gauss-Newton / Marquardt
    steps)
Date: 04/27/21   Time: 15:57
Sample (adjusted): 12 81
Included observations: 70 after adjustments
Failure to improve likelihood (non-zero gradients) after 8 iterations
Coefficient covariance computed using outer product of gradients
MA Backcast: 4 11

Variable	Coefficient	Std. Error	t-Statistic	Prob.
C	-0.001884	0.005364	-0.351318	0.7265
AR(11)	0.364426	0.121116	3.008898	0.0037
MA(8)	-0.252539	0.128095	-1.971500	0.0528

R-squared	0.214591	Mean dependent var	-0.002363
Adjusted R-squared	0.191146	S.D. dependent var	0.040295
S.E. of regression	0.036240	Akaike info criterion	-3.755398
Sum squared resid	0.087993	Schwarz criterion	-3.659034
Log likelihood	134.4389	Hannan-Quinn criter.	-3.717121
F-statistic	9.152963	Durbin-Watson stat	2.083499
Prob(F-statistic)	0.000306		

Inverted AR Roots	.91	.77+.49i	.77-.49i	.38-.83i
	.38+.83i	-.13-.90i	-.13+.90i	-.60+.69i
	-.60-.69i	-.88+.26i	-.88-.26i	
Inverted MA Roots	.84	.60-.60i	.60+.60i	-.00-.84i
	-.00+.84i	-.60-.60i	-.60-.60i	-.84

Fig. 6.7   ARIMA Estimates

EViews provides two options for forecasting, namely static and
dynamic. The ARMA (11, 8) model forecasting estimates for both
static and dynamic methods are shown in Fig. 6.11 (a) and (b). Theil
U2 coefficients values are higher than 1 in both the cases. Higher
values of the Theil U2 coefficients indicate that more sophisticated
modelling is needed for forecasting. The large values of the variance

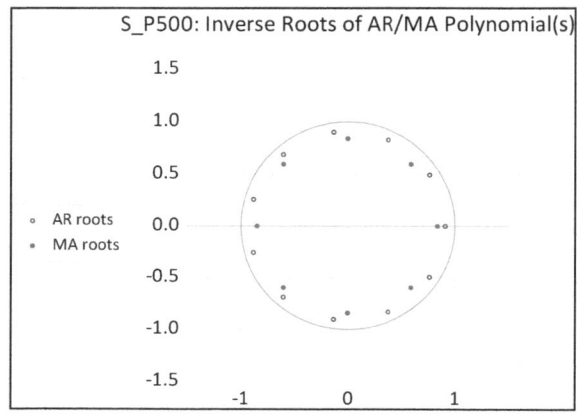

Fig. 6.8   Inverted AR and MA roots plot

proportion indicates that the forecasts are not tracking the varia-tion in the actual S&P 500 series. Thus, the ARMA models do not account for the volatility clustering.

Illustration 3: To examine the presence of the ARCH effect in the daily mean return of S&P 500 index between the period 22 January 2020 and 11 April 2020.

EViews Stepwise Implementations

Step 1: Import data into the EViews Workfile window.
Step 2: Double click on the series to test on the Workfile window.
Step 3: Plot the graph as shown in the Fig. 6.12.
Step 4: Then click on Quick → Estimate Equation → The Equa-tion Estimation Window will appear → Type "s_p500 c s_p500(-1)" in the equation specification as shown in Fig. 6.13 → Click the OK button → Estimation Window will appear as shown below in Fig. 6.14.
    Next, perform the ARCH test to check whether ARCH effect is present in the residuals obtained from the AR(1) regressions as shown in Fig. 6.15.
Step 5: Next, check for the ARCH effect in the residuals of the estimated AR(1) model. ARCH Estimation Window → Residual

Date: 04/27/21   Time: 16:39
Sample (adjusted): 12 81
Q-statistic probabilities adjusted for 2 ARMA terms

Autocorrelation	Partial Correlation		AC	PAC	Q-Stat	Prob
		1	-0.046	-0.046	0.1541	
		2	-0.147	-0.149	1.7543	
		3	-0.061	-0.078	2.0360	0.154
		4	0.097	0.069	2.7521	0.253
		5	-0.121	-0.136	3.8799	0.275
		6	-0.188	-0.192	6.6561	0.155
		7	0.082	0.037	7.1967	0.206
		8	-0.032	-0.114	7.2811	0.296
		9	0.120	0.125	8.4647	0.293
		10	0.006	0.021	8.4679	0.389
		11	0.040	0.009	8.6065	0.474
		12	-0.029	-0.009	8.6813	0.563
		13	0.171	0.188	11.252	0.422
		14	-0.160	-0.166	13.548	0.331
		15	-0.059	0.044	13.867	0.383
		16	0.130	0.126	15.442	0.349
		17	-0.019	-0.064	15.476	0.418
		18	-0.125	-0.065	16.993	0.386
		19	-0.071	-0.030	17.497	0.421
		20	0.122	-0.049	19.007	0.391
		21	-0.210	-0.201	23.548	0.214
		22	-0.074	-0.105	24.115	0.237
		23	0.100	0.017	25.186	0.239
		24	0.114	0.021	26.600	0.227
		25	0.047	0.096	26.847	0.263
		26	-0.008	-0.028	26.855	0.311
		27	0.052	0.054	27.176	0.347
		28	-0.059	-0.013	27.588	0.379
		29	0.015	0.010	27.618	0.431
		30	-0.027	0.104	27.709	0.480
		31	-0.025	0.063	27.787	0.529
		32	0.002	0.011	27.788	0.582

Fig. 6.9   Q Statistics Estimates

Diagnostics → Heteroskedasticity Tests → Heteroskedasticity Tests
Window will appear → Select test type as ARCH → Click OK →
Heteroskedasticity Tests estimates Window will appear as shown in
the Fig. 6.15.

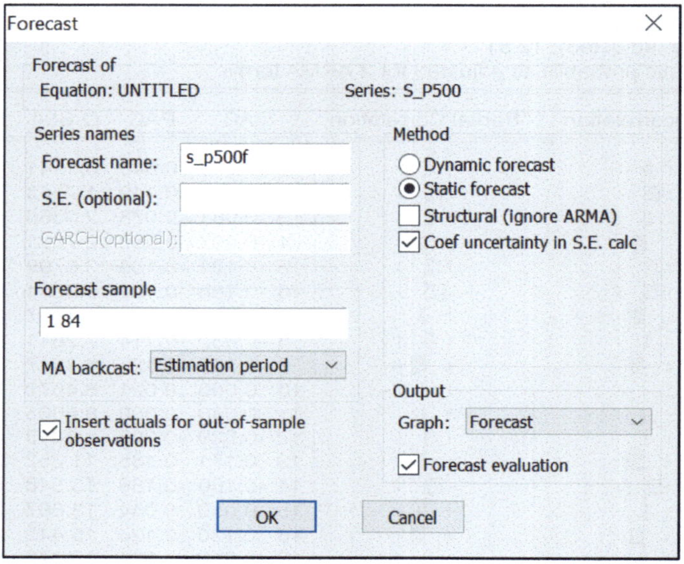

Fig. 6.10   Forecast Window Specification

The Obs* R squared statistics find to be statistically significant. That confirms the presence of the ARCH effect in the S&P 500 in the daily mean returns.

Illustration 4: To estimate the GARCH model for the daily mean return of S&P 500 index between the period 22 January 2020 and 11 April 2020.

EViews Stepwise Implementations

Step 1: Import data into the EViews Workfile window.
Step 2: Then click on Quick → Estimate Equation → The Equation Estimation Window will appear → Write "s_p500 c s_p500(-1)" in the equation specification and select method as the ARCH from the drop down list as shown in Fig. 6.16.
Step 3: Select all necessary GARCH specification → Click OK → Estimated GARCH model Window will appear as shown in Fig. 6.17.

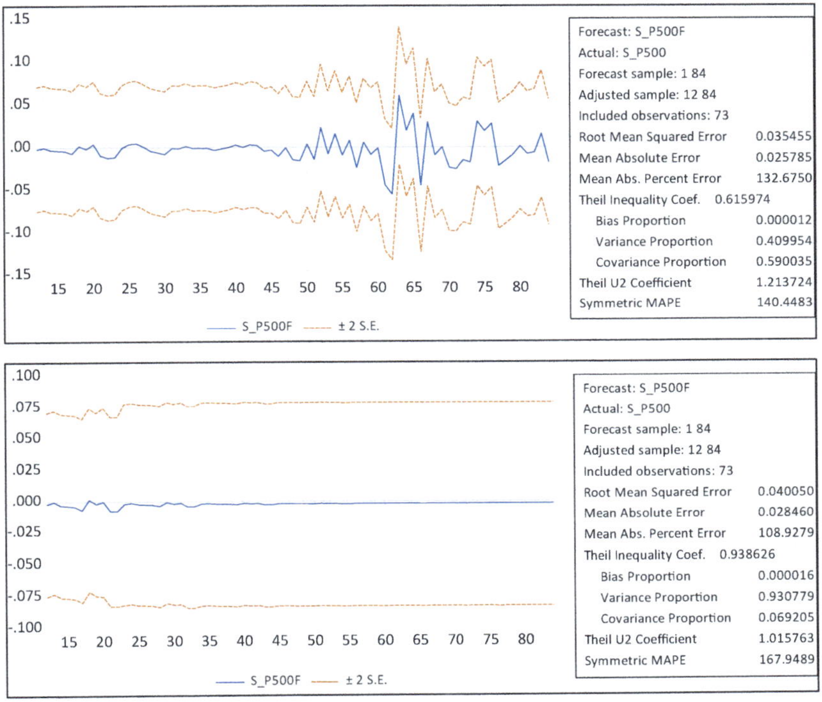

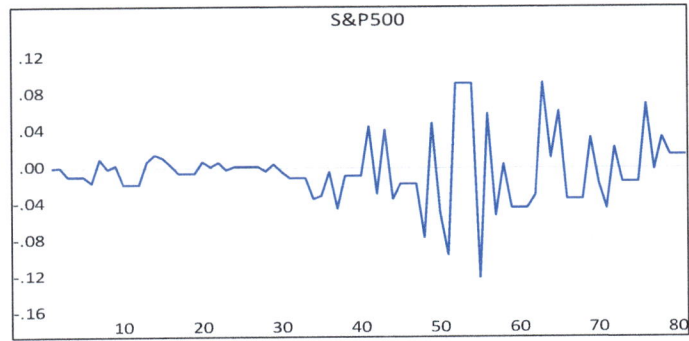

Forecast: S_P500F		
Actual: S_P500		
Forecast sample: 1 84		
Adjusted sample: 12 84		
Included observations: 73		
Root Mean Squared Error		0.035455
Mean Absolute Error		0.025785
Mean Abs. Percent Error		132.6750
Theil Inequality Coef.	0.615974	
Bias Proportion		0.000012
Variance Proportion		0.409954
Covariance Proportion		0.590035
Theil U2 Coefficient		1.213724
Symmetric MAPE		140.4483

Forecast: S_P500F		
Actual: S_P500		
Forecast sample: 1 84		
Adjusted sample: 12 84		
Included observations: 73		
Root Mean Squared Error		0.040050
Mean Absolute Error		0.028460
Mean Abs. Percent Error		108.9279
Theil Inequality Coef.	0.938626	
Bias Proportion		0.000016
Variance Proportion		0.930779
Covariance Proportion		0.069205
Theil U2 Coefficient		1.015763
Symmetric MAPE		167.9489

Fig. 6.11 (a) Static method and (b) Dynamic method

Fig. 6.12 S&P daily return plot

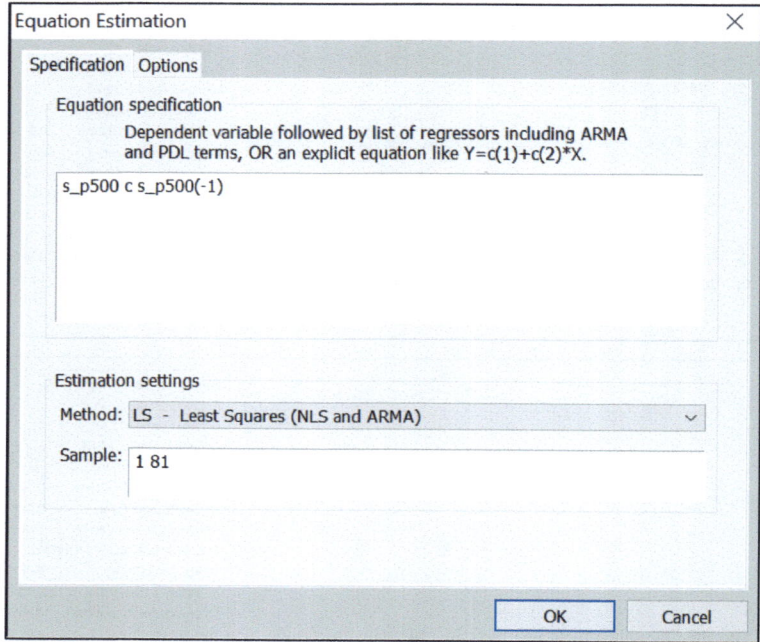

Fig. 6.13 Equation Estimation Window

The GARCH (1, 1) model estimates show that both the lagged squared residual and lagged conditional variance coefficients are highly statistically significant. That confirms the presence of the volatility clustering in the S&P 500 daily mean returns. Further, the coefficients values of both the lagged squared residual and lagged conditional variance terms are closer to 1. This indicates that the volatility shocks are quite persistent in the S&P 500 daily mean returns.

Illustration 5: To estimate a VAR model with the EUR_USD, GBP_USD, and USD_JPY.

Data description: Daily exchange rates between the period 31 December 2019 and 22 July 2020.

Dependent Variable: S_P500 Method: Least Squares Date: 04/27/21 Time: 22:16 Sample (adjusted): 2 81 Included observations: 80 after adjustments				
Variable	Coefficient	Std. Error	t-Statistic	Prob.
C	-0.003208	0.004245	-0.755700	0.4521
S_P500(-1)	-0.107856	0.112716	-0.956889	0.3416
R-squared	0.011603	Mean dependent var		-0.002878
Adjusted R-squared	-0.001069	S.D. dependent var		0.037820
S.E. of regression	0.037840	Akaike info criterion		-3.686222
Sum squared resid	0.111685	Schwarz criterion		-3.626671
Log likelihood	149.4489	Hannan-Quinn criter.		-3.662346
F-statistic	0.915636	Durbin-Watson stat		1.987600
Prob(F-statistic)	0.341580			

Fig. 6.14 Estimation output

EViews Stepwise Implementations

Step 1: Import data into the EViews Workfile window.

Step 2: Estimate the log values: Click on Quick → Generate Series → The Generate Series by Equation Window will appear as shown in Fig. 6.18 → Type "leu = log(eur_usd)" in the field enter equation and click OK → Generated new series will be added into the EViews Workfile. Similarly, following the same procedure estimate the log values for the other variables.

[Note: LEU represent log(EUR_USD); LGU represents log(GBP_USD); and LUJ represents log(USD_JPY)].

Step 3: Estimate the VAR equation: Quick → Estimate VAR → The VAR specification Window will appear → Type "d(leu) d(lgu) d(luj)" in the Endogenous variables, set lag to 1, select VAR type as the Standard VAR as shown in Fig. 6.19 → Click the OK button → The VAR Estimation Window will appear as shown below in Fig. 6.20.

Note: Log series are not stationary. Thus, d(log) series are used for the VAR analysis.

Heteroskedasticity Test: ARCH				
F-statistic	46.41055	Prob. F(1,77)		0.0000
Obs*R-squared	29.70924	Prob. Chi-Square(1)		0.0000

Test Equation:
Dependent Variable: RESID^2
Method: Least Squares
Date: 04/26/21   Time: 22:09
Sample (adjusted): 3 81
Included observations: 79 after adjustments

Variable	Coefficient	Std. Error	t-Statistic	Prob.
C	0.000550	0.000274	2.005906	0.0484
RESID^2(-1)	0.612788	0.089950	6.812529	0.0000
R-squared	0.376066	Mean dependent var		0.001413
Adjusted R-squared	0.367963	S.D. dependent var		0.002719
S.E. of regression	0.002161	Akaike info criterion		-9.411215
Sum squared resid	0.000360	Schwarz criterion		-9.351229
Log likelihood	373.7430	Hannan-Quinn criter.		-9.387183
F-statistic	46.41055	Durbin-Watson stat		2.425662
Prob(F-statistic)	0.000000			

Fig. 6.15 ARCH Test estimates

The Second column of the VAR estimates (Fig. 6.20) represents
EUR_USD equation. Similarly, column third and fourth belongs to
the GBP_USD and USD_JPY, respectively. Only D[LGU(-1)] coefficient appears to be statistically significant in all three equations.
Thus, it indicates that the higher growth of D[LGU(-1)] during
period $t - 1$ leads to higher growth of D[LEU], D[LGU]; and
D[LUJ] in period t. The estimated VAR model can be used for
forecasting.

Step 4: Granger Causality Test: VAR Estimation Window → Lag
Structure → Granger Causality/Block Exogeneity Test → VAR
Granger Causality Test Estimation Window will appear as shown
below in Fig. 6.21.

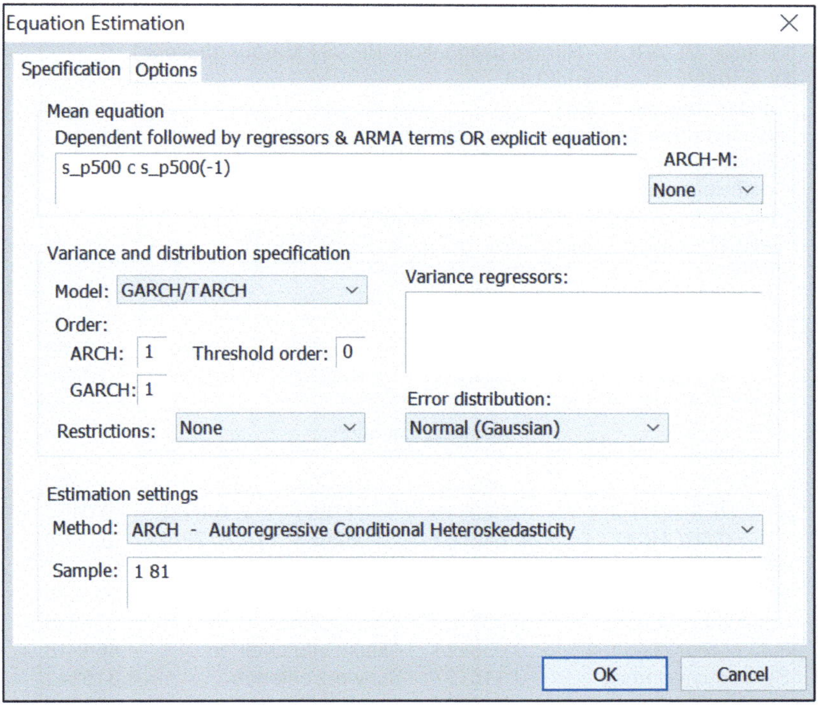

Fig. 6.16 Equation Estimation Window

Read the above VAR Granger Causality Test estimates as following.

Dependable Variable (EUR_USD)
D[LGU] → D[LEU] implies D[LGU] Granger causes D[LEU]
D[LUJ] ⇏ D[LEU] implies D[LUJ] doesn't Granger cause D[LEU]
D[LGU], D[LUJ] → D[LEU] implies D[LGU] & D[LUJ] jointly Granger cause D[LEU]

Dependable Variable (GBP_USD)
D[LEU] ⇏ D[LGU] implies D[LEU] doesn't Granger cause D[LGU]

```
Dependent Variable: S_P500
Method: ML ARCH - Normal distribution (BFGS / Marquardt steps)
Date: 04/26/21   Time: 22:18
Sample (adjusted): 2 81
Included observations: 80 after adjustments
Convergence achieved after 28 iterations
Coefficient covariance computed using outer product of gradients
Presample variance: backcast (parameter = 0.7)
GARCH = C(3) + C(4)*RESID(-1)^2 + C(5)*GARCH(-1)
```

Variable	Coefficient	Std. Error	z-Statistic	Prob.
C	0.000536	0.001592	0.336767	0.7363
S_P500(-1)	0.044384	0.135332	0.327965	0.7429
Variance Equation				
C	1.90E-06	5.86E-06	0.323910	0.7460
RESID(-1)^2	0.522399	0.211653	2.468185	0.0136
GARCH(-1)	0.646603	0.082085	7.877272	0.0000

R-squared	-0.019124	Mean dependent var	-0.002878
Adjusted R-squared	-0.032189	S.D. dependent var	0.037820
S.E. of regression	0.038424	Akaike info criterion	-4.464018
Sum squared resid	0.115157	Schwarz criterion	-4.315141
Log likelihood	183.5607	Hannan-Quinn criter.	-4.404329
Durbin-Watson stat	2.285867		

Fig. 6.17   GARCH Estimates

D[LUJ] $\nrightarrow$ D[LGU] implies D[LUJ] doesn't Granger cause D[LGU]
D[LEU], D[LUJ] $\nrightarrow$ D[LGU] implies D[LGU] & D[LUJ] do not jointly Granger cause D[LGU]

Dependable Variable (USD_JPY)
D[LEU] $\nrightarrow$ D[LUJ] implies D[LEU] doesn't Granger cause D[LUJ]
D[LGU] $\rightarrow$ D[LUJ] implies D[LGU] Granger causes D[LUJ]
D[LEU], D[LGU] $\rightarrow$ D[LUJ] implies D[LEU] & D[LGU] jointly Granger cause D[LUJ]

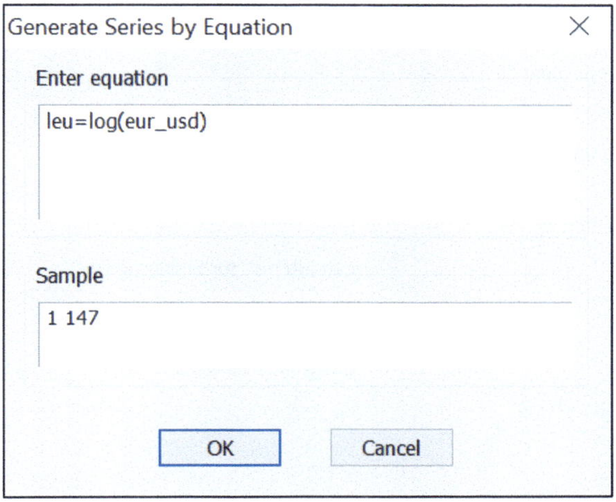

Fig. 6.18   Generate Series by Equation Window

Thus, the conclusion derived from the Granger Causality test esti-mates show similar inference as the VAR estimates (Fig. 6.20).

Step 5: VAR stability conditional check: View → Lag Structure → AR Roots Table → Estimates will appear as shown in Fig. 6.22. The VAR satisfies the stability condition.

Step 6: Lag Length Selection: View → Lag Structure → Lag length criteria → Lag Specification Window will appear, include number of lag as 6 and click OK → Estimates will appear as shown in Fig. 6.23.

The obtained lag length selection estimates show that the FPE, AIC, and HQ all selected lag order of one. Whereas SC selected the lag order of zero. All of these estimates justify our selection of the lag order of one.

Step 7: Autocorrelation LM Test: View → Residual Test → Autocor-relation LM Test → Lag Specification Window will appear, include number of lag as 6 and click OK → Estimates will appear as shown in Fig. 6.24.

The VAR residual serial correlation LM tests estimates show that there is no serial correlation in the VAR model.

Step 8: Impulse Response: View → Impulse Response → The Impulse Response Specification Window will appear (as shown in

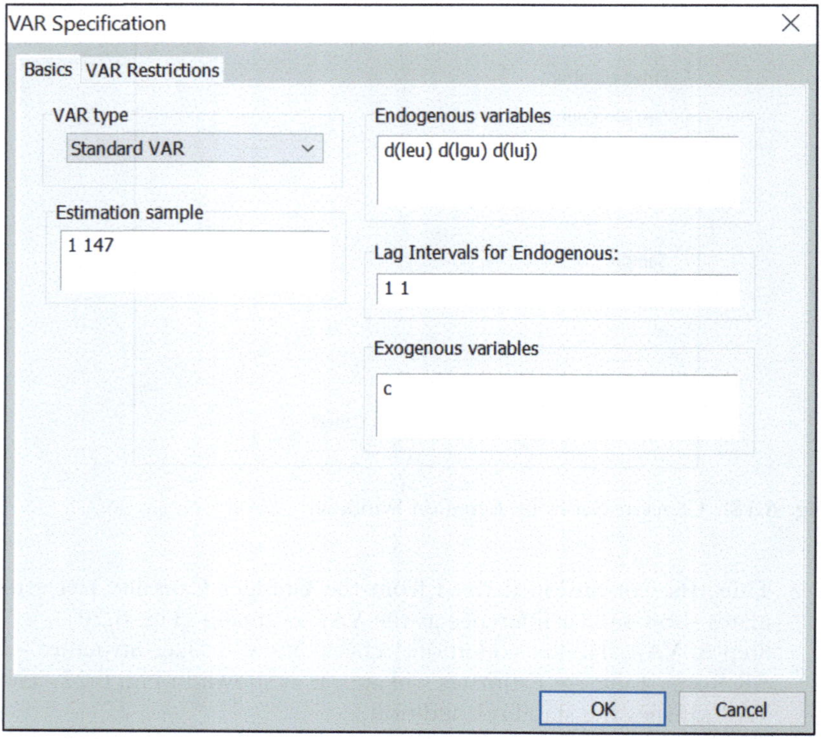

Fig. 6.19   VAR specification Window

Fig. 6.25), select the specification details and click OK → Estimates will appear as shown in Fig. 6.26.

The solid lines in the diagram represent the response of the various endogenous variables to shocks. Whereas the dotted lines represent the upper and lower limits of the statistical significance. The impulse response diagram indicates the amount of time required by the endogenous variables to return back to its long run equilibrium states.

Step 9: Variance Decomposition: View → Variance Decomposition → The Variance Decomposition Specification Window will appear (as shown in Fig. 6.27), select the specification details and click OK → Estimates will appear as shown in Fig. 6.28.

	D(LEU)	D(LGU)	D(LUJ)
Vector Autoregression Estimates Date: 04/28/21 Time: 10:38 Sample (adjusted): 3 147 Included observations: 145 after adjustments Standard errors in ( ) & t-statistics in [ ]			
D(LEU(-1))	0.091964 (0.10436) [0.88126]	0.263020 (0.15755) [1.66940]	-0.041208 (0.12206) [-0.33760]
D(LGU(-1))	0.219363 (0.06399) [3.42787]	0.192899 (0.09662) [1.99655]	-0.307572 (0.07485) [-4.10901]
D(LUJ(-1))	0.104697 (0.07924) [1.32133]	0.093056 (0.11963) [0.77788]	-0.113270 (0.09268) [-1.22214]
C	0.000248 (0.00041) [0.60573]	-0.000271 (0.00062) [-0.43771]	-0.000203 (0.00048) [-0.42265]
R-squared	0.120573	0.087075	0.141139
Adj. R-squared	0.101862	0.067651	0.122865
Sum sq. resids	0.003425	0.007807	0.004686
S.E. equation	0.004929	0.007441	0.005765
F-statistic	6.443908	4.482880	7.723617
Log likelihood	566.6260	506.8921	543.8992
Akaike AIC	-7.760359	-6.936443	-7.446886
Schwarz SC	-7.678242	-6.854326	-7.364769
Mean dependent	0.000199	-0.000287	-0.000123
S.D. dependent	0.005200	0.007706	0.006155
Determinant resid covariance (dof adj.)	2.58E-14		
Determinant resid covariance	2.37E-14		
Log likelihood	1657.312		
Akaike information criterion	-22.69395		
Schwarz criterion	-22.44760		
Number of coefficients	12		

Fig. 6.20 VAR Estimates

VAR Granger Causality/Block Exogeneity Wald Tests Date: 04/28/21 Time: 10:44 Sample: 1 147 Included observations: 145			
Dependent variable: D(LEU)			
Excluded	Chi-sq	df	Prob.
D(LGU)	11.75026	1	0.0006
D(LUJ)	1.745907	1	0.1864
All	12.51313	2	0.0019
Dependent variable: D(LGU)			
Excluded	Chi-sq	df	Prob.
D(LEU)	2.786909	1	0.0950
D(LUJ)	0.605091	1	0.4366
All	2.798128	2	0.2468
Dependent variable: D(LUJ)			
Excluded	Chi-sq	df	Prob.
D(LEU)	0.113970	1	0.7357
D(LGU)	16.88397	1	0.0000
All	22.69683	2	0.0000

Fig. 6.21 VAR Granger Causality Test estimates

The variance decomposition diagram provides important information on the percentage forecasting errors of a variable due to the unanticipated shocks. The unanticipated shocks may result due to the variable itself or from the other interrelated variables. The variance decomposition diagram

Roots of Characteristic Polynomial Endogenous variables: D(LEU) D(LGU) D(LUJ) Exogenous variables: C Lag specification: 1 1 Date: 04/28/21 Time: 10:47	
Root	Modulus
0.291006 -0.149722 0.030310	0.291006 0.149722 0.030310
No root lies outside the unit circle. VAR satisfies the stability condition.	

Fig. 6.22   VAR Stability Estimates

VAR Lag Order Selection Criteria
Endogenous variables: D(LEU) D(LGU) D(LUJ)
Exogenous variables: C
Date: 04/28/21   Time: 10:50
Sample: 1 147
Included observations: 140

Lag	LogL	LR	FPE	AIC	SC	HQ
0	1582.119	NA	3.20e-14	-22.55884	-22.49581*	-22.53323
1	1597.930	30.71941	2.91e-14*	-22.65615*	-22.40401	-22.55369*
2	1599.248	2.503138	3.24e-14	-22.54640	-22.10515	-22.36709
3	1608.237	16.69491	3.24e-14	-22.54625	-21.91590	-22.29009
4	1616.259	14.55411	3.29e-14	-22.53228	-21.71282	-22.19927
5	1624.298	14.24009	3.34e-14	-22.51855	-21.50998	-22.10870
6	1634.221	17.15242*	3.31e-14	-22.53173	-21.33406	-22.04503

* indicates lag order selected by the criterion
LR: sequential modified LR test statistic (each test at 5% level)
FPE: Final prediction error
AIC: Akaike information criterion
SC: Schwarz information criterion
HQ: Hannan-Quinn information criterion

Fig. 6.23   Lag Length Selection Estimates

| VAR Residual Serial Correlation LM Tests |
| Date: 04/28/21   Time: 10:53 |
| Sample: 1 147 |
| Included observations: 145 |

Null hypothesis: No serial correlation at lag h

Lag	LRE* stat	df	Prob.	Rao F-stat	df	Prob.
1	2.181166	9	0.9883	0.240600	(9, 331.1)	0.9883
2	3.538069	9	0.9391	0.391071	(9, 331.1)	0.9391
3	12.40571	9	0.1914	1.389594	(9, 331.1)	0.1914
4	17.60703	9	0.0400	1.987708	(9, 331.1)	0.0400
5	12.86996	9	0.1686	1.442602	(9, 331.1)	0.1686
6	15.00549	9	0.0908	1.687387	(9, 331.1)	0.0908

Null hypothesis: No serial correlation at lags 1 to h

Lag	LRE* stat	df	Prob.	Rao F-stat	df	Prob.
1	2.181166	9	0.9883	0.240600	(9, 331.1)	0.9883
2	17.52732	18	0.4872	0.975545	(18, 376.7)	0.4874
3	28.72617	27	0.3743	1.068676	(27, 380.3)	0.3749
4	38.48870	36	0.3575	1.074648	(36, 376.0)	0.3587
5	49.28788	45	0.3057	1.103133	(45, 369.2)	0.3076
6	69.09702	54	0.0810	1.306777	(54, 361.3)	0.0825

| *Edgeworth expansion corrected likelihood ratio statistic. |

Fig. 6.24 Autocorrelation LM Test Estimates

estimate for the D[LEU] shows that more than 90% of the forecast error variations is due its own shocks even in longer period (10).

Summary

This chapter briefly introduced the various econometrics techniques used to deal with the time series. The STL (Seasonal and Trend decomposition using LOESS) techniques to decompose a time series into its various

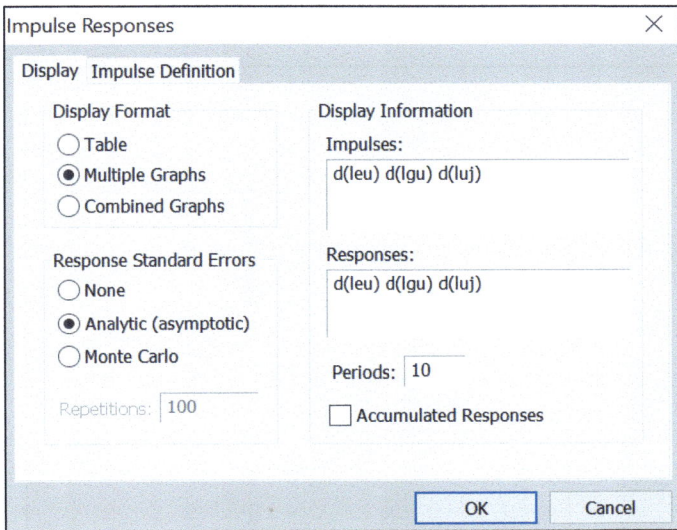

Fig. 6.25 Impulse Responses Specification Window

components is covered in detail. The ARIMA models are discussed in detail. The Correlogram diagrams are discussed in detail for lag selections. ARCH and GARCH models are discussed in detail. Then VAR models are covered along with its usefulness. Finally, each of these econometrics techniques is illustrated with EViews stepwise implementations along with its interpretations.

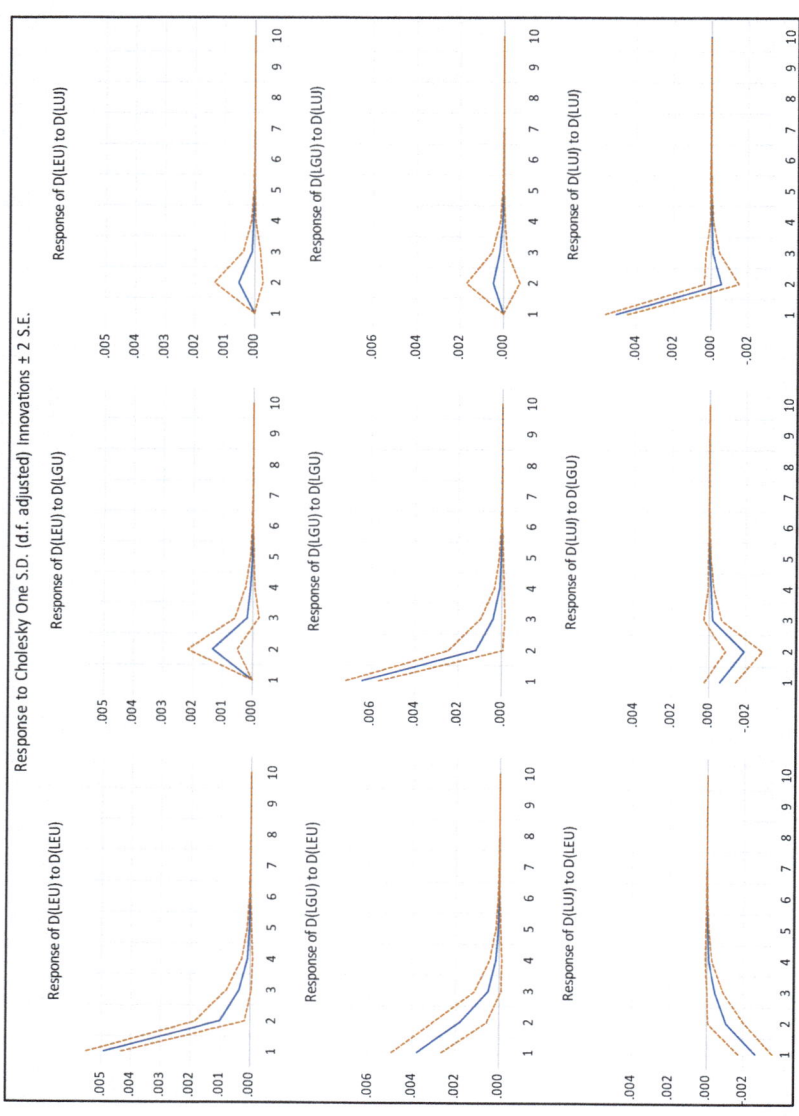

Fig. 6.26 Impulse response analysis

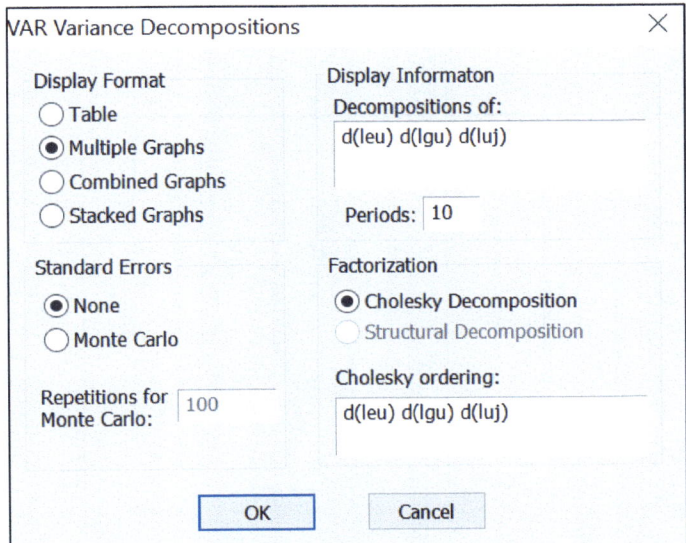

Fig. 6.27 Variance Decomposition Specification Window

Analysts/Investors Corner

The random walk models are not always efficient in capturing the autocorrelations that exist in the time series. To deal with the time series, it is necessary to have the stationary time series. The ARMA models are efficient to a greater extent for handling such autocorrelation problems. However, ARMA models do not account for the volatility clustering or conditional heteroscedasticity that exists in the time series. Thus, for modelling the volatility clustering requires more sophisticated techniques such as the ARCH and GARCH modelling. To deal with the multivariate time series, VAR models are useful. While if the time series is not stationary but cointegrated, then VECM models may be useful. The VAR models may be also useful for impulse response analysis and variance decomposition of the variables.

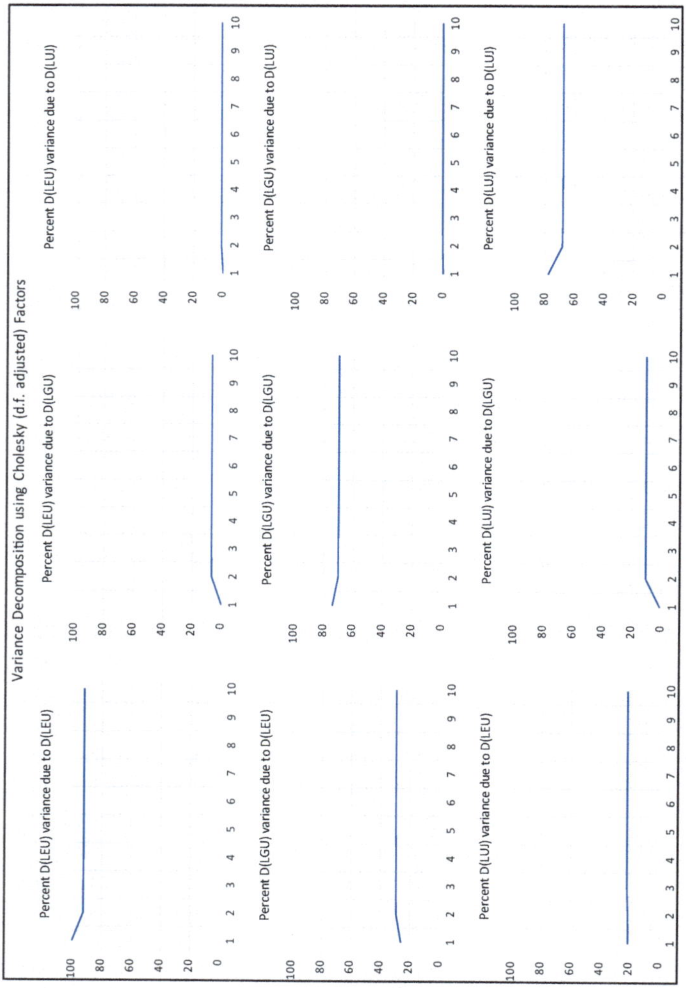

Fig. 6.28 Variance Decomposition Analysis

6.3   Exercises

6.3.1   *Multiple Choice Questions*

1. ARIMA stands for

   (a) Auto Regressive Integer Moving Average
   (b) Auto Regressive Integrated Moving Average
   (c) Auto Regressive Independent Moving Average
   (d) None

2. In ARIMA modelling "I" stands for

   (a) Independent
   (b) Integer
   (c) Integrated
   (d) Integration

3. The ARMA models are used for forecasting the _____ time series.

   (a) Stationary
   (b) Non Stationary
   (c) Both
   (d) None of the above

4. The acronym for STL is

   (a) Seasonal Time series Loss
   (b) Seasonal and Trend Loss
   (c) Seasonal and Trend decomposition using LOESS
   (d) Seasonal and Trend decomposition using LOSS

5. The acronym for LOESS is

   (a) locally estimated scales smoothing
   (b) locally estimated scatterplot smoothing
   (c) large of errors scatterplot smoothing
   (d) local error scatterplot smoothing

6. GARCH stands for

   (a) Geometric autoregressive conditional homoskedasticity
   (b) Generalized autoregressive conditional heteroskedasticity
   (c) Generalized autoregressive conditional homoskedasticity
   (d) Geometric autoregressive conditional heteroskedasticity

7. The acronym for VECM is

   (a) Vector Error Correction Model
   (b) Vector Error Correction Method
   (c) Variance Error Correction Model
   d) Variance Error Correction Method

8. The VAR models are useful for modelling the _____ time series.

   (a) Multi Scale
   (b) Multivariate
   (c) Multiple
   (d) Multi frequency

9. In ARMA model lagged values are selected based on the

   (a) ACF
   (b) PACF
   (c) Both ACF and PACF
   (d) None of the above

10. A time series can be decomposed into which of the following component(s)

   (a) Trend
   (b) Season
   (c) Remainder
   (d) All of the above

6.3.2   Fill in the Blanks

1. The ARIMA (p, 0, q) model is same as the _____ model if the original time series is stationary.
2. The _____ and _____ techniques are used widely for modelling the volatility.
3. _____ test is used to examine causality among the variables.
4. If the variables are not stationary but cointegrated then _____ may be useful.
5. The VAR stands for _____.
6. The ARMA models do not account for the _____.

7. The _____ method is used for decomposing a time series into its various components.
8. The STL decomposes the time series into different components using an _____ function.
9. The LOESS is a _____ technique.
10. The ARIMA stands for _____.

6.3.3 Long Answer Questions

1. Define STL method for time series decomposition using suitable examples?
2. Define ARIMA forecasting modelling using suitable examples?
3. What is ARCH effect and its implications?
4. How ARCH and GARCH modelling are dissimilar explain it with suitable examples?
5. Comment on the following statement: The ARCH and GARCH are more sophisticated modelling techniques as compared to the ARIMA.
6. Define VAR modelling with suitable examples?
7. List the various advantages and disadvantages associated with the VAR technique.
8. What is VECM and its implications?
9. Explain the term stationarity with respect to the time series. Why stationarity assumption of a time series is essential for modelling?
10. What is the importance of VAR Granger Causality Test? How it is different from regressions?
11. What is impulse response analysis of the variables? How impulse response analysis of the variables is different from the variance decomposition of the variables?
12. What is Correlogram diagram and its significance in econometric modelling?
13. What is Q statistics for ARMA and its significance?
14. What is ARCH test and its significance?
15. What are inverted AR and MA roots, and its relevance?

6.3.4   Real-World Tasks

1. A professor asks his/her student to test the ARCH effect during the COVID-19 first and second phase impact on the European stock markets ? Assume yourself as the student and perform the task. Then prepare a detailed report of the analysis to be submitted to the professor.
2. A researcher wants to develop the ARIMA forecasting models for the top five cryptocurrencies during the noble Corona virus pandemic. Assume yourself as the researcher: perform the mentioned task in details and develop the analysis report.
3. An analyst wants to model the volatility of the world indices before, and during the COVID-19 pandemic. Help him/her to perform the said analysis and prepare the report.
4. A student needs to develop a VAR model for the variables GDP, Money supply and Income as his/her project dissertation. Help the student to complete his/her project dissertation successfully and satisfactorily.
5. A senior manager of the Reserve bank of India (RBI) asked an intern working under him/her to develop a precise GDP forecasting model of India. Help the intern in analysing and developing the final report for timely submission to the senior RBI manager.
6. An investor wants to examine if there exists any volatility clustering in the Herzfeld Caribbean Basin Fund (CUBA) average daily returns. Help the investors to examine the CUBA fund volatility clustering.

6.3.5   Case Studies

1. The figure below represents the STL decomposition diagram for the VIX daily returns between the period 3 January 2020 and 31 March 2020. Based on this information comment on the each components of the decomposed series.

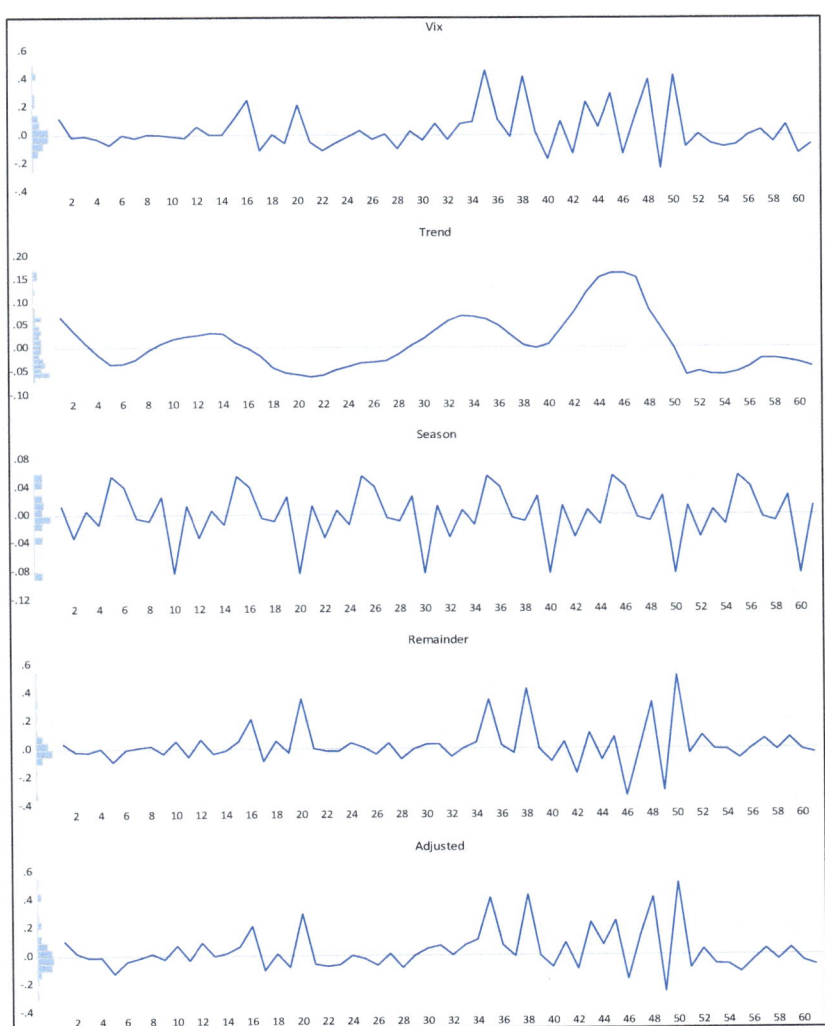

2. Comment on the ARCH Test Estimates Obtained for the Gold Daily Average Returns Between the Period 2 January 2020 and 18 June 2020.

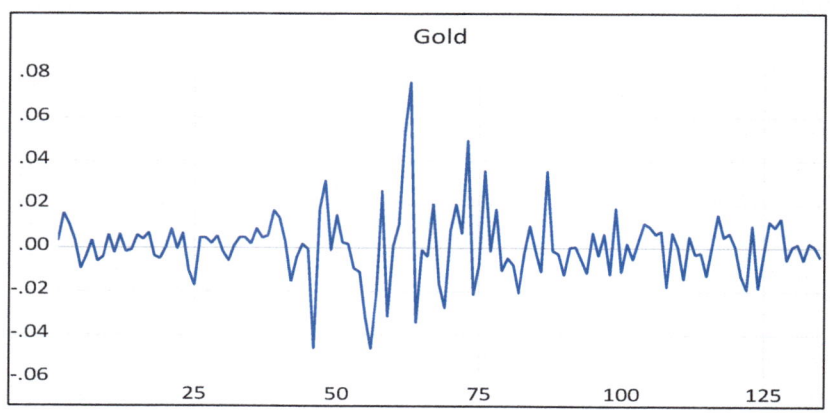

```
Dependent Variable: GOLD
Method: Least Squares
Date: 04/29/21   Time: 09:59
Sample (adjusted): 2 135
Included observations: 134 after adjustments
```

Variable	Coefficient	Std. Error	t-Statistic	Prob.
C	0.000992	0.001384	0.716792	0.4748
GOLD(-1)	0.068170	0.086865	0.784783	0.4340

R-squared	0.004644	Mean dependent var		0.001069
Adjusted R-squared	-0.002896	S.D. dependent var		0.015957
S.E. of regression	0.015980	Akaike info criterion		-5.420189
Sum squared resid	0.033706	Schwarz criterion		-5.376938
Log likelihood	365.1527	Hannan-Quinn criter.		-5.402613
F-statistic	0.615884	Durbin-Watson stat		1.983273
Prob(F-statistic)	0.433987			

```
Heteroskedasticity Test: ARCH
```

F-statistic	28.66243	Prob. F(1,131)	0.0000
Obs*R-squared	23.87602	Prob. Chi-Square(1)	0.0000

```
Test Equation:
Dependent Variable: RESID^2
Method: Least Squares
Date: 04/29/21   Time: 09:57
Sample (adjusted): 3 135
Included observations: 133 after adjustments
```

Variable	Coefficient	Std. Error	t-Statistic	Prob.
C	0.000144	5.36E-05	2.695724	0.0079
RESID^2(-1)	0.423900	0.079179	5.353731	0.0000

R-squared	0.179519	Mean dependent var	0.000252
Adjusted R-squared	0.173256	S.D. dependent var	0.000630
S.E. of regression	0.000573	Akaike info criterion	-12.07704
Sum squared resid	4.30E-05	Schwarz criterion	-12.03358
Log likelihood	805.1234	Hannan-Quinn criter.	-12.05938
F-statistic	28.66243	Durbin-Watson stat	1.900741
Prob(F-statistic)	0.000000		

3. Comment on the GARCH Test Estimates Obtained for the Gold Daily Average Returns Between the Period 2 January 2020 and 18 June 2020.

Dependent Variable: GOLD
Method: ML ARCH - Normal distribution (BFGS / Marquardt steps)
Date: 04/29/21   Time: 10:03
Sample (adjusted): 2 135
Included observations: 134 after adjustments
Convergence achieved after 22 iterations
Coefficient covariance computed using outer product of gradients
Presample variance: backcast (parameter = 0.7)
GARCH = C(3) + C(4)*RESID(-1)^2 + C(5)*GARCH(-1)

Variable	Coefficient	Std. Error	z-Statistic	Prob.
C	0.000702	0.001231	0.570184	0.5686
GOLD(-1)	0.032829	0.119068	0.275720	0.7828

Variance Equation				
C	7.79E-06	4.62E-06	1.684342	0.0921
RESID(-1)^2	0.172918	0.082517	2.095551	0.0361
GARCH(-1)	0.804663	0.071662	11.22853	0.0000

R-squared	0.002966	Mean dependent var	0.001069
Adjusted R-squared	-0.004588	S.D. dependent var	0.015957
S.E. of regression	0.015993	Akaike info criterion	-5.743923
Sum squared resid	0.033763	Schwarz criterion	-5.635795
Log likelihood	389.8429	Hannan-Quinn criter.	-5.699983
Durbin-Watson stat	1.917516		

4. Below shows ADF test and Correlogram estimates for the Gold daily returns between the period 2 January 2020 and 18 June 2020. Based on these information develop an appropriate ARMA model for gold.

Null Hypothesis: GOLD has a unit root Exogenous: Constant Lag Length: 0 (Automatic - based on SIC, maxlag=12)		t-Statistic	Prob.*
Augmented Dickey-Fuller test statistic		-10.72736	0.0000
Test critical values:	1% level	-3.479656	
	5% level	-2.883073	
	10% level	-2.578331	
*MacKinnon (1996) one-sided p-values.			

Date: 04/29/21   Time: 10:17
Sample (adjusted): 1 135
Included observations: 135 after adjustments

Autocorrelation	Partial Correlation		AC	PAC	Q-Stat	Prob
		1	0.068	0.068	0.6403	0.424
		2	-0.078	-0.083	1.4765	0.478
		3	-0.021	-0.010	1.5405	0.673
		4	-0.041	-0.045	1.7751	0.777
		5	0.021	0.025	1.8360	0.871
		6	-0.296	-0.311	14.386	0.026
		7	-0.283	-0.263	25.983	0.001
		8	-0.054	-0.104	26.406	0.001
		9	-0.020	-0.097	26.467	0.002
		10	0.216	0.183	33.349	0.000
		11	0.116	0.111	35.371	0.000
		12	-0.079	-0.149	36.310	0.000
		13	0.198	0.078	42.280	0.000
		14	0.114	-0.000	44.251	0.000
		15	0.116	0.098	46.324	0.000
		16	-0.163	-0.091	50.462	0.000
		17	-0.270	-0.113	61.906	0.000
		18	-0.014	-0.035	61.936	0.000
		19	-0.109	-0.118	63.841	0.000
		20	-0.123	-0.100	66.265	0.000
		21	-0.085	-0.084	67.428	0.000
		22	0.072	0.109	68.281	0.000
		23	0.025	-0.219	68.382	0.000
		24	0.098	-0.073	69.971	0.000
		25	0.053	-0.111	70.447	0.000
		26	0.133	0.046	73.428	0.000
		27	-0.083	-0.136	74.610	0.000
		28	0.010	-0.006	74.629	0.000
		29	0.059	0.031	75.243	0.000
		30	-0.069	-0.013	76.071	0.000
		31	-0.051	0.012	76.527	0.000
		32	-0.028	0.022	76.670	0.000
		33	0.034	0.033	76.880	0.000
		34	0.069	0.108	77.758	0.000
		35	-0.077	-0.142	78.867	0.000
		36	0.088	0.091	80.326	0.000

5. Decompose the daily mean returns of the BSE 500 index for the last five years into different components. Also comment on the each components of the decomposed series.

Then perform the following set of analysis on the daily mean returns of the BSE 500 index for the last five years.

(a) Unit Root Test
(b) ARCH and GARCH Test
(c) ARIMA modelling

6. Comment on the obtained VAR model estimates for the Crude oil, Gold, and Silver daily average returns between the period 02 January 2020 and 18 June 2020.

VAR Estimates

Vector Autoregression Estimates			
Date: 04/29/21 Time: 16:47			
Sample (adjusted): 3 135			
Included observations: 133 after adjustments			
Standard errors in ( ) & t-statistics in [ ]			
	OIL	GOLD	SILVER
OIL(-2)	-0.110511	-0.007136	-0.008315
	(0.08866)	(0.00347)	(0.00574)
	[-1.24649]	[-2.05378]	[-1.44800]
GOLD(-2)	0.736653	-0.257861	-0.354910
	(3.19580)	(0.12525)	(0.20700)
	[0.23051]	[-2.05873]	[-1.71454]
SILVER(-2)	0.853563	0.152483	0.415394
	(1.92379)	(0.07540)	(0.12461)
	[0.44369]	[2.02236]	[3.33358]
C	-0.041482	0.000941	0.000101
	(0.03495)	(0.00137)	(0.00226)
	[-1.18699]	[0.68689]	[0.04481]

R-squared	0.016829	0.057900	0.091470
Adj. R-squared	-0.006035	0.035990	0.070341
Sum sq. resids	20.62749	0.031685	0.086542
S.E. equation	0.399879	0.015672	0.025901
F-statistic	0.736040	2.642703	4.329203
Log likelihood	-64.78114	366.0410	299.2231
Akaike AIC	1.034303	-5.444225	-4.439445
Schwarz SC	1.121231	-5.357297	-4.352517
Mean dependent	-0.036379	0.000955	0.000125
S.D. dependent	0.398677	0.015962	0.026863

Determinant resid covariance (dof adj.)	1.19E-08
Determinant resid covariance	1.08E-08
Log likelihood	653.6024
Akaike information criterion	-9.648156
Schwarz criterion	-9.387373
Number of coefficients	12

VAR Stability Condition Checks

VAR Granger Causality/Block Exogeneity Wald Tests
Date: 04/29/21   Time: 16:51
Sample: 1 136
Included observations: 133

Dependent variable: OIL

Excluded	Chi-sq	df	Prob.
GOLD	0.053133	1	0.8177
SILVER	0.196859	1	0.6573
All	0.863149	2	0.6495

Dependent variable: GOLD			
Excluded	Chi-sq	df	Prob.
OIL	4.218010	1	0.0400
SILVER	4.089921	1	0.0431
All	7.098736	2	0.0287
Dependent variable: SILVER			
Excluded	Chi-sq	df	Prob.
OIL	2.096691	1	0.1476
GOLD	2.939648	1	0.0864
All	4.582579	2	0.1011

VAR Granger Causality Test Estimates

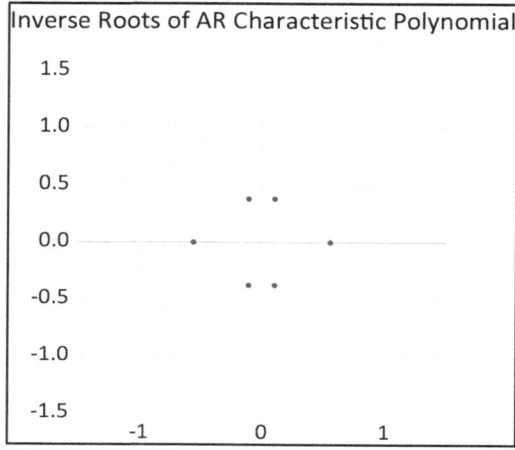

Lag Length Selection

VAR Lag Order Selection Criteria
Endogenous variables: OIL GOLD SILVER
Exogenous variables: C
Date: 04/29/21   Time: 16:55
Sample: 1 136
Included observations: 130

Lag	LogL	LR	FPE	AIC	SC	HQ
0	623.6914	NA	1.43e-08	-9.549099	-9.482925*	-9.522210*
1	632.6254	17.31809	1.43e-08	-9.548082	-9.283387	-9.440528
2	645.8823	25.08614*	1.34e-08*	-9.613573*	-9.150356	-9.425353
3	649.3858	6.468084	1.46e-08	-9.529012	-8.867274	-9.260126
4	651.6261	4.032529	1.62e-08	-9.425017	-8.564756	-9.075464
5	659.6406	14.05626	1.65e-08	-9.409856	-8.351074	-8.979637

* indicates lag order selected by the criterion
LR: sequential modified LR test statistic (each test at 5% level)
FPE: Final prediction error
AIC: Akaike information criterion
SC: Schwarz information criterion
HQ: Hannan-Quinn information criterion

Autocorrelation LM Test

```
VAR Residual Serial Correlation LM Tests
Date: 04/29/21   Time: 17:03
Sample: 1 136
Included observations: 133
```

Null hypothesis: No serial correlation at lag h

Lag	LRE* stat	df	Prob.	Rao F-stat	df	Prob.
1	23.60198	9	0.0050	2.695183	(9, 301.9)	0.0050
2	4.436636	9	0.8804	0.490867	(9, 301.9)	0.8804
3	2.414482	9	0.9831	0.266253	(9, 301.9)	0.9831
4	2.761029	9	0.9730	0.304640	(9, 301.9)	0.9730

Null hypothesis: No serial correlation at lags 1 to h

Lag	LRE* stat	df	Prob.	Rao F-stat	df	Prob.
1	23.60198	9	0.0050	2.695183	(9, 301.9)	0.0050
2	27.83976	18	0.0645	1.572978	(18, 342.7)	0.0646
3	30.71095	27	0.2832	1.146193	(27, 345.3)	0.2838
4	43.94847	36	0.1703	1.237229	(36, 340.5)	0.1714

*Edgeworth expansion corrected likelihood ratio statistic.

Impulse Response Analysis

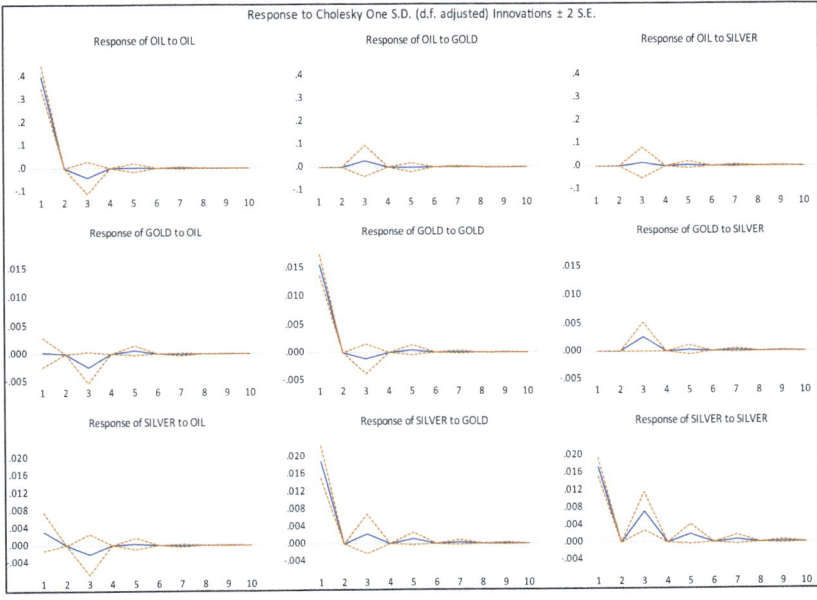

Variance Decomposition

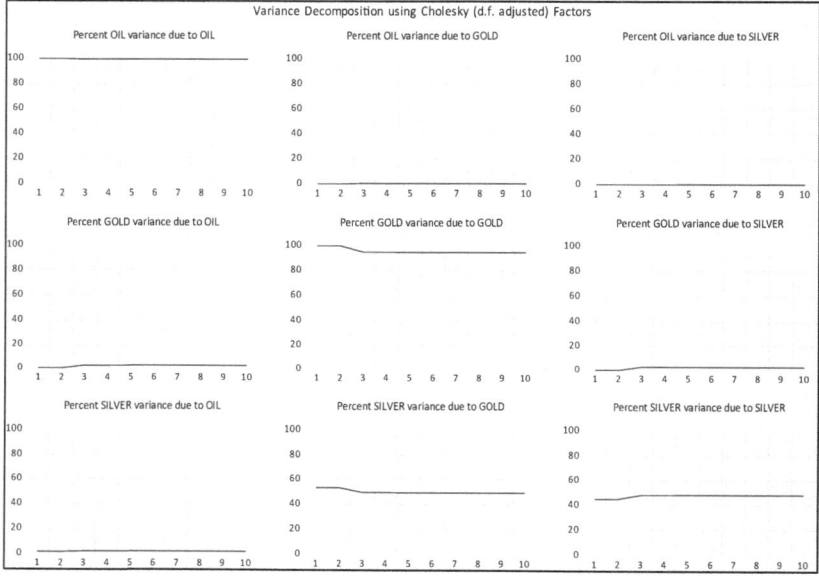

7. Comment on the obtained VAR model forecasting estimates for the Crude oil, Gold, and Silver daily average returns between the period 2 January 2020 and 18 June 2020.

Forecast Evaluation
Date: 04/29/21   Time: 17:08
Sample: 1 136
Included observations: 136

Variable	Inc. obs.	RMSE	MAE	MAPE	Theil
GOLD	135	0.015910	0.010478	1075.030	0.939839
OIL	135	0.397174	0.102912	281.0562	0.912167
SILVER	135	0.026777	0.016669	15461.75	0.986481

RMSE: Root Mean Square Error
MAE: Mean Absolute Error
MAPE: Mean Absolute Percentage Error
Theil: Theil inequality coefficient

REFERENCES

Bollerslev, T. (1986). Generalized autoregressive conditional heteroskedasticity. *Journal of Econometrics, 31*(3), 307–327.

Cleveland, R., Cleveland, W., McRae, J., & Terpenning, I. (1990). STL: A seasonal-trend decomposition procedure based on Loess. *Journal of Official Statistics, 6*(1), 3–73.

Engle, R. F. (1982). Autoregressive conditional heteroscedasticity with estimates of the variance of United Kingdom inflation. *Econometrica: Journal of the econometric society*, 987–1007.

Engle, R. F. (1983). Estimates of the variance of US inflation based upon the ARCH Model. *Journal of Money, Credit and Banking, 15*(3), 286–301.

CHAPTER 7

Introduction to Fat Tails

Key Topics Covered

- *Skewness*
- *Kurtosis*
- *Fat Tails*
- *Quantile Regression*
- *EViews Illustrations on OLS Versus Quantile Regression*
- *EViews Illustrations on Plotting Residual Graphs*

7.1 BACKGROUND

In developing economies stock markets are not developed or advanced like the developed countries and hence expected to have different characteristics of the stock market in terms of risk and return relationships (Maiti, 2020). Most of the financial studies assume that the security or portfolio average returns follow a normal distribution. In reality the security or portfolio average returns does not follow a normal distribution rather they are kurtotic and skewed. Kurtosis provides measure on how heavy is the tail of a distribution whereas skewness provides information on the asymmetry of the distribution.

If the random distribution follows a normal distribution then there will be no skewness. The mean, median, and mode all measures lie in the same line. The distribution on both sides of the line is symmetric as shown in Fig. 7.1. The random distribution which is not symmetric or distorted then such distribution is said to be skewed distribution. If the distribution is not symmetric and distorted towards the left with its tail on the right is said to be the positive skewness. Likewise if the distribution distorted towards the right with its tail on the left is said to be the negative skewness. The Pearson measures for the skewness (first and second coefficients) can be obtained using the below expressions.

$$\text{Skewness} = \frac{\overline{x} - \text{Mode Value}}{\sigma} \tag{7.1}$$

$$\text{Skewness} = \frac{3\overline{x} - \text{Median Value}}{\sigma} \tag{7.2}$$

Similarly, if the distribution follows a normal distribution then there will be no kurtosis and said to be mesokurtic as shown in Fig. 7.2. The leptokurtic distribution represents positive excess kurtosis. The leptokurtic distribution signifies heavy tails or outliers or higher risk on either side of the distribution while platykurtic distribution signifies negative excess kurtosis. Large kurtosis value represents higher risk whereas small kurtosis value represents moderate or low risk.

$$\text{Excess Kurtosis} = \text{Kurtosis} \pm 3 \tag{7.3}$$

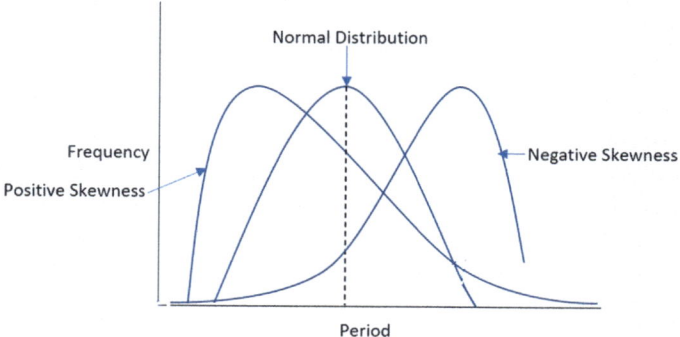

Fig. 7.1 Skewness

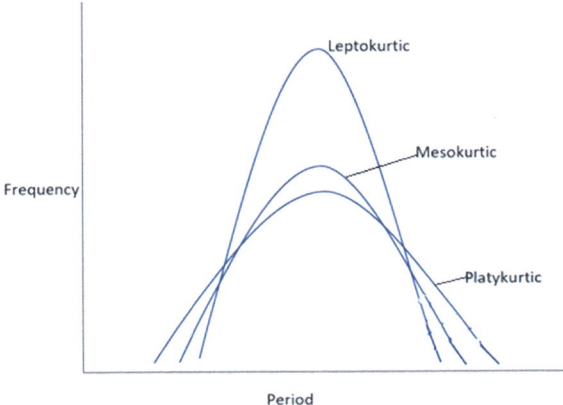

Fig. 7.2 Kurtosis

There often materializes a misconception that the highly unpredictable stocks have a higher tail probability. Thus it has a higher excess kurtosis rating. However, this is not the case always. In finance, kurtosis is a very useful measurement for quantifying the tail risk though the skewness is used in conjunction with kurtosis to assess the likelihood of events occurring in the distribution's tails.

Financial data series distributions usually have higher kurtosis and skewness values. Presence of excess kurtosis and skewness in the random distribution leads to the fat tails as shown in Fig. 7.3. Fat tails can exist on both sides of the distribution namely at the lower and higher ends. However, market participants and investors are more concerned about the lower end that contains information on the unexpected losses than the gains. Tail events are rare and risks associated with the tail events are often referred to as the tail risk. Typically all established finance theories and models are based on the idea that the security or portfolio average returns follow a normal distribution. However, reality is far more complex and tail events do have large impact on the security or portfolio average returns. Tail events are important in portfolio management not only in theory but also in practice. At least the last few decades witness serious episodes of tail events, namely bond crisis, Asian financial crisis, subprime crisis, COVID-19 pandemic, and others. Ignoring tail events can potentially lead to the overestimation of alphas. Ordinary least square (OLS)

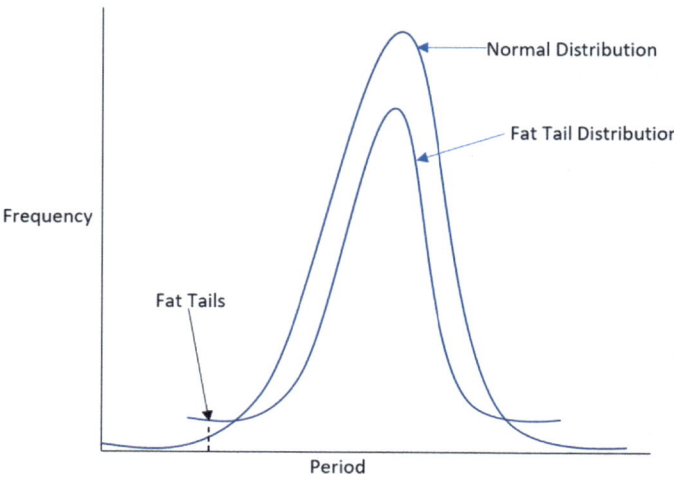

Fig. 7.3   Fat tails

regression is least effective in handling the tail events as compared to the quantile regression (Maiti, 2019, 2021).

Quantile Regression
Quantile regression is familiarized by Koenker and Bassett (1978). The ordinary least square (OLS) regression is based on the mean estimates while quantile regression estimates are based on the median. The median estimator function of quantile regression estimates the conditional median function by reducing the sum of absolute errors. Likewise the other conditional quantile function can be estimated by reducing the asymmetric weight of the absolute errors. Thus, conditional quantile function can be seen as the well-structured optimization problem. The solution to the problem of decreasing the sum squares of residuals defined as the sample mean. Likewise solution to the problem of decreasing the sum squares of absolute residuals defined as the median. The aim of the conditional quantile function is to reduce the sum of square of residuals or absolute errors. If there are an equivalent number of positive and negative residuals above and below the median line, the sum of absolute residuals is said to be minimized. Other quantile functions can be obtained in

the same way by assigning different weights to the negative and positive residuals, i.e. by minimizing the asymmetric weights of the residuals.

Mathematically the loss function can be represented as shown below:

$$\varrho_T = \begin{cases} Tu & \text{if } u > 0 \\ (T-1)u & \text{if } u \leq 0 \end{cases} \tag{7.4}$$

Tth quantile residual (ξ) can be minimized as shown below:

$$R(\xi) = \sum_{i=1}^{n} \varrho_T(Y_i - \xi) \tag{7.5}$$

The above function is not differentiable however has directional right and left derivatives as described below:

Right derivative

$$\begin{aligned} R'(\xi+) &= \text{Lim}_{(h \to 0+)} \left[R(\xi+h) - R(\xi) \right] / h \\ &= \text{Lim}_{(h \to 0+)} \sum_{i=1}^{n} \frac{\varrho_T(y - \xi - h) - \varrho_T(y - \xi)}{h} \\ &= \sum_{i=1}^{n} \left(I(Y_i \leq \xi) - T \right) \end{aligned} \tag{7.6}$$

Left derivative

$$\begin{aligned} R'(\xi-) &= \text{Lim}_{(h \to 0+)} \left[R(\xi-h) - R(\xi) \right] / h \\ &= \text{Lim}_{(h \to 0+)} \sum_{i=1}^{n} \frac{\varrho_T(y - \xi + h) - \varrho_T(y - \xi)}{h} \\ &= \sum_{i=1}^{n} \left(T - I(Y_i < \xi) \right) \end{aligned} \tag{7.7}$$

Tth quantile residual (ξ) is said to be minimized by the conditional quantile function if it satisfies the condition of $R'(\xi +) \geq 0$ and $R'(\xi -) \geq 0$ (see Fig. 7.4).

The unconditional quantiles of the optimization problem can now easily be defined as the conditional quantiles analogously. The ordinary least square (OLS) regression can be used further for modelling. For instance assume following random samples of $[Y_1, Y_2, ..., Y_n]$.

$$R(\mu) = \sum_{i=1}^{n} \varrho_T(Y_i - \mu)^2 \tag{7.8}$$

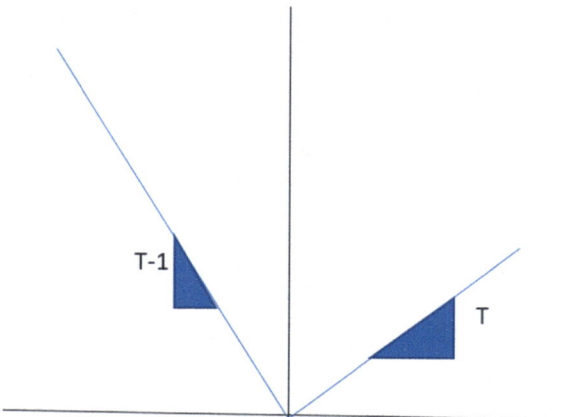

Fig. 7.4 Conditional quantile function

Equation 7.8 above represents the sample mean estimates for the unconditional population mean. Now replace the scalar variable (μ) with the parametric function $\mu\,(x, \beta)$ in the above equation we get

$$R(\mu) = \sum_{i=1}^{n} \varrho_T \left(Y_i - \mu\left(x, \beta\right) \right)^2 \tag{7.9}$$

Likewise the conditional median function can be obtained by replacing the scalar variable (ξ) with the parametric function $\xi\,(x, \beta)$ and setting the Tth quantile as $1/2$. Similarly, values of the other conditional quantile functions can be obtained by replacing those absolute values by $\varrho_T\,(*)$:

$$R(\xi) = \sum_{i=1}^{n} \varrho T \left(Yi - \xi\left(x, \beta\right) \right)^2 \tag{7.10}$$

Finally by applying linear programming (LP) the minimizing problem can easily be solved by formulating $\xi\,(x, \beta)$ as linear parameters.

7.2   Finance in Action

Illustration 1: To compare the OLS and quantile regression in Indian context. Based on the obtained regression estimates comment on these two regression models.

Data Description:
BSE 500 companies are used to construct the study portfolios based on the size and value factors by means of the Fama–French (1993) technique. For risk free rate 91 days T-bills returns are used. BSE-200 index mean excess returns used as proxy for the market. The study period is between July 2000 and June 2014. All data points are in monthly frequency.

Regression models used is as follows:

Fama–French three factor model

$$E(r_i) - r_f = \alpha_i + \beta_{im} * (r_m - r_f) + \beta_{is} * (\text{Size}) + \beta_{iv} * (\text{Value}) + \varepsilon_i$$

EViews stepwise implementations
Above regression can be executed easily in EViews by following the below steps.

Step 1: Import data into the EViews Workfile window.
Step 2: Then click on Quick → Estimate Equation → The Equation Estimation window will appear as shown in Fig. 7.5.
Step 3: Under the equation specification space write dependable variable followed by list of regressors as shown below. Hence, dependable variables are portfolios P1 to P25. Whereas regressors are the risk factors (market, size, and value) and c is the regression intercept.

Fama–French three factor model: P1 c Rm Size Value.

Choose Methods as Least Square (from the drop down list).

Then click OK button. The OLS Regression estimates will appear as shown in Fig. 7.6.
Step 4: Quantile regression estimates: Quick → Estimate Equation → The Equation Estimation window will appear → Use the same equation as OLS → Choose Methods as Quantile Regression (from the drop down list) and select required quantile as shown in Fig. 7.7.
Step 5: Click OK. Quantile regression estimates will appear as shown in Fig. 7.8. Figure 7.8 shows quantile regression estimates for portfolios 1 and 25 for quantiles 0.05 and 0.95.

The OLS estimates for portfolio 1 show that all risk factors (Rm, Size, and Value) coefficients are positive and are statistically significant at 5% level. The quantile regression estimates for quantiles 0.05 and 0.95 also show similar results. Quantile estimates further show that at the lower

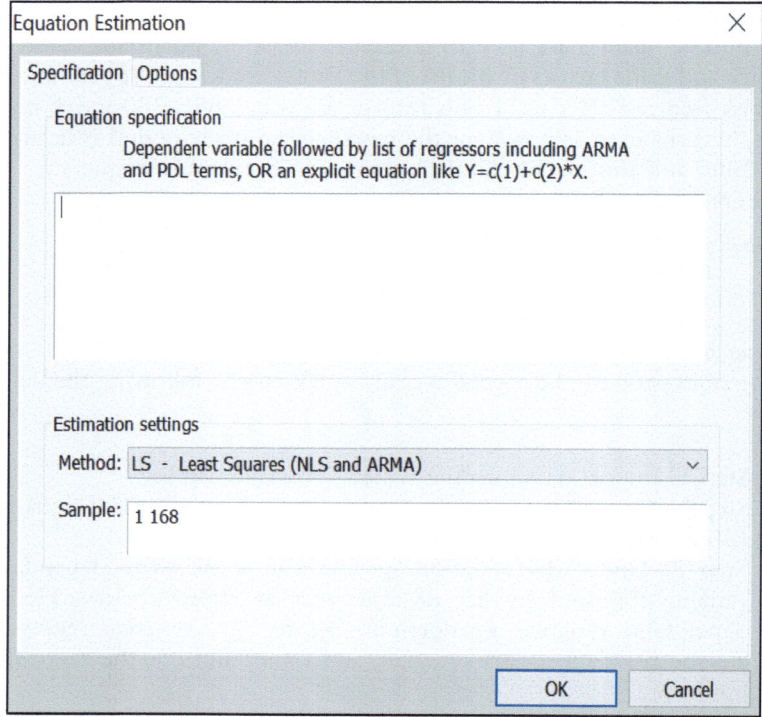

Fig. 7.5 OLS Regression Equation Estimation window

Dependent Variable: P1
Method: Least Squares
Date: 05/06/21   Time: 10:14
Sample: 1 168
Included observations: 168

Variable	Coefficient	Std. Error	t-Statistic	Prob.
C	0.007402	0.007908	0.936008	0.3506
RM	1.008077	0.098808	10.20239	0.0000
SIZE	2.245479	0.221148	10.15374	0.0000
VALUE	1.254280	0.152632	8.217682	0.0000

R-squared	0.711899	Mean dependent var		0.066953
Adjusted R-squared	0.706629	S.D. dependent var		0.171525
S.E. of regression	0.092904	Akaike info criterion		-1.890969
Sum squared resid	1.415523	Schwarz criterion		-1.816589
Log likelihood	162.8414	Hannan-Quinn criter.		-1.860782
F-statistic	135.0817	Durbin-Watson stat		1.913764
Prob(F-statistic)	0.000000			

Dependent Variable: P25
Method: Least Squares
Date: 05/06/21   Time: 10:15
Sample: 1 168
Included observations: 168

Variable	Coefficient	Std. Error	t-Statistic	Prob.
C	-0.000611	0.002179	-0.280657	0.7793
RM	1.015497	0.027221	37.30519	0.0000
SIZE	0.148553	0.060926	2.438264	0.0158
VALUE	-0.265910	0.042050	-6.323715	0.0000

R-squared	0.898755	Mean dependent var		0.005333
Adjusted R-squared	0.896902	S.D. dependent var		0.079713
S.E. of regression	0.025595	Akaike info criterion		-4.469323
Sum squared resid	0.107436	Schwarz criterion		-4.394943
Log likelihood	379.4232	Hannan-Quinn criter.		-4.439136
F-statistic	485.2753	Durbin-Watson stat		2.095334
Prob(F-statistic)	0.000000			

Fig. 7.6 Fama–French three factor model OLS estimates for Portfolios 1 and 25

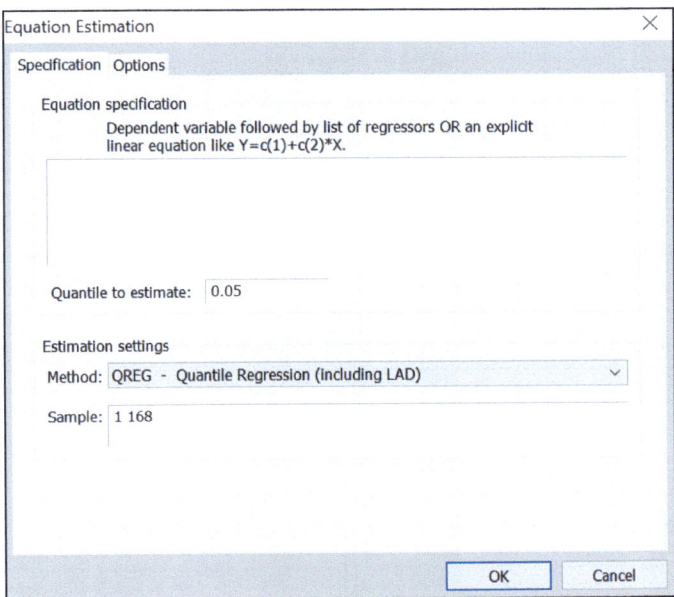

Fig. 7.7 Quantile Regression Equation Estimation window

quartile (0.05) weights of all risk factors (Rm, Size, and Value) coefficients are less positive as compared to the mean estimates of OLS. For portfolio 25 OLS estimates show that all risk factors coefficients are positive except Value and are statistically significant at 5% level. The quantile regression estimates for portfolio 25 at lower quantile (0.05) also show similar results. However, at the higher quantile (0.95) notably the coefficient of Size (risk factor) becomes negative and statistically not significant at 5% level. Following the above steps, estimates for other portfolios can be obtained and compared.

Illustration 2: To plot the residual graphs obtained from the above OLS and quantile regressions (Illustration 1). Based on the obtained regression residual graphs comment on these two regression models.

Data Description:
BSE 500 companies are used to construct the study portfolios based on the size and value factors by means of the Fama–French (1993) technique.

Dependent Variable: P1				
Method: Quantile Regression (tau = 0.05)				
Date: 05/06/21 Time: 10:04				
Sample: 1 168				
Included observations: 168				
Huber Sandwich Standard Errors & Covariance				
Sparsity method: Kernel (Epanechnikov) using residuals				
Bandwidth method: Hall-Sheather, bw=0.038464				
Estimation successfully identifies unique optimal solution				

Variable	Coefficient	Std. Error	t-Statistic	Prob.
C	-0.052953	0.008436	-6.277030	0.0000
RM	1.024997	0.074994	13.66778	0.0000
SIZE	1.582089	0.192230	8.230173	0.0000
VALUE	0.559612	0.143277	3.905802	0.0001

Pseudo R-squared	0.546369	Mean dependent var	0.066953
Adjusted R-squared	0.538071	S.D. dependent var	0.171525
S.E. of regression	0.132349	Objective	0.946191
Quantile dependent var	-0.131288	Restr. objective	2.085819
Sparsity	0.427402	Quasi-LR statistic	112.2697
Prob(Quasi-LR stat)	0.000000		

Dependent Variable: P25				
Method: Quantile Regression (tau = 0.05)				
Date: 05/06/21 Time: 10:06				
Sample: 1 168				
Included observations: 168				
Huber Sandwich Standard Errors & Covariance				
Sparsity method: Kernel (Epanechnikov) using residuals				
Bandwidth method: Hall-Sheather, bw=0.038464				
Estimation successfully identifies unique optimal solution				

Variable	Coefficient	Std. Error	t-Statistic	Prob.
C	-0.031771	0.002529	-12.56224	0.0000
RM	0.999069	0.025004	39.95623	0.0000
SIZE	0.185202	0.067878	2.728469	0.0071
VALUE	-0.546819	0.069041	-7.920221	0.0000

Pseudo R-squared	0.767484	Mean dependent var	0.005333
Adjusted R-squared	0.763231	S.D. dependent var	0.079713
S.E. of regression	0.046639	Objective	0.372406
Quantile dependent var	-0.119173	Restr. objective	1.601638
Sparsity	0.125556	Quasi-LR statistic	412.2250
Prob(Quasi-LR stat)	0.000000		

Dependent Variable: P1				
Method: Quantile Regression (tau = 0.95)				
Date: 05/06/21 Time: 10:05				
Sample: 1 168				
Included observations: 168				
Huber Sandwich Standard Errors & Covariance				
Sparsity method: Kernel (Epanechnikov) using residuals				
Bandwidth method: Hall-Sheather, bw=0.038464				
Estimation successfully identifies unique optimal solution				

Variable	Coefficient	Std. Error	t-Statistic	Prob.
C	0.099208	0.011349	8.741797	0.0000
RM	1.288610	0.116220	11.08768	0.0000
SIZE	2.181266	0.408823	5.335481	0.0000
VALUE	1.229178	0.218548	5.624287	0.0000

Pseudo R-squared	0.539499	Mean dependent var	0.066953
Adjusted R-squared	0.531075	S.D. dependent var	0.171525
S.E. of regression	0.133991	Objective	1.817911
Quantile dependent var	0.312162	Restr. objective	3.947680
Sparsity	0.545973	Quasi-LR statistic	164.2470
Prob(Quasi-LR stat)	0.000000		

Dependent Variable: P25				
Method: Quantile Regression (tau = 0.95)				
Date: 05/06/21 Time: 10:08				
Sample: 1 168				
Included observations: 168				
Huber Sandwich Standard Errors & Covariance				
Sparsity method: Kernel (Epanechnikov) using residuals				
Bandwidth method: Hall-Sheather, bw=0.038464				
Estimation successfully identifies unique optimal solution				

Variable	Coefficient	Std. Error	t-Statistic	Prob.
C	0.046835	0.007685	6.094681	0.0000
RM	1.027059	0.044660	22.99726	0.0000
SIZE	-0.064528	0.144122	-0.447733	0.6549
VALUE	-0.207664	0.079483	-2.612677	0.0098

Pseudo R-squared	0.661069	Mean dependent var	0.005333
Adjusted R-squared	0.654869	S.D. dependent var	0.079713
S.E. of regression	0.053386	Objective	0.515193
Quantile dependent var	0.124902	Restr. objective	1.520053
Sparsity	0.286581	Quasi-LR statistic	147.6370
Prob(Quasi-LR stat)	0.000000		

Fig. 7.8 Fama–French three factor model Quantile (0.05 & 0.95) estimates for Portfolios 1 and 25

For risk free rate 91 days T-bills returns are used. BSE-200 index mean excess returns used as proxy for the market. The study period is between July 2000 and June 2014. All data points are in monthly frequency.

Regression models used are as follows:

Fama–French three factor model

$$E(r_i) - r_f = \alpha_i + \beta_{im} * (r_m - r_f) + \beta_{is} * (\text{Size}) + \beta_{iv} * (\text{Value}) + \varepsilon_i$$

EViews stepwise implementations.
Regression estimates Window → View → Actual, Fitted, Residual → Residual Graph → Output will be displayed as shown in Fig. 7.9.Dotted

OLS Residuals

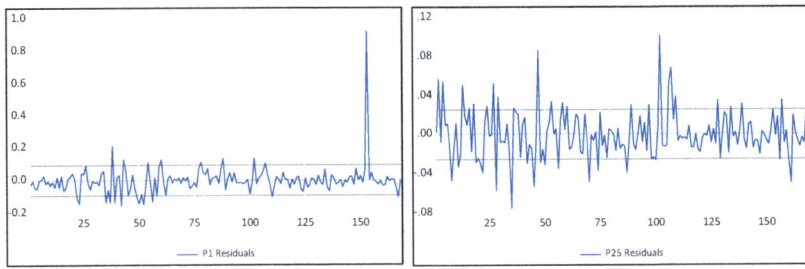

Quantile regression Residuals (0.05)

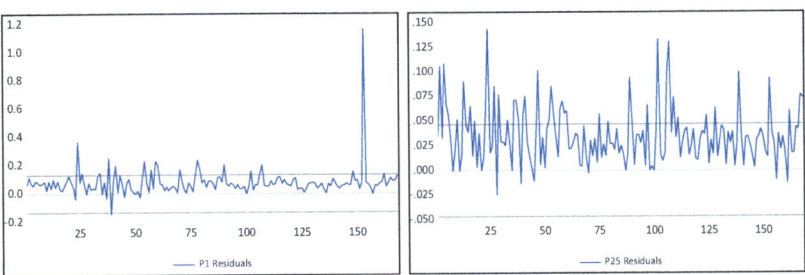

Quantile regression Residuals (0.95)

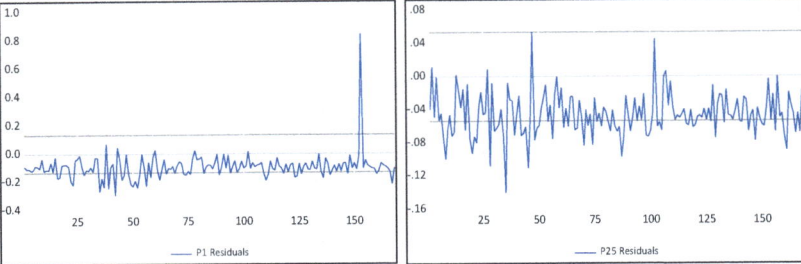

Fig. 7.9 OLS and quantile regression residuals graph

lines in the above Fig. 7.9 represent lower and upper limits. Peaks outside this region indicate that the value of residuals is not zero or close to zero. The residual graphs of portfolios 1 and 25 obtained from the OLS show several peaks that lie outside the upper and lower limits. The residual graphs of portfolios 1 and 25 obtained from the quantile regression at lower quantile (0.05) show no peak that lies outside the upper and lower limits. Similar results are obtained in case of the higher quantile (0.95), except one peak is observed in case of the portfolio 1 that lies outside the upper limit as shown in Fig. 7.9. The residual graphs estimates clearly indicate the superiority of quantile regression over OLS in extreme events. Following the above steps, residual graphs for other portfolios can be plotted and compared.

Summary

This chapter briefly introduced the topics skewness and kurtosis. Importance of skewness and kurtosis in finance is discussed. Then it is also discussed how excess values of skewness and kurtosis can lead to fat tails. What is fat tails and its implications are covered in detail. Tail events are rare but have significant effects in the overall investment performance. Last few decades witness such episodes of tail events that lead to serious disasters. Ordinary least square regression is inefficient over quantile regression dealing with such tail events. EViews stepwise implementations and estimation interpretations of OLS and quantile regressions are discussed plausibly. Residual graph plot using EViews is also disused with illustrations.

Analysts/Investors Corner

Skewness and kurtosis are two very important measures for analysing the tail risk. Surplus values of skewness and kurtosis convey important information related to the tail data. Though tail events are rare but certainly it should not be ignored in portfolio management. On several occasions history shows that tail events can be serious. Tail risks are very important particularly while analysing the hedge fund returns. Tail events are not well captured by the

OLS. To deal with the tail events more sophisticated modelling techniques such as quantile regression had better to be implemented. The quantile regression approach should not be reflected as the regular practice as quantile regression deals with the median estimates. The quantile regression is used for certain purposes and should be dealt with cautions on case-to-case basis.

7.3   EXERCISES

7.3.1   *Multiple Choice Questions*

1. A zero value of skewness indicates that the distribution is

    a. Not skewed
    b. Skewed
    c. Positively skewed
    d. Negatively skewed

2. A zero value of kurtosis indicates that the distribution is

    a. Leptokurtic distribution
    b. Mesokurtic distribution
    c. Platykurtic distribution
    d. None of the above

3. A positive excess value of kurtosis indicates that the distribution is

    a. Mesokurtic distribution
    b. Leptokurtic distribution
    c. Gaussian distribution
    d. Platykurtic distribution

4. A negative excess value of kurtosis indicates that the distribution is

    a. Gaussian distribution
    b. Platykurtic distribution
    c. Mesokurtic distribution
    d. Leptokurtic distribution

5. Which of the following distribution have higher tail risk ?

a. Mesokurtic distribution
b. Gaussian distribution
c. Leptokurtic distribution
d. Platykurtic distribution

6. The mean, median, and mode values of a normal distribution are

a. Equal
b. Distinct
c. Zero
d. One

7. Which of the following term(s) is/are related to the tail risk?

a. Fat tails
b. Extreme events
c. Tail events are rare
d. All of the above

8. Which of the following distribution is wide and flat?

a. Mesokurtic distribution
b. Gaussian distribution
c. Leptokurtic distribution
d. Platykurtic distribution

9. Which among the following technique is more effective dealing with the tail risk?

a. Ordinary least square regression
b. Quantile regression
c. Panel regression
d. Logit regression

10. Tail risk

a. Can be hedged
b. Cannot be hedged
c. Does not exists in practice
d. Are frequent events

7.3.2   *Fill in the Blanks*

1. The _____ & _____ are the measure of shape of the random distribution.
2. The _____, _____, & _____ are the measures of central tendency.
3. The mean, median, and mode values are equal for the _____ distribution.
4. _____, _____, & _____ are the examples of tail events.
5. Excess Kurtosis = Kurtosis ± _____.
6. A zero value of kurtosis indicates that the distribution is a _____.
7. The _____ graphs/plots are used to find problems with regressions.
8. Fat tailed distributions are the random distributions that have higher values of _____ & _____.
9. Investors are more concerned about the _____ of the tailed distribution.
10. A _____ distribution has tails that are heavier than an exponential distribution.

7.3.3   *Long Answer Questions*

1. Define skewness and its implications with suitable examples?
2. Define kurtosis and its implications with suitable examples?
3. Define three types of the kurtosis and its implications ? Explain it in brief.
4. Show that lognormal distributions have fat tails.
5. Which distribution among the two have heavier tail: lognormal distribution or gamma distribution? Explain it in brief with suitable examples.
6. Is there any difference between the heavy tail and fat tail distribution, or they are the same?
7. Why fat tails are important in finance?
8. Is it possible to eliminate the fat tails through portfolio diversifications?
9. Efficient market hypothesis can deal with the fat tails. Discuss it briefly.

10. What is your understanding on tail risk? Why one should pay more attention to it ? How to handle tail risk?
11. Comment on: How fat is fat tails ? Likewise how heavy is heavy tails?
12. Discuss fat tails with respect to the asset pricing models?
13. Discuss the impact of COVID-19 pandemic on the tail risk?
14. Comment on the tail risk contagion among the global financial markets during the COVID-19 pandemic crisis?

7.3.4   Real-World Tasks

1. A professor asks his/her student to analyse the shape of the random distribution during the COVID-19 first and second phase impact on the European stock markets ? Assume yourself as the student and perform the task. Then prepare a detailed report of the analysis to be submitted to the professor.
2. A researcher want to analyse whether the top seven cryptocurrencies returns have fat tails during the noble coronavirus pandemic. Assume yourself as the researcher: perform the mentioned task in details and develop the analysis report.
3. An analyst want to examine whether the world indices before, during, and after the first phase of COVID-19 have tail risk contagion. Help him/her to perform the said analysis and prepare the report.
4. A scholar need to examine the presence of fat tails for the three major currency pairs daily exchange rate during the last three years as his/her project dissertation. Additionally he/she need to comment on how good is the efficient market hypothesis to deal with the fat tails ? Help the scholar to complete his/her project dissertation successfully and satisfactorily.
5. A senior manager of the Reserve Bank of India (RBI) asked an intern working under him/her to analyse the tail risk for all the technological securities traded in the NSE during the first phase of COVID-19 pandemic. Help the intern in analysing and developing the final report for timely submission to the senior RBI manager.
6. An investor is evaluating his/her investing option as the hedge funds during early 2020. Help the investors to examine the hedge fund with respect to the extreme events and help him/her to make investment decision.

7. Conduct a simple empirical research to show that the tail events are important.
8. Conduct a simple empirical research that evidences all random distribution does not have fat tails.
9. Conduct a simple empirical research to show the difference between the heavy tail and fat tail

7.3.5 Case Studies

1. The figures below show the regression coefficients obtained from the CAPM and Fama–French three factor model using OLS and quantile regressions. Based on these information comment on the relationship between the risk factors and expected returns.

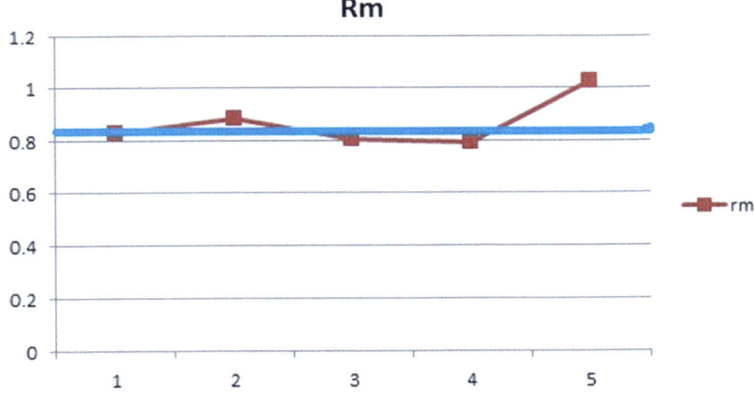

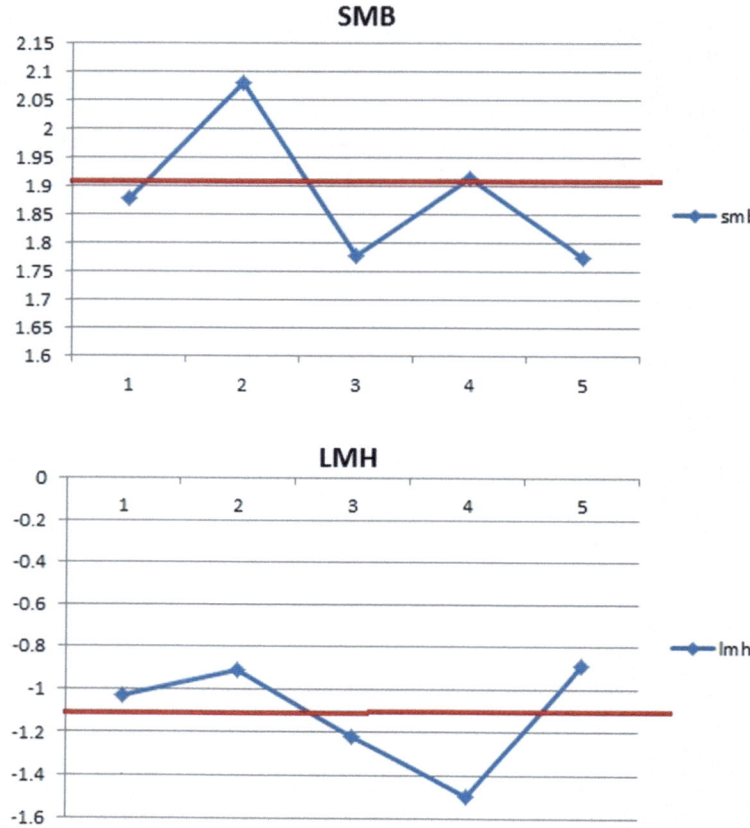

2. The figures below show the regression residual graphs obtained from the CAPM and Fama–French three factor model using OLS and quantile regressions for portfolio A. Based on these information comment on the model performances.

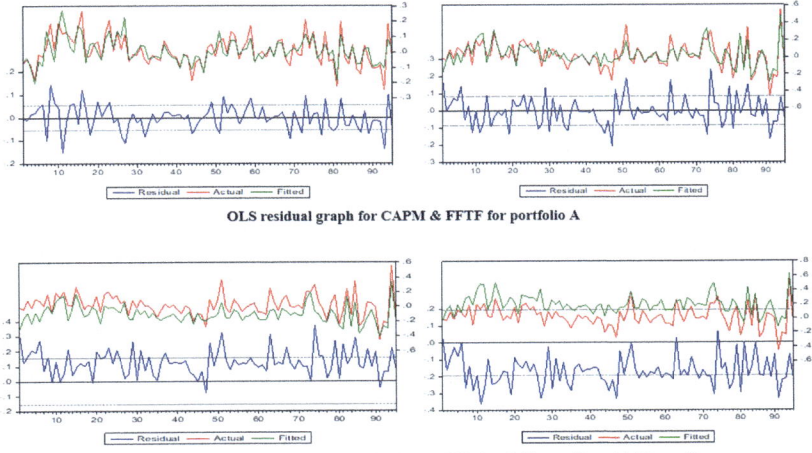

OLS residual graph for CAPM & FFTF for portfolio A

Quantile regression residual graph for FFTF for portfolio A at 0.05 quantile and 0.95 quantile

REFERENCES

Koenker, R., & Bassett Jr, G. (1978). Regression quantiles. *Econometrica: Journal of the Econometric Society*, 33–50.

Maiti, M. (2019). OLS versus quantile regression in extreme distributions. *Contaduría y Administración, 64*(2), 12.

Maiti, M. (2020). A critical review on evolution of risk factors and factor models. *Journal of Economic Surveys, 34*(1), 175–184.

Maiti, M. (2021). Quantile regression, asset pricing and investment decision. *IIMB Management Review.*

CHAPTER 8

Threshold Autoregression

Key Topics Covered

- *Non-linearity*
- *Threshold Autoregressive models*
- *BDS test for Independence*
- *TAR and STAR*
- *Testing of TAR models using EViews.*

8.1 Background

It is very difficult to generalize the theory of non-linearity of time series. There could be several reasons for non-linear behaviour of the time series such as the presence of asymmetric cycle (Thanh et al., 2020), breaks, thresholds, time varying variances (Vukovic et al., 2019), excess volatility, and others. Presence of such distinct non-linear characteristics in a time series is often uncaptured and unnoticed (Vukovic et al., 2020). Non-linear time series do encompasses several important information useful for making the investment decision. Hence, to capture such behaviour there is the need for an appropriate statistical model. Traditional linear models often failed to recognize the distinctive features of the financial assets and as results it demands for the more critical analytical models (Maiti,

M. Maiti, *Applied Financial Econometrics*, https://doi.org/10.1007/978-981-16-4063-6_8

Vyklyuk et al., 2020). Tong (1990) proposed Threshold Autoregressive (here after TAR) for non-linear time series. Subsequently Teräsvirta (1994); Li and Lam (1995); Hansen (2000); Chen et al. (2019); Maiti, Grubisic et al. (2020); and others are among the notable studies that use threshold regression. These studies also indicate that threshold regressions are as simple as the simple linear regressions yet have the ability to capture the non-linear phenomena of the time series. However, TAR models are challenged on several grounds such as issues related to the mistakes in measurements and documentations of appropriate threshold values. To address these issues to a great extent less restrictive TAR variation models are developed also known as the STAR models.

Mathematical expression for Threshold Autoregression

Threshold Autoregression can be represented by a simple mathematical model as shown below in Eq. 8.1:

$$Y_t = \alpha + \beta_0 X_t + \beta_1 X_t h(q_t; \theta) + \varepsilon_t \qquad (8.1)$$

where

β_0 and β_1 represent K * 1 vectors
q_t threshold variable
θ represents vector of parameters
$h(q_t; \theta)$ represents a transition function
ε_t represents the disturbance terms.

STAR models are also very popular among the Threshold Autoregression. STAR models essentially work with continuous transition function unlike TAR. STAR models transition functions basically could be any one these as explained below:

Logistic

$$G(s; c, \gamma) = (1 + exp(-\gamma(s - c))) - 1$$

It could also be in the form of second-order logistic function.

Exponential

$$G(s; c, \gamma) = 1 - exp(-\gamma(s - c)^2)$$

where

s: threshold variable
c: threshold value
γ: represents slope.

8.2   FINANCE IN ACTION

The pandemic as a result of the COVID-19 virus spread has affected all financial markets worldwide. Investors globally have become highly risk averse as a consequence of this pandemic. Some industry sectors may have gotten hit harder than others, the price of their stock may have dropped to such deep discounts that their price to book value ratio may have gotten extremely low. This implies that for some cases, it is cheaper for an investor to own the stock than the owners of the company itself. The investor would find an opportunity to acquire the stock at prices even lower than the cost of the company. That risk premium can be obtained from the ratio of the price of the stock today versus the price at which the stock was quoting at the declaration of the pandemic status. On the other hand, precious metal (such as Gold & Silver) shows unprecedented fluctuation that trying to navigate a new environment during COVID-19 pandemic. Economic instability and uncertainty due to COVID-19 pandemic stimulates extraordinary fluctuations in premiums and demand for precious metal gold and silver, respectively. Before COVID-19 pandemic these precious metals such as gold and silver were abundant but COVID-19 pandemic disturbed the whole global supply chains due to which it creates a severe shortage of these products. Other factors could be cash crunch among the traders and investors leads to reduction in trading desk risk appetite and volume of trading. Among the precious metals during COVID-19 pandemic gold price surges significantly possibly due to the risk off sentiment and safe haven asset nature of the yellow metal. Similarly silver white metal due to its nature of precious and industrial metal do exhibits some unique properties of risk appetite and dynamics. The nature of volatility and risk appetite of these two precious metals (gold and silver) prices differ during COVID-19.

Also, recently news headline "oil futures went negative" creates turmoil among the global investors. Possible explanation for this event could be due to the consequence of lack of demand for the oil and the excess offer by the oil producers. Uncertainty and volatility in the crude oil prices may trigger investments in the other assets like precious metals. It is interesting to check that how much correlated is crude oil with precious metals during COVID-19 pandemic? Experts say that COVID-19 pandemic affected world economies much more than the financial crisis of 2008–2009.

Let's address the following:

Analyse the behaviour of the crude oil, gold, and silver during COVID-19 crisis to check whether the daily average return series of the crude oil, gold, and silver are linear or non-linear in nature. If there exists any non-linearity in the series then analyse the characteristics of such non-linear series using threshold regression models.

8.3   EVIEWS IMPLEMENTATION AND INTERPRETATIONS

This section discusses how to implement the above-mentioned task stepwise using EViews.

8.3.1   Data

Gold (GC), Silver (SI), and Crude oil (CL) daily closing price data are obtained from Yahoo Finance website. Data consists of daily closing prices for a period from 31 December 2019 to 18 June 2020, and daily average returns are obtained using these data.

8.3.2   Methodology

To execute the above-mentioned task and derive the results following methods are deployed: Test of stationarity (ADF test); Test of linearity (BDS independence test) and Threshold autoregressions.

8.3.3   Test of Stationarity

Dickey–Fuller test (1979) is deployed to check the presence of unit root in the series.

8.3.4   BDS Test for Independence

Brock et al. (1996) test for independence is used to check the time series linear characteristics.

8.3.5   Threshold Autoregression

Following Hansen (2011) a two-regime (lower and higher) threshold regression with AR (11) in each regime is deployed. For estimating threshold values Bai and Perron (1998) techniques are used. In general, model selection criteria are determined using the sum squared residual values obtained from the various threshold autoregression models. Here logistic function chosen as the transition function.

8.3.6   Stepwise Implementation and Interpretations

Step 1: *Import data to EViews.*
Step 2: *Preliminary analysis: Descriptive Statistics; Correlation analysis; and graphs plots.*

Descriptive Statistics

To obtain the descriptive statistics of the Crude oil (CL), Silver (SI), and Gold (GC) daily return series using EViews following steps are deployed:

Go to EViews work file and then select three series (Gold (GC), Silver (SI), and Crude oil (CL)). On right clicking on it a new selection list open will appear → Select as Group → Group Workfile Window will appear → View → Descriptive Stats → Individual samples → Then estimates will appear as shown below in Fig. 8.1.

Descriptive statistics shows that all the time series have high kurtosis and oil series have high negative skewness. To check correlation between the variables click view → Covariance Analysis → Covariance Analysis new window will appear → Select required specifications → click OK button. On clicking OK, covariance analysis estimates appears as shown in Fig. 8.2.

Correlation analysis shows that there exists higher correlation between gold and silver series, and statistically significant. Next let's plot the series using graph features of EViews. View → Graph → In Graph Options Window, select Line & Symbol and Multiple graphs. Then on clicking

	OIL	SILVER	GOLD
Mean	-0.035599	0.000223	0.001085
Median	-0.003416	0.000113	0.000947
Maximum	0.484010	0.110799	0.076411
Minimum	-4.330882	-0.122183	-0.046281
Std. Dev.	0.395746	0.026674	0.015898
Skewness	-9.714549	-0.632424	0.793323
Kurtosis	104.8613	10.24003	7.821080
Jarque-Bera	60486.80	303.8501	144.9014
Probability	0.000000	0.000000	0.000000
Sum	-4.805901	0.030083	0.146476
Sum Sq. Dev.	20.98644	0.095343	0.033868
Observations	135	135	135

Fig. 8.1 Descriptive statistics

Covariance Analysis: Ordinary
Date: 04/06/21   Time: 07:13
Sample: 1 135
Included observations: 135

Correlation Probability	OIL	SILVER	GOLD
OIL	1.000000		

SILVER	0.141801	1.000000	
	0.1009	-----	
GOLD	0.035323	0.730016	1.000000
	0.6842	0.0000	-----

Fig. 8.2 Correlation estimates

OK button, similar graphs will appear as shown in Fig. 8.3. In general, Silver and Gold seem to be more volatile as compared to Oil.

Step 3: *Unit root test.*

To check unit root in EViews: Select the series, click view and Unit Root Test (View ➔ Unit Root Test ➔ In Unit Root Test, select required specifications ➔ click OK).

On clicking the OK button, unit root test estimates will look as shown in Fig. 8.4. Fig. 8.4 shows ADF test statistics for all series. ADF test estimates show that all-time series (Crude oil, Silver, and Gold) daily return series are stationary.

Step 4: *Linearity test: BDS independence test.*

Likewise to check linearity in EViews: Select the series, click view and BDS independence test (View ➔ BDS Independence Test ➔ BDS Test Statistics new Window will appear as shown in Fig. 8.5).

On clicking OK, BDS independence test estimates following window will look as shown in Fig. 8.6. BDS test statistics show that Silver and

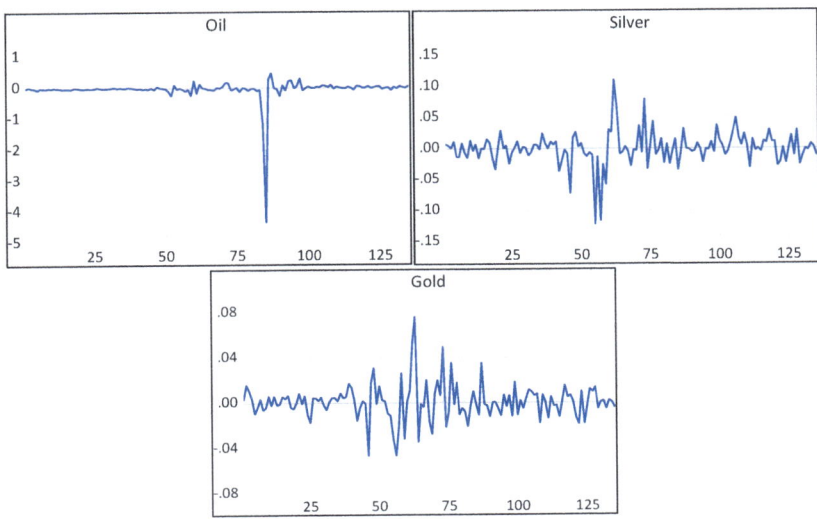

Fig. 8.3 Plot of daily average return pattern of gold, silver and crude oil

	t-Statistic	Prob.*

Null Hypothesis: OIL has a unit root
Exogenous: Constant
Lag Length: 0 (Automatic - based on SIC, maxlag=12)

		t-Statistic	Prob.*
Augmented Dickey-Fuller test statistic		-9.564065	0.0000
Test critical values:	1% level	-3.479656	
	5% level	-2.883073	
	10% level	-2.578331	

*MacKinnon (1996) one-sided p-values.

Null Hypothesis: SILVER has a unit root
Exogenous: Constant
Lag Length: 1 (Automatic - based on SIC, maxlag=12)

		t-Statistic	Prob.*
Augmented Dickey-Fuller test statistic		-5.873233	0.0000
Test critical values:	1% level	-3.480038	
	5% level	-2.883239	
	10% level	-2.578420	

*MacKinnon (1996) one-sided p-values.

Null Hypothesis: GOLD has a unit root
Exogenous: Constant
Lag Length: 0 (Automatic - based on SIC, maxlag=12)

		t-Statistic	Prob.*
Augmented Dickey-Fuller test statistic		-10.72736	0.0000
Test critical values:	1% level	-3.479656	
	5% level	-2.883073	
	10% level	-2.578331	

*MacKinnon (1996) one-sided p-values.

Fig. 8.4 EViews Unit Root Test estimates

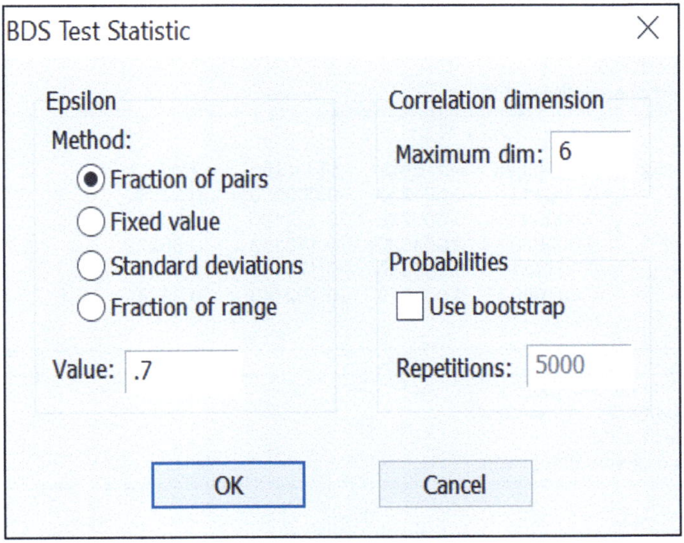

Fig. 8.5 EViews BDS Independence Test statistic estimation window

Gold reject the null hypothesis of "Data in a time series is independently and identically distributed (iid)"

Fig. 8.6 shows BDS independence test statistics for linearity. Estimates clearly indicate that both gold and silver series exhibit high non-linear and chaotic nature. Whereas in case of oil series BDS test estimates fail to reject the null hypothesis of "Data in a time series is independently and identically distributed (iid)".

```
BDS Test for OIL
Date: 04/06/21   Time: 07:41
Sample: 1 135
Included observations: 135
```

Dimension	BDS Statistic	Std. Error	z-Statistic	Prob.
2	-0.000111	0.001233	-0.089659	0.9286
3	-0.000333	0.002729	-0.122120	0.9028
4	-0.000670	0.004520	-0.148153	0.8822
5	-0.001121	0.006549	-0.171188	0.8641
6	-0.001689	0.008779	-0.192443	0.8474

```
BDS Test for SILVER
Date: 04/06/21   Time: 07:42
Sample: 1 135
Included observations: 135
```

Dimension	BDS Statistic	Std. Error	z-Statistic	Prob.
2	0.007718	0.009153	0.843193	0.3991
3	0.031355	0.014642	2.141422	0.0322
4	0.041839	0.017557	2.383081	0.0172
5	0.043650	0.018429	2.368495	0.0179
6	0.041638	0.017902	2.325913	0.0200

```
BDS Test for GOLD
Date: 04/06/21   Time: 07:43
Sample: 1 135
Included observations: 135
```

Dimension	BDS Statistic	Std. Error	z-Statistic	Prob.
2	0.033011	0.009203	3.586980	0.0003
3	0.067202	0.014736	4.560410	0.0000
4	0.090921	0.017687	5.140648	0.0000
5	0.103897	0.018584	5.590708	0.0000
6	0.108767	0.018070	6.019380	0.0000

Fig. 8.6 EViews BDS independence Test estimates

Step 5: *Estimation of Non-linear models.*

Threshold Autoregression (TAR)

BDS estimates indicate that both the Gold and Silver daily returns are highly non-linear and chaotic in nature. To study such non-linearity and messy characteristics of the Gold and Silver daily returns primarily a TAR model is deployed to identify the critical threshold values that are responsible for the multi-regime switching regimes. Following Hansen (2011) a multi-regime threshold autoregression with AR (11) for each regime is deployed. Threshold variable specifications list includes lags between -2 and -7.

To run the Threshold Autoregression (TAR) in EViews, go to Quick ➜ Estimate Equation and following window will appears as shown in Figs. 8.7 and 8.8. Then include the following inputs to the respective fields as follows:

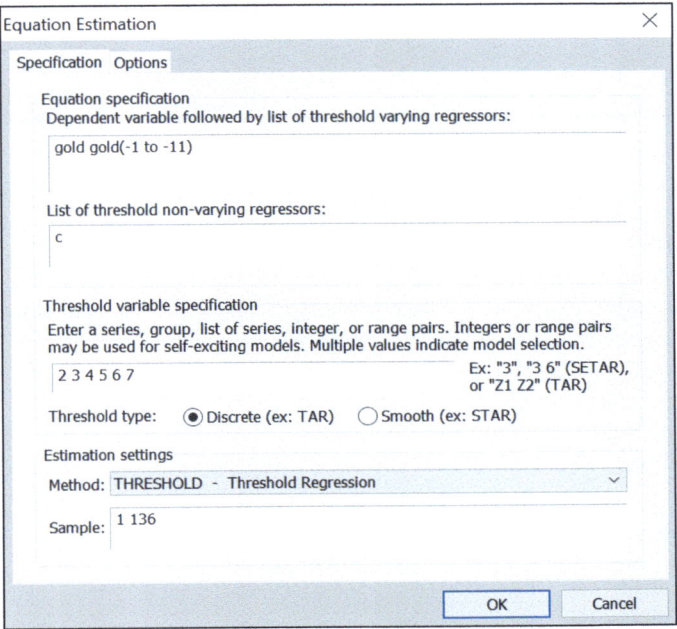

Fig. 8.7 TAR equation specification tab (Equation Estimation)

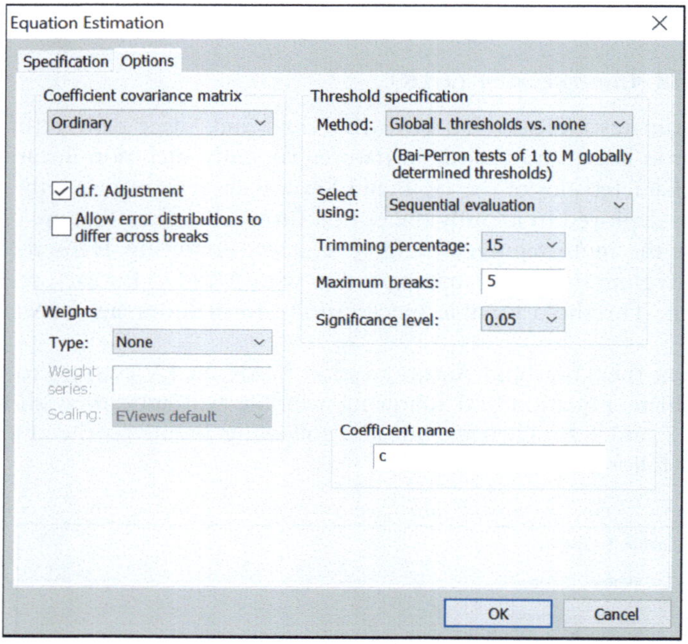

Fig. 8.8 TAR equation options tab (Equation Estimation)

Specification tab:

Dependent Variable followed by list of threshold varying regressors:
gold gold(-1 to -11)
List of threshold non-varying regressors: c
Threshold variable specification: 2 3 4 5 6 7
Threshold type: Discrete (ex: TAR).
Method: THRESHOLD-Threshold Regression.

Options tab:
Method: Global L thresholds versus none.

Then on clicking OK, TAR estimates will appear as shown below in
Fig. 8.9. Similarly by following the above steps obtain the TAR esti-

Dependent Variable: GOLD
Method: Discrete Threshold Regression
Date: 04/06/21   Time: 07:54
Sample (adjusted): 12 135
Included observations: 124 after adjustments
Variable chosen: GOLD(-2)
Selection: Sequential evaluation, Trimming 0.15, Max. thresholds 5, Sig.
    level 0.05
Threshold variables considered: GOLD(-2) GOLD(-3) GOLD(-4) GOLD(
    -5) GOLD(-6) GOLD(-7)

Variable	Coefficient	Std. Error	t-Statistic	Prob.
	GOLD(-2) < -0.01067776 -- 22 obs			
GOLD(-1)	-0.037553	0.188911	-0.198788	0.8431
GOLD(-2)	0.032195	0.148325	0.217054	0.8289
GOLD(-3)	0.719603	0.159748	4.504623	0.0000
GOLD(-4)	-0.024409	0.304020	-0.080287	0.9363
GOLD(-5)	0.359440	0.176569	2.035689	0.0464
GOLD(-6)	-0.093684	0.258408	-0.363704	0.7174
GOLD(-7)	-0.082288	0.155865	-0.527818	0.5997
GOLD(-8)	0.228835	0.157132	1.456321	0.1508
GOLD(-9)	0.049773	0.164450	0.302664	0.7632
GOLD(-10)	1.052738	0.161330	6.525351	0.0000
GOLD(-11)	0.583211	0.187863	3.104445	0.0030
	-0.01067776 <= GOLD(-2) < -0.00137885 -- 20 obs			
GOLD(-1)	-0.145747	0.221464	-0.658109	0.5131
GOLD(-2)	0.252061	0.707823	0.356108	0.7231
GOLD(-3)	-0.349633	0.454828	-0.768714	0.4452
GOLD(-4)	-0.056105	0.212286	-0.264291	0.7925
GOLD(-5)	-0.025334	0.256479	-0.098775	0.9217
GOLD(-6)	-0.322252	0.227738	-1.415012	0.1625
GOLD(-7)	-0.361817	0.303680	-1.191442	0.2384
GOLD(-8)	-0.136693	0.169368	-0.808259	0.4223
GOLD(-9)	-0.078630	0.184580	-0.425992	0.6717
GOLD(-10)	-0.063542	0.187169	-0.339489	0.7355
GOLD(-11)	-0.240533	0.271520	-0.885874	0.3794
	-0.00137885 <= GOLD(-2) < 0.001899457 -- 18 obs			
GOLD(-1)	-0.431969	0.218397	-1.977910	0.0528
GOLD(-2)	-13.52515	4.433246	-3.050845	0.0035
GOLD(-3)	-0.953072	0.305187	-3.122915	0.0028
GOLD(-4)	-0.088121	0.248325	-0.354863	0.7240
GOLD(-5)	-0.398032	0.239705	-1.660510	0.1023
GOLD(-6)	-0.375053	0.297038	-1.262642	0.2119
GOLD(-7)	-0.195793	0.221907	-0.882320	0.3813
GOLD(-8)	-0.147291	0.286162	-0.514710	0.6087
GOLD(-9)	-0.362216	0.387251	-0.935351	0.3536
GOLD(-10)	0.963419	0.356337	2.703872	0.0090
GOLD(-11)	0.275585	0.318306	0.865784	0.3902
	0.001899457 <= GOLD(-2) < 0.006483777 -- 22 obs			
GOLD(-1)	0.546917	0.380932	1.435735	0.1565
GOLD(-2)	-0.478687	0.786181	-0.608876	0.5450
GOLD(-3)	0.007195	0.288676	0.024923	0.9802
GOLD(-4)	-0.112981	0.301684	-0.374502	0.7094
GOLD(-5)	-0.036566	0.267958	-0.136461	0.8919
GOLD(-6)	0.246480	0.335617	0.734409	0.4657
GOLD(-7)	0.188194	0.241349	0.779760	0.4388
GOLD(-8)	0.265897	0.320640	0.829270	0.4104
GOLD(-9)	-0.039328	0.312831	-0.125710	0.9004
GOLD(-10)	0.397304	0.354547	1.120597	0.2672
GOLD(-11)	0.145166	0.301635	0.481263	0.6322
	0.006483777 <= GOLD(-2) < 0.01229147 -- 18 obs			
GOLD(-1)	-0.288052	0.362379	-0.794893	0.4300
GOLD(-2)	-0.083836	0.426868	-0.196398	0.8450
GOLD(-3)	-0.018576	0.374567	-0.049594	0.9608
GOLD(-4)	-0.713330	0.327266	-2.179660	0.0334
GOLD(-5)	0.700256	0.384512	1.821152	0.0738
GOLD(-6)	-0.086986	0.398776	-0.218134	0.8281
GOLD(-7)	-0.313471	0.308832	-1.015020	0.3144
GOLD(-8)	-0.780260	0.343559	-2.271107	0.0269
GOLD(-9)	-0.691678	0.250376	-2.762556	0.0077
GOLD(-10)	0.001540	0.200351	0.007684	0.9939
GOLD(-11)	0.276407	0.370535	0.745967	0.4588
	0.01229147 <= GOLD(-2) -- 18 obs			
GOLD(-1)	-0.182558	0.185421	-0.984559	0.3290
GOLD(-2)	-0.168910	0.139199	-1.213440	0.2300
GOLD(-3)	-0.010806	0.188029	-0.056408	0.9552
GOLD(-4)	0.145350	0.172547	-0.842376	0.4031
GOLD(-5)	0.392024	0.201808	1.942556	0.0570
GOLD(-6)	-0.125118	0.172705	-0.724458	0.4717
GOLD(-7)	0.107236	0.161031	0.665934	0.5081
GOLD(-8)	-0.112804	0.326750	-0.345230	0.7312
GOLD(-9)	-0.237672	0.260185	-0.913475	0.3648
GOLD(-10)	0.511031	0.156356	3.268376	0.0018
GOLD(-11)	0.152759	0.190218	0.803074	0.4253
	Non-Threshold Variables			
C	0.002518	0.002445	1.029529	0.3078

R-squared	0.821627	Mean dependent var		0.001024
Adjusted R-squared	0.615089	S.D. dependent var		0.016451
S.E. of regression	0.010206	Akaike info criterion		-6.028234
Sum squared resid	0.005937	Schwarz criterion		-4.504372
Log likelihood	440.7505	Hannan-Quinn criter.		-5.409206
F-statistic	3.978098	Durbin-Watson stat		2.062344
Prob(F-statistic)	0.000000			

Dependent Variable: SILVER
Method: Discrete Threshold Regression
Date: 04/06/21   Time: 07:58
Sample (adjusted): 12 135
Included observations: 124 after adjustments
Variable chosen: SILVER(-6)
Selection: Sequential evaluation, Trimming 0.15, Max. thresholds 5, Sig.
    level 0.05
Threshold variables considered: SILVER(-2) SILVER(-3) SILVER(-4)
    SILVER(-5) SILVER(-6) SILVER(-7)

Variable	Coefficient	Std. Error	t-Statistic	Prob.
	SILVER(-6) < -0.01454511 -- 20 obs			
SILVER(-1)	0.102174	0.202264	0.505152	0.6154
SILVER(-2)	-0.441463	0.233644	-1.889469	0.0639
SILVER(-3)	0.131867	0.204323	0.645532	0.5212
SILVER(-4)	-0.004461	0.195816	-0.022781	0.9819
SILVER(-5)	0.371149	0.465984	0.796484	0.4291
SILVER(-6)	-0.091546	0.154539	-0.592384	0.5559
SILVER(-7)	-0.534356	0.244244	-2.187799	0.0328
SILVER(-8)	-0.419001	0.245295	-1.708150	0.0930
SILVER(-9)	0.123680	0.228634	0.540951	0.5906
SILVER(-10)	0.562703	0.262391	2.144519	0.0363
SILVER(-11)	-0.321069	0.276902	-1.159506	0.2511
	-0.01454511 <= SILVER(-6) < -0.00554107 -- 21 obs			
SILVER(-1)	0.896521	0.332600	2.695496	0.0092
SILVER(-2)	0.521694	0.152143	3.428960	0.0011
SILVER(-3)	-0.771523	0.251330	-3.069764	0.0033
SILVER(-4)	-0.117255	0.191201	-0.613256	0.5421
SILVER(-5)	-0.106164	0.127484	-0.832766	0.4085
SILVER(-6)	0.398587	0.630920	0.631756	0.5301
SILVER(-7)	-0.079013	0.196858	-0.403420	0.6881
SILVER(-8)	0.509105	0.230213	2.211449	0.0310
SILVER(-9)	-0.602911	0.296624	-2.032575	0.0468
SILVER(-10)	-0.285296	0.215284	-1.325209	0.1904
SILVER(-11)	0.290936	0.274257	1.060816	0.2932
	-0.00554107 <= SILVER(-6) < 0.001666475 -- 27 obs			
SILVER(-1)	-0.487534	0.287303	-1.696932	0.0952
SILVER(-2)	-0.010118	0.180424	-0.056082	0.9555
SILVER(-3)	1.047787	0.629823	1.663621	0.1017
SILVER(-4)	0.846373	0.375282	2.255301	0.0280
SILVER(-5)	-0.128259	0.390674	-0.328303	0.7438
SILVER(-6)	-1.817868	2.004957	-0.906687	0.3684
SILVER(-7)	0.176347	0.278454	0.633309	0.5291
SILVER(-8)	-0.226204	0.252865	-0.894565	0.3748
SILVER(-9)	0.196756	0.106573	0.756526	0.4524
SILVER(-10)	0.385595	0.188345	2.047276	0.0453
SILVER(-11)	0.433266	0.154209	2.809605	0.0068
	0.001666475 <= SILVER(-6) < 0.009018385 -- 18 obs			
SILVER(-1)	0.186111	0.289054	0.643864	0.5222
SILVER(-2)	0.333408	0.510254	0.653417	0.5161
SILVER(-3)	0.132083	0.344377	0.383541	0.7027
SILVER(-4)	-0.137586	0.297189	-0.462960	0.6452
SILVER(-5)	-0.003543	0.317312	-0.011167	0.9911
SILVER(-6)	0.484170	0.538257	0.899515	0.3722
SILVER(-7)	0.214840	0.329897	0.651234	0.5175
SILVER(-8)	0.739174	0.491040	1.505323	0.1378
SILVER(-9)	-0.098514	0.306007	-0.321935	0.7487
SILVER(-10)	-0.052198	0.327000	-0.159596	0.8738
SILVER(-11)	0.473025	0.285628	1.656087	0.1032
	0.009018385 <= SILVER(-6) < 0.01781912 -- 18 obs			
SILVER(-1)	0.262492	0.209373	1.253706	0.2151
SILVER(-2)	0.210950	0.347617	0.606845	0.5464
SILVER(-3)	0.132083	0.344377	0.383541	0.7027
SILVER(-4)	-0.137586	0.297189	-0.462960	0.6452
SILVER(-5)	-0.003543	0.317312	-0.011167	0.9911
SILVER(-6)	0.484170	0.165115	-0.032159	0.9745
SILVER(-7)	-0.066106	0.161293	-0.409853	0.6835
SILVER(-8)	0.056199	0.180760	0.310904	0.7570
SILVER(-9)	-0.287437	0.289529	-0.992777	0.3250
SILVER(-10)	-0.164549	0.217731	-0.755743	0.4529
SILVER(-11)	0.194939	0.227543	0.856711	0.3952
	0.01781912 <= SILVER(-6) -- 20 obs			
SILVER(-1)	-0.302277	0.416239	-0.726210	0.4707
SILVER(-2)	-0.263666	0.420813	-0.626563	0.5334
SILVER(-3)	-0.021830	0.249569	-0.087473	0.9306
SILVER(-4)	-0.053296	0.272049	-0.195907	0.8454
SILVER(-5)	-0.243238	0.178993	-1.358925	0.1795
SILVER(-6)	0.005310	0.165115	-0.032159	0.9745
SILVER(-7)	-0.066106	0.161293	-0.409853	0.6835
SILVER(-8)	0.056199	0.180760	0.310904	0.7570
SILVER(-9)	-0.287437	0.289529	-0.992777	0.3250
SILVER(-10)	-0.164549	0.217731	-0.755743	0.4529
SILVER(-11)	0.194939	0.227543	0.856711	0.3952
	Non-Threshold Variables			
C	-0.001224	0.004002	-0.305832	0.7608

R-squared	0.801224	Mean dependent var		0.000217
Adjusted R-squared	0.571062	S.D. dependent var		0.027682
S.E. of regression	0.018130	Akaike info criterion		-4.879073
Sum squared resid	0.018736	Schwarz criterion		-3.355211
Log likelihood	369.5025	Hannan-Quinn criter.		-4.260044
F-statistic	3.481130	Durbin-Watson stat		1.629699
Prob(F-statistic)	0.000002			

Fig. 8.9 EViews TAR Estimates

mates for Silver. Threshold Autoregression (TAR) models' estimates are represented in Fig. 8.9, for gold and silver, respectively. Bai and Perron (1998) techniques are used for estimating the threshold variables. TAR estimates (Fig. 8.9) show that it splits the regimes into two based on the six different threshold values. In case of the Gold TAR model with lag 2 is selected whereas for Silver lag 4 is chosen as the optimal. All associated statistical values associated with the variables gold and silver are represented in the Fig. 8.9. In this part summary all obtained statistical values are self-explanatory and a p value less than 0.05 represents that the respective threshold variable is statistical significance at 5% level. At the end part the Fig. 8.9 shows results for the non-threshold variables estimates.

To cross-check the model validation plot the sum squares of residuals are shown in Fig. 8.10. Fig. 8.10 clearly indicates that gold (-2) and silver (-6) are the best model fit. These figures could be obtained from EViews by following the steps below:

TAR estimation result window ➔ View ➔ Model Selection Summary ➔ Criteria Graph).

Step 6: *Smooth Transition Autoregressive (STAR).*

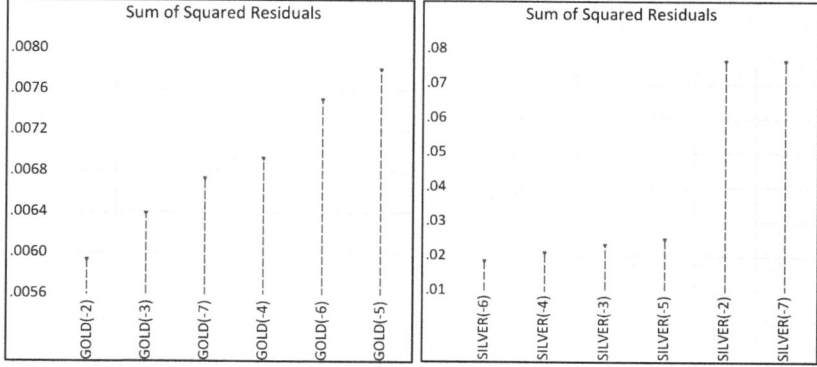

Fig. 8.10   TAR sum squares of residuals plot

Smooth Transition Autoregressive (STAR)

To run Smooth Threshold Autoregression (STAR) in EViews, go to Quick ➜ Estimate Equation and following window will appears as shown in Fig. 8.11. Then include the following inputs to the respective fields as follows:

Specification tab:

> Dependent Variable followed by list of threshold varying regressors: gold gold (-1 to -6).
> List of threshold non-varying regressors: c
> Threshold variable specification: 2 3 4 5 6 7
> Threshold type: SMOOTH (ex: STAR)
> Method: THRESHOLD-Threshold Regression.

> Options tab:
> Threshold Type: Logistic

Then on clicking OK following window will appears with STAR estimates as shown in Fig. 8.12. Similarly by following the above steps STAR estimates for any other series could also be obtained.

The above estimates show two-regime (linear and non-linear) smooth transition autoregressive model with six thresholds varying regressors in each regime for Gold and Silver with a lag of 4 and 3, respectively. STAR model estimates for gold and silver are shown in Fig. 8.12. STAR estimates show that estimation converge after 11 and 10 iterations for gold and silver, respectively. In this part summary all obtained statistical values are self-explanatory and a p value of less than 0.05 represents that the respective threshold variable is statistical significance at 5% level. At the end part the Fig. 8.12 shows results for the non-threshold variables estimates.

Fig. 8.13 shows the non-linear distribution of threshold weights function. The median transition weight lies near the values -0.0219747 & 0.000862521 for gold and silver, respectively. These figures could be obtained from EViews by following steps:

STAR estimation result window ➜ View ➜ Threshold Smoothing Weights.

Model selection criteria for STAR (least value of SSR) are lag four for both gold and silver. However, EViews based on its pre-defined criteria

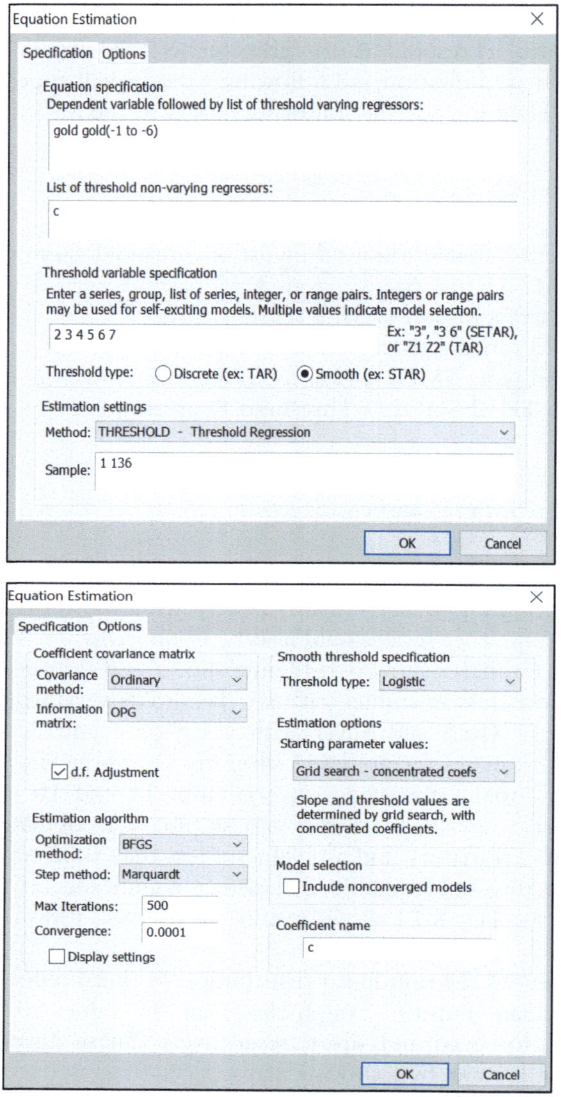

Fig. 8.11 STAR Equation Estimation in EViews

Dependent Variable: GOLD
Method: Smooth Threshold Regression
Transition function: Logistic
Date: 04/06/21   Time: 08:26
Sample (adjusted): 7 135
Included observations: 129 after adjustments
Threshold variable chosen: GOLD(-4)
Threshold variables considered: GOLD(-2) GOLD(-3) GOLD(-4) GOLD(-5) GOLD(-6) GOLD(-7)
Starting values: Grid search with concentrated regression coefficients
Note: final equation sample is larger than selection sample
Ordinary standard errors & covariance using outer product of gradients
Convergence achieved after 11 iterations

Variable	Coefficient	Std. Error	t-Statistic	Prob.
Threshold Variables (linear part)				
GOLD(-1)	1.964741	0.387306	5.072845	0.0000
GOLD(-2)	5.130571	1.456114	3.523468	0.0006
GOLD(-3)	-2.116474	1.027330	-2.060169	0.0417
GOLD(-4)	2.307307	0.797759	2.892234	0.0046
GOLD(-5)	0.057331	0.336071	0.170592	0.8648
GOLD(-6)	0.641658	0.413210	1.552864	0.1232
Threshold Variables (nonlinear part)				
GOLD(-1)	-1.996925	0.395075	-5.054550	0.0000
GOLD(-2)	-5.358387	1.458091	-3.674934	0.0004
GOLD(-3)	2.020514	1.030127	1.961422	0.0523
GOLD(-4)	-2.214502	0.803040	-2.757649	0.0068
GOLD(-5)	-0.153886	0.348632	-0.441400	0.6598
GOLD(-6)	-0.961473	0.420102	-2.288665	0.0239
Non-Threshold Variables				
C	0.000359	0.001208	0.297163	0.7669
Slopes				
SLOPE	1965.146	2096.504	0.937344	0.3506
Thresholds				
THRESHOLD	-0.021975	0.000848	-25.91491	0.0000

R-squared	0.439634	Mean dependent var	0.000971
Adjusted R-squared	0.370817	S.D. dependent var	0.016154
S.E. of regression	0.012813	Akaike info criterion	-5.767691
Sum squared resid	0.018717	Schwarz criterion	-5.435155
Log likelihood	387.0161	Hannan-Quinn criter.	-5.632575
F-statistic	6.388458	Durbin-Watson stat	1.920314
Prob(F-statistic)	0.000000		

Dependent Variable: SILVER
Method: Smooth Threshold Regression
Transition function: Logistic
Date: 04/06/21   Time: 09:19
Sample (adjusted): 7 135
Included observations: 129 after adjustments
Threshold variable chosen: SILVER(-3)
Threshold variables considered: SILVER(-2) SILVER(-3) SILVER(-4) SILVER(-5) SILVER(-6) SILVER(-7)
Starting values: Grid search with concentrated regression coefficients
Note: final equation sample is larger than selection sample
Ordinary standard errors & covariance using outer product of gradients
Convergence achieved after 10 iterations

Variable	Coefficient	Std. Error	t-Statistic	Prob.
Threshold Variables (linear part)				
SILVER(-1)	0.227833	0.193347	1.178362	0.2411
SILVER(-2)	0.989955	0.588168	1.683115	0.0951
SILVER(-3)	0.010908	0.181476	0.060106	0.9522
SILVER(-4)	-0.060801	0.242534	-0.250689	0.8025
SILVER(-5)	-0.581000	0.236882	-2.452694	0.0157
SILVER(-6)	-0.185295	0.270288	-0.685545	0.4944
Threshold Variables (nonlinear part)				
SILVER(-1)	-0.193219	0.410033	-0.471228	0.6384
SILVER(-2)	-1.447072	0.868558	-1.666063	0.0984
SILVER(-3)	0.145923	0.315296	0.462812	0.6444
SILVER(-4)	-0.103606	0.440599	-0.235148	0.8145
SILVER(-5)	0.877848	0.496502	1.768066	0.0797
SILVER(-6)	0.132457	0.480589	0.275615	0.7833
Non-Threshold Variables				
C	0.000376	0.002471	0.152125	0.8794
Slopes				
SLOPE	41.71300	32.61986	1.278761	0.2036
Thresholds				
THRESHOLD	0.000863	0.021672	0.039798	0.9683

R-squared	0.288980	Mean dependent var	0.000217
Adjusted R-squared	0.201662	S.D. dependent var	0.027213
S.E. of regression	0.024315	Akaike info criterion	-4.486541
Sum squared resid	0.067396	Schwarz criterion	-4.154004
Log likelihood	304.3819	Hannan-Quinn criter.	-4.351425
F-statistic	3.309501	Durbin-Watson stat	2.147058
Prob(F-statistic)	0.000188		

Fig. 8.12 EViews STAR estimates

chooses lag 3 over lag 4 (among the lags 2, 3, 4, 5, 6, and 7) for Silver model estimation. These figures (Fig. 8.14) could be obtained from EViews by following steps:

STAR estimation result window ➔ View ➔ Model Selection Summary ➔ Criteria Graph/Table.

Linearity Test

For robustness check additional linearity test could be performed in EViews as discussed below.

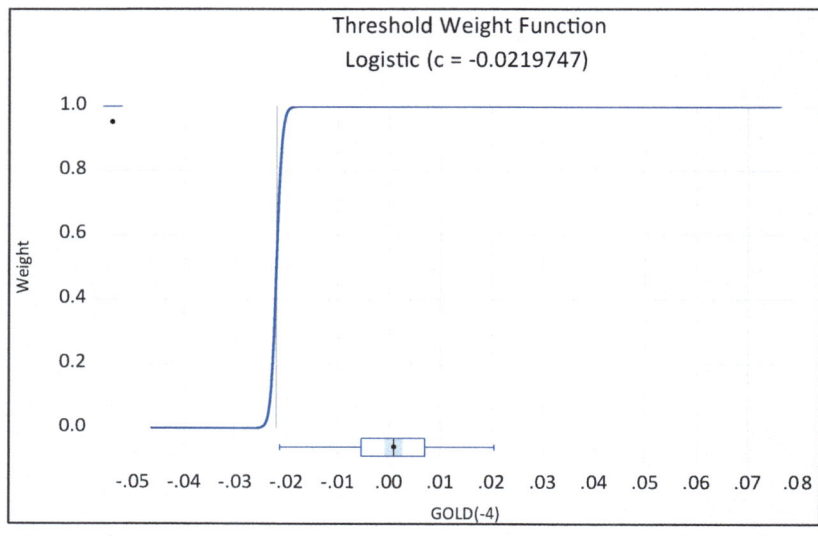

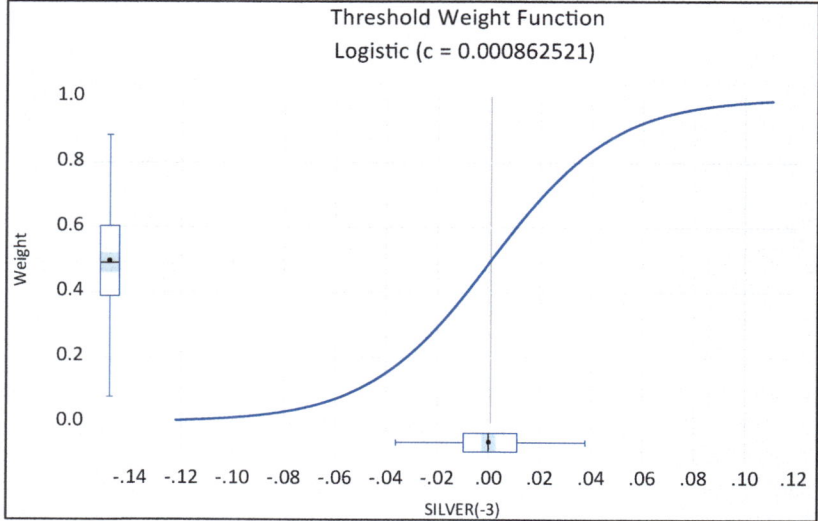

Fig. 8.13 Threshold weights view and shape of the smoothing function

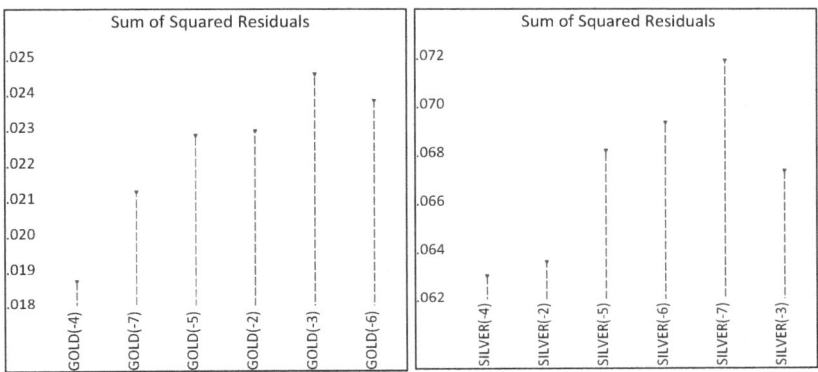

Fig. 8.14   STAR sum of squared residuals plot

Linearity test could be performed in the EViews by following steps: STAR estimation result window ➔ View ➔ Stability Diagnostics ➔ Linearity Test. Fig. 8.15 shows three different test estimates obtained for smooth threshold linearity tests for gold and silver. Estimates show that null hypothesis of linearity is rejected by all tests at 5% significant level for both gold and silver. Estimates also show that chosen preferred transition function as logistic (LSTAR) models are preferred over exponential (ESTAR) models for Gold and Silver.

Remaining non-linearity test

EViews also offers to test whether there is additional unmodelled non-linearity. Remaining non-linearity test could be performed in the EViews by following steps:

STAR estimation result window ➔ View➔ Stability Diagnostics ➔ Remaining Non-Linearity Test ➔ Encapsulated Non-linearity Test.

The remaining non-linearity using encapsulated non-linearity tests and obtained estimates are shown in Fig. 8.16. Encapsulated non-linearity test estimates confirm that the developed STAR model is passable in explaining the non-linear dynamics of the time series.

Smooth Threshold Linearity Tests			
Date: 04/06/21 Time: 09:05			
Sample: 1 135			
Included observations: 129			
Test for nonlinearity using GOLD(-4) as the threshold variable			
Taylor series alternatives: b0 + b1*s [+ b2*s^2 + b3*s^3 + b4*s^4]			

| | Linearity Tests | | |
Null Hypothesis	F-statistic	d.f.	p-value
H04: b1=b2=b3=b4=0	3.213706	(24, 98)	0.0000
H03: b1=b2=b3=0	2.882234	(18, 104)	0.0004
H02: b1=b2=0	3.849806	(12, 110)	0.0001
H01: b1=0	6.137300	(6, 116)	0.0000

The H0i test uses the i-th order Taylor expansion (bj=0 for all j>i).

| | Terasvirta Sequential Tests | | |
Null Hypothesis	F-statistic	d.f.	p-value
H3: b3=0	0.962738	(6, 104)	0.4543
H2: b2=0 | b3=0	1.426820	(6, 110)	0.2108
H1: b1=0 | b2=b3=0	6.137300	(6, 116)	0.0000

All tests are based on the third-order Taylor expansion (b4=0).
Linear model is rejected at the 5% level using H03.
Recommended model: first-order logistic.
. Pr(H1) <= Pr(H2)

| | Escribano-Jorda Tests | | |
Null Hypothesis	F-statistic	d.f.	p-value
H0L: b2=b4=0	2.253930	(12, 98)	0.0145
H0E: b1=b3=0	2.822913	(12, 98)	0.0023

All tests are based on the fourth-order Taylor expansion.
Linear model is rejected at the 5% level using H04.
Recommended model: first-order logistic with nonzero threshold.
. Pr(H0L) >= Pr(H0E) with Pr(H0L) < .05

Smooth Threshold Linearity Tests			
Date: 04/06/21 Time: 09:35			
Sample: 1 135			
Included observations: 129			
Test for nonlinearity using SILVER(-3) as the threshold variable			
Taylor series alternatives: b0 + b1*s [+ b2*s^2 + b3*s^3 + b4*s^4]			

| | Linearity Tests | | |
Null Hypothesis	F-statistic	d.f.	p-value
H04: b1=b2=b3=b4=0	1.820886	(24, 98)	0.0214
H03: b1=b2=b3=0	1.710360	(18, 104)	0.0488
H02: b1=b2=0	2.176885	(12, 110)	0.0175
H01: b1=0	3.811938	(6, 116)	0.0017

The H0i test uses the i-th order Taylor expansion (bj=0 for all j>i).

| | Terasvirta Sequential Tests | | |
Null Hypothesis	F-statistic	d.f.	p-value
H3: b3=0	0.820044	(6, 104)	0.5568
H2: b2=0 | b3=0	0.617291	(6, 110)	0.7161
H1: b1=0 | b2=b3=0	3.811938	(6, 116)	0.0017

All tests are based on the third-order Taylor expansion (b4=0).
Linear model is rejected at the 5% level using H03.
Recommended model: first-order logistic.
. Pr(H3) <= Pr(H2) or Pr(H1) <= Pr(H2)

| | Escribano-Jorda Tests | | |
Null Hypothesis	F-statistic	d.f.	p-value
H0L: b2=b4=0	1.434924	(12, 98)	0.1632
H0E: b1=b3=0	2.312001	(12, 98)	0.0121

All tests are based on the fourth-order Taylor expansion.
Linear model is rejected at the 5% level using H04.
Recommended model: first-order logistic with zero threshold.
. Pr(H0L) >= Pr(H0E) with Pr(H0L) >= .05 and Pr(H0E) < .05).

Fig. 8.15 STAR linearity test estimates

Summary

This chapter introduces Threshold Autoregression using EViews. Here we investigated the behaviour of gold, silver, and crude oil daily average return time series patterns during COVID-19 period. Estimates show that the behaviour of gold and silver daily average return time series patterns is highly non-linear and chaotic in nature unlike crude oil. To further investigate the gold and silver non-linear time series rich dynamics both TAR and STAR models are deployed. TAR estimates favour following modelling specifications: for gold TAR models with lag 2 and 6 regimes, whereas for silver TAR models with lag 4 and 6 regimes are chosen. Whereas STAR estimates display best results with a lag of 4 and 3 for gold and silver daily return time series, respectively. Further linearity and remaining non-linearity estimates confirm robustness check, chooses

Smooth Threshold Remaining Nonlinearity Tests
Date: 04/06/21 Time: 09:38
Sample: 1 135
Included observations: 129
Encapsulated nonlinearity tests using GOLD(-4) as the threshold variable
Taylor series alternatives: b0 + b1*s [+ b2*s^2 + b3*s^3 + b4*s^4]

Encapsulated Nonlinearity Tests			
Null Hypothesis	F-statistic	d.f.	p-value
H04: b1=b2=b3=b4=0	1.382184	(30, 85)	0.1257
H03: b1=b2=b3=0	1.503816	(24, 91)	0.0866
H02: b1=b2=0	1.661955	(18, 97)	0.0599
H01: b1=0	0.894244	(11, 104)	0.5486

The H0i test uses the i-th order Taylor expansion (bj=0 for all j>i).

Terasvirta Sequential Tests			
Null Hypothesis	F-statistic	d.f.	p-value
H3: b3=0	1.022468	(6, 91)	0.4159
H2: b2=0	b3=0	2.706913	(7, 97)	0.0132
H1: b1=0	b2=b3=0	0.894244	(11, 104)	0.5486

All tests are based on the third-order Taylor expansion (b4=0).
Original model is not rejected at the 5% level using H03.

Escribano-Jorda Tests			
Null Hypothesis	F-statistic	d.f.	p-value
H0L: b2=b4=0	2.219841	(6, 91)	0.0481
H0E: b1=b3=0	2.917852	(6, 91)	0.0120

All tests are based on the fourth-order Taylor expansion.
Original model is not rejected at the 5% level using H04.

Smooth Threshold Remaining Nonlinearity Tests
Date: 04/06/21 Time: 09:37
Sample: 1 135
Included observations: 129
Encapsulated nonlinearity tests using SILVER(-3) as the threshold variable
Taylor series alternatives: b0 + b1*s [+ b2*s^2 + b3*s^3 + b4*s^4]

Encapsulated Nonlinearity Tests			
Null Hypothesis	F-statistic	d.f.	p-value
H04: b1=b2=b3=b4=0	1.311023	(37, 77)	0.1587
H03: b1=b2=b3=0	1.157660	(35, 79)	0.2915
H02: b1=b2=0	1.096336	(24, 90)	0.3643
H01: b1=0	0.642137	(12, 102)	0.8016

The H0i test uses the i-th order Taylor expansion (bj=0 for all j>i).

Terasvirta Sequential Tests			
Null Hypothesis	F-statistic	d.f.	p-value
H3: b3=0	1.225525	(11, 79)	0.2845
H2: b2=0	b3=0	1.511866	(12, 90)	0.1345
H1: b1=0	b2=b3=0	0.642137	(12, 102)	0.8016

All tests are based on the third-order Taylor expansion (b4=0).
Original model is not rejected at the 5% level using H03.

Escribano-Jorda Tests			
Null Hypothesis	F-statistic	d.f.	p-value
H0L: b2=b4=0	1.452681	(13, 77)	0.1554
H0E: b1=b3=0	1.472608	(13, 77)	0.1473

All tests are based on the fourth-order Taylor expansion.
Original model is not rejected at the 5% level using H04.

Fig. 8.16   STAR Encapsulated non-linearity test estimates

preferred transition function as logistic (LSTAR) models over exponential (ESTAR) models and chosen models are adequate to capture the non-linear dynamics of gold and silver. The main message here is that both gold and silver show distinctive features during COVID-19. Likewise during any other crisis financial time series might be non-linear and chaotic. To study such distinct non-linear and chaotic nature of the time series, TAR models could be a substantial solutions.

Analyst/Investor Corners

Descriptive statistics show crude oil has average negative returns. Then gold, silver, and crude oil time series are highly kurtotic. BDS independence test confirms that both the gold and silver daily average returns are highly non-linear and chaotic in nature unlike crude oil. To study the non-linear dynamics of gold and silver daily returns time series threshold regressions are deployed. TAR estimates favour following modelling specifications: for gold TAR model with lag 2 and 6 regimes, whereas for silver TAR model with lag 4 and 6 regimes are chosen. Further sum squares of residuals plots also confirm and validate the best model fit for TAR. STAR estimates show that estimation converge after 11 and 13 iterations for gold and silver, respectively. STAR estimates display best results with a lag of 4 and 3 for gold and silver daily return time series, respectively. Further linearity and remaining non-linearity estimates confirm that preferred transition function as logistic (LSTAR) models are preferred over exponential (ESTAR) models and current models are acceptable to capture the non-linear dynamics of gold and silver.

Estimated results support strong argument in favour of the claim that gold is being used to manipulate precious metal markets. Obtained estimates show that risk appetite differs significantly across these gold, silver, and crude oil assets. Gold could be regarded as the safe heaven asset during crisis periods. Investors those whose are looking to invest in the white assets specially during crisis need to be more cautious as it is a risky asset. The main message here is that both gold and silver show distinctive features during COVID-19 pandemic. To study such distinctive features of a non-linear time series TAR models would give an additional edge.

8.4   Exercises

8.4.1   Multiple Choice Questions

1. STAR stands for

   (a) Smooth Transition Auto Regression
   (b) Smooth Transition Autoregressive
   (c) Simple Transition Autoregressive
   (d) Simple Transition Auto Regression

2. Which of the following common transition function is not used in STAR models?

(a) Logistic
(b) Normal
(c) Exponential
(d) Brownian

3. Which of the following is not a Threshold Autoregression model?

(a) ESTAR
(b) LSTAR
(c) MSTAR
(d) STAR

4. For determining the thresholds in EViews which methods is used?

(a) Bai and Perron test
(b) BDS Independence test
(c) Phillips–Perron test
(d) KPSS test

5. Which of the following is associated with the linearity test?

(a) Variance ratio test
(b) Wald (Chi-Square)joint tests
(c) Chow-Denning maximum $|z|$ joint tests
(d) BDS Independence test

6. Which of the following term is not associated with the non-linearity?

(a) Structural breaks
(b) Regimes
(c) Cycles
(d) None of the above

7. In EViews linearity test provides which of the following test(s) estimates:

(a) *Teräsvirta* Sequential tests
(b) Escribano and Jorda tests
(c) Linearity tests
(d) All of the above

8. Which of the following TAR model is a discrete model?

    (a) STAR
    (b) ESTAR
    (c) SETAR
    (d) LSTAR

9. SETAR stands for

    (a) Super Exciting Threshold Autoregression
    (b) Self-Exciting Threshold Autoregression
    (c) Smooth Exciting Threshold Autoregression
    (d) Simple Exciting Threshold Autoregression

10. SSR stands for

    (a) Second squares of the residuals
    (b) Sum of squared residuals
    (c) Simple squares of the residuals
    (d) None of the above

8.4.2   Fill in the Blanks

1. Model selection criteria are generally based on the _____.
2. LSTAR stands for _____.
3. _____ is a discrete TAR model.
4. The _____ is used for testing the linearity of a time series.
5. Bai and Perron test is used for determining the _____.
6. Two well-*known* non-linear *Threshold Autoregressive models are* _____ *&* _____.

8.4.3   Long Answer Questions

1. Define non-linearity with the help of suitable examples?
2. What are *Threshold Autoregressive models*?
3. Why *Threshold Autoregressive models are not often used in financial studies*?
4. How one can determine whether the selected threshold type in a STAR model is precise?
5. Comment on the following statement:

Sum of squared residuals (SSR)—small values with huge influence.
6. How TAR and STAR models are different? Explain it taking suitable examples?

8.4.4 Real-World Tasks

1. A professor asks his/her student to test whether US commodities returns follow a non-linear pattern during the COVID-19 first and second phase ? Assume yourself as the student and perform the task. Then prepare a detailed report of the analysis to be submitted to the professor.
2. A researcher want to analyse whether the top seven cryptocurrencies returns are chaotic and non-linear during the noble coronavirus pandemic period. Assume yourself as the researcher perform the mentioned task in detail and develop the analysis report.
3. An analyst wants to examine the world indices non-linear dynamics before, during, and after the first phase of COVID-19. Help him/her to perform the said analysis and prepare the report.
4. A scholar needs to test the different threshold autoregression models for modelling the major three currency pairs daily exchange rate for the last three years as his/her project dissertation. Help the scholar to complete his/her project dissertation successfully and satisfactorily.
5. A senior manager of the Reserve Bank of Australia asked an intern working under him/her to conduct test of linearity for all the technological securities traded in the Australian Securities Exchange during the first phase of COVID-19 pandemic. Help the intern in analysing and developing the final report for timely submission to the senior manager.
6. Conduct a simple empirical research that evidences non-linearity and chaotic movements in the security average returns ?

8.4.5 Case Study

A researcher conducts a research to uncover the hidden non-linear characteristics of the USD_JPY daily exchange rates returns between the period

1 January 2020 and 22 July 2020. Few of the important estimates that the researcher obtained are shown below.

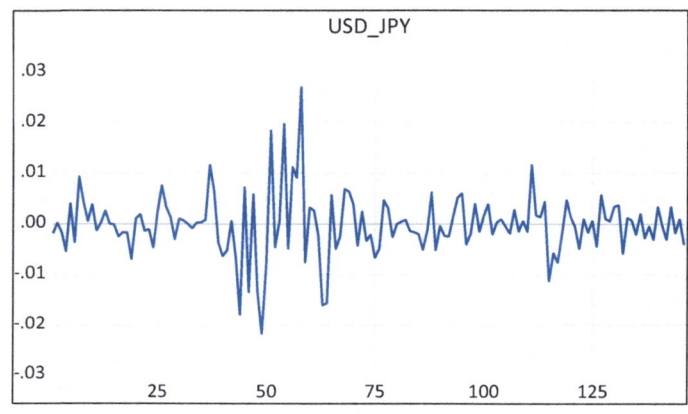

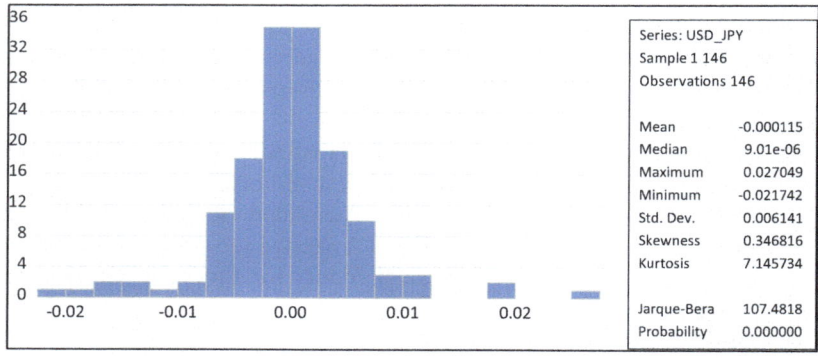

Null Hypothesis: USD_JPY has a unit root
Exogenous: Constant
Lag Length: 0 (Automatic - based on SIC, maxlag=13)

		t-Statistic	Prob.*
Augmented Dickey-Fuller test statistic		-11.33748	0.0000
Test critical values:	1% level	-3.475819	
	5% level	-2.881400	
	10% level	-2.577439	

*MacKinnon (1996) one-sided p-values.

BDS Test for USD_JPY
Date: 04/06/21   Time: 17:20
Sample: 1 146
Included observations: 146

Dimension	BDS Statistic	Std. Error	z-Statistic	Prob.
2	0.043858	0.008755	5.009519	0.0000
3	0.082325	0.014014	5.874573	0.0000
4	0.104428	0.016814	6.210774	0.0000
5	0.117654	0.017661	6.661974	0.0000
6	0.121558	0.017165	7.081561	0.0000

Raw epsilon	0.007397		
Pairs within epsilon	15048.00	V-Statistic	0.705949
Triples within epsilon	1715020.	V-Statistic	0.551075

Dimension	C(m,n)	c(m,n)	C(1,n-(m-1))	c(1,n-(m-1))	c(1,n-(m-1))^k
2	5624.000	0.538697	7344.000	0.703448	0.494839
3	4398.000	0.427156	7220.000	0.701243	0.344831
4	3491.000	0.343839	7102.000	0.699498	0.239412
5	2844.000	0.284088	6994.000	0.698632	0.166434
6	2335.000	0.236575	6883.000	0.697366	0.115017

Dependent Variable: USD_JPY
Method: Discrete Threshold Regression
Date: 04/06/21 Time: 17:25
Sample (adjusted): 12 146
Included observations: 135 after adjustments
Variable chosen: USD_JPY(-7)
Selection: Sequential evaluation, Trimming 0.15, Max. thresholds 5, Sig. level 0.05
Threshold variables considered: USD_JPY(-2) USD_JPY(-3) USD_JPY(-4) USD_JPY(-5) USD_JPY(-6) USD_JPY(-7)

Variable	Coefficient	Std. Error	t-Statistic	Prob.
USD_JPY(-7) < -0.003978971 -- 27 obs				
USD_JPY(-1)	-0.132615	0.127201	-1.042561	0.3008
USD_JPY(-2)	0.040048	0.095609	0.418878	0.6766
USD_JPY(-3)	-0.422545	0.162342	-2.602807	0.0113
USD_JPY(-4)	0.156177	0.091098	1.714393	0.0910
USD_JPY(-5)	0.032151	0.131769	0.243995	0.8080
USD_JPY(-6)	0.326193	0.101221	3.222566	0.0020
USD_JPY(-7)	-0.236529	0.148425	-1.593599	0.1157
USD_JPY(-8)	-0.385558	0.113465	-3.398323	0.0011
USD_JPY(-9)	0.228664	0.144192	1.585833	0.1174
USD_JPY(-10)	-0.268671	0.142372	-1.887097	0.0634
USD_JPY(-11)	-0.384628	0.124100	-3.099351	0.0028
-0.003978971 <= USD_JPY(-7) < -0.001485526 -- 24 obs				
USD_JPY(-1)	-0.050545	0.508428	-0.099415	0.9211
USD_JPY(-2)	0.417429	0.210564	1.982427	0.0515
USD_JPY(-3)	0.489012	0.325946	1.500285	0.1382
USD_JPY(-4)	0.417168	0.305855	1.363940	0.1771
USD_JPY(-5)	0.305719	0.328678	0.930148	0.3556
USD_JPY(-6)	-0.123011	0.327522	-0.375581	0.7084
USD_JPY(-7)	-0.047381	0.599748	-0.079002	0.9373
USD_JPY(-8)	0.005064	0.328338	0.015394	0.9878
USD_JPY(-9)	-0.085617	0.251516	-0.340403	0.7346
USD_JPY(-10)	-0.061905	0.212355	-0.291517	0.7715
USD_JPY(-11)	0.337264	0.213072	1.582864	0.1181
-0.001485526 <= USD_JPY(-7) < 0.0003717225 -- 20 obs				
USD_JPY(-1)	0.003367	0.244898	0.013750	0.9891
USD_JPY(-2)	-0.473143	0.237744	-1.990133	0.0506
USD_JPY(-3)	-0.018116	0.274275	-0.066051	0.9475
USD_JPY(-4)	-0.517653	0.241879	-2.140133	0.0359
USD_JPY(-5)	0.135888	0.296166	0.458825	0.6478
USD_JPY(-6)	-1.021774	0.427442	-2.390438	0.0196
USD_JPY(-7)	-1.328600	1.484582	-0.894932	0.3740
USD_JPY(-8)	-1.229825	0.547499	-2.246258	0.0279
USD_JPY(-9)	-0.906397	0.580091	-1.565957	0.1220
USD_JPY(-10)	-0.286145	0.418104	-0.684387	0.4961
USD_JPY(-11)	0.111407	0.290484	0.383523	0.7025
0.0003717225 <= USD_JPY(-7) < 0.001425762 -- 20 obs				
USD_JPY(-1)	0.555868	0.223492	2.487197	0.0153
USD_JPY(-2)	1.185454	0.668537	1.773207	0.0807
USD_JPY(-3)	-0.036741	0.510971	-0.071904	0.9429
USD_JPY(-4)	-0.475361	0.551541	-0.861878	0.3918
USD_JPY(-5)	0.265500	0.275433	0.963968	0.3385
USD_JPY(-6)	0.297057	0.250843	1.184235	0.2404
USD_JPY(-7)	-1.213490	2.819489	-0.430394	0.6683
USD_JPY(-8)	0.044672	0.331926	0.134583	0.8933
USD_JPY(-9)	0.491925	0.371806	1.323068	0.1902
USD_JPY(-10)	2.220767	0.645766	3.438965	0.0010
USD_JPY(-11)	0.569642	0.364707	1.561916	0.1229
0.001425762 <= USD_JPY(-7) < 0.00471509 -- 23 obs				
USD_JPY(-1)	-0.459113	0.359330	-1.277691	0.2057
USD_JPY(-2)	-0.152618	0.315974	-0.483009	0.6306
USD_JPY(-3)	0.311194	0.273405	1.138216	0.2590
USD_JPY(-4)	-0.425990	0.228258	-1.866262	0.0663
USD_JPY(-5)	-0.029619	0.236596	-0.125189	0.9007
USD_JPY(-6)	0.067748	0.240663	0.281507	0.7792
USD_JPY(-7)	0.528034	0.548813	0.962138	0.3394
USD_JPY(-8)	-0.098720	0.287735	-0.343092	0.7326
USD_JPY(-9)	-0.158912	0.201869	-0.787246	0.4339
USD_JPY(-10)	-0.176257	0.210182	-0.838596	0.4046
USD_JPY(-11)	-0.056106	0.242500	-0.231366	0.8177
0.00471509 <= USD_JPY(-7) -- 21 obs				
USD_JPY(-1)	0.170275	0.187660	0.907408	0.3674
USD_JPY(-2)	-0.094173	0.297119	-0.316953	0.7523
USD_JPY(-3)	0.298794	0.142516	2.096566	0.0398
USD_JPY(-4)	0.405698	0.236826	1.713063	0.0913
USD_JPY(-5)	-0.177845	0.163683	-1.086522	0.2811
USD_JPY(-6)	-0.472862	0.183543	-2.576294	0.0122
USD_JPY(-7)	0.092016	0.160621	0.571806	0.5693
USD_JPY(-8)	0.194668	0.172229	1.130285	0.2623
USD_JPY(-9)	-0.235682	0.189169	-1.245883	0.2171
USD_JPY(-10)	-0.528818	0.204721	-2.583118	0.0119
USD_JPY(-11)	0.072354	0.227144	0.318638	0.7511
Non-Threshold Variables				
C	-0.001226	0.001147	-1.069698	0.2885

R-squared	0.801706	Mean dependent var	-0.000192
Adjusted R-squared	0.609244	S.D. dependent var	0.006275
S.E. of regression	0.003923	Akaike info criterion	-7.937302
Sum squared resid	0.001046	Schwarz criterion	-6.495425
Log likelihood	602.7879	Hannan-Quinn criter.	-7.351383
F-statistic	4.165531	Durbin-Watson stat	2.080708
Prob(F-statistic)	0.000000		

Dependent Variable: USD_JPY
Method: Smooth Threshold Regression
Transition function: Exponential
Date: 04/06/21 Time: 17:28
Sample (adjusted): 7 146
Included observations: 140 after adjustments
Threshold variable chosen: USD_JPY(-2)
Threshold variables considered: USD_JPY(-2) USD_JPY(-3) USD_JPY(-4) USD_JPY(-5) USD_JPY(-6) USD_JPY(-7)
Starting values: Grid search with concentrated regression coefficients
Note: final estimation sample is larger than selection sample
Ordinary standard errors & covariance using outer product of gradients
Convergence achieved after 9 iterations

Variable	Coefficient	Std. Error	t-Statistic	Prob.
Threshold Variables (linear part)				
USD_JPY(-1)	0.218943	0.115701	1.892326	0.0608
USD_JPY(-2)	-0.202990	0.165374	-1.227455	0.2220
USD_JPY(-3)	0.456903	0.113325	4.031787	0.0001
USD_JPY(-4)	-0.230703	0.105400	-2.188838	0.0305
USD_JPY(-5)	-0.101757	0.099296	-1.024778	0.3074
USD_JPY(-6)	-0.203890	0.098082	-2.078768	0.0397
Threshold Variables (nonlinear part)				
USD_JPY(-1)	-0.705665	0.341095	-2.068822	0.0406
USD_JPY(-2)	0.726715	0.349053	2.081964	0.0394
USD_JPY(-3)	-2.077691	0.769040	-2.701670	0.0079
USD_JPY(-4)	1.269858	0.464535	2.733609	0.0072
USD_JPY(-5)	0.444190	0.367429	1.208913	0.2290
USD_JPY(-6)	0.085994	0.426995	0.201394	0.8407
Non-Threshold Variables				
C	-0.000566	0.000480	-1.179619	0.2404
Slopes				
SLOPE	5042.704	2874.200	1.754472	0.0818
Thresholds				
THRESHOLD	-0.001922	0.000709	-2.710329	0.0077

R-squared	0.344921	Mean dependent var	-6.41E-05
Adjusted R-squared	0.271552	S.D. dependent var	0.006236
S.E. of regression	0.005322	Akaike info criterion	-7.532866
Sum squared resid	0.003541	Schwarz criterion	-7.217690
Log likelihood	542.3006	Hannan-Quinn criter.	-7.404788
F-statistic	4.701183	Durbin-Watson stat	2.131459
Prob(F-statistic)	0.000001		

Note: SSR for TAR and STAR

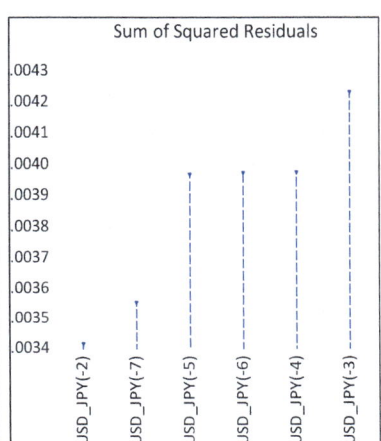

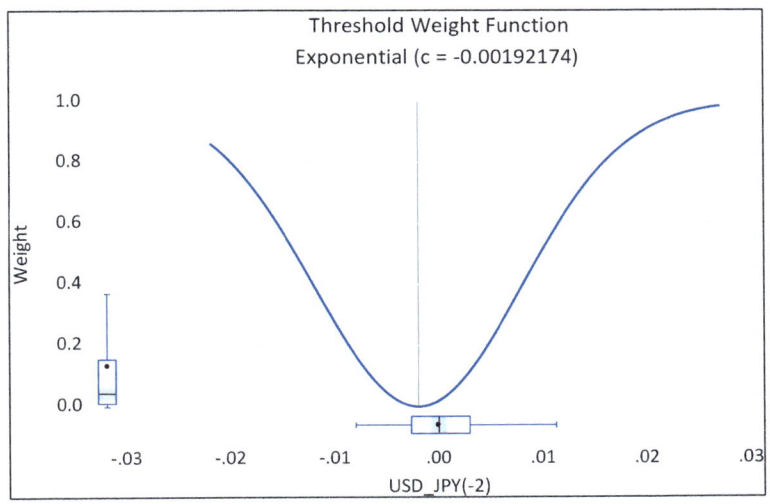

Smooth Threshold Linearity Tests Date: 04/06/21 Time: 17:33 Sample: 1 146 Included observations: 140 Test for nonlinearity using USD JPY(-2) as the threshold variable Taylor series alternatives: b0 + b1*s [+ b2*s^2 + b3*s^3 + b4*s^4]

Null Hypothesis	Linearity Tests F-statistic	d.f.	p-value
H04: b1=b2=b3=b4=0	4.278218	(24, 109)	0.0000
H03: b1=b2=b3=0	5.373744	(18, 115)	0.0000
H02: b1=b2=0	7.218697	(12, 121)	0.0000
H01: b1=0	2.176891	(6, 127)	0.0494

The H0i test uses the i-th order Taylor expansion (bj=0 for all j>i).

Null Hypothesis	Terasvirta Sequential Tests F-statistic	d.f.	p-value
H3: b3=0	1.398530	(6, 115)	0.2212
H2: b2=0	b3=0	11.21041	(6, 121)	0.0000
H1: b1=0	b2=b3=0	2.176891	(6, 127)	0.0494

All tests are based on the third-order Taylor expansion (b4=0).
Linear model is rejected at the 5% level using H03.
Recommended model: exponential.
. Pr(H2) < Pr(H3) and Pr(H2) < Pr(H1))

Null Hypothesis	Escribano-Jorda Tests F-statistic	d.f.	p-value
H0L: b2=b4=0	5.032232	(12, 109)	0.0000
H0E: b1=b3=0	2.407501	(12, 109)	0.0083

All tests are based on the fourth-order Taylor expansion.
Linear model is rejected at the 5% level using H04.
Recommended model: exponential with nonzero threshold.
. Pr(H0L) < Pr(H0E) with Pr(H0E) < .05

Smooth Threshold Remaining Nonlinearity Tests Date: 04/06/21 Time: 17:34 Sample: 1 146 Included observations: 140 Encapsulated nonlinearity tests using USD_JPY(-2) as the threshold variable Taylor series alternatives: b0 + b1*s [+ b2*s^2 + b3*s^3 + b4*s^4]

Null Hypothesis	Encapsulated Nonlinearity Tests F-statistic	d.f.	p-value
H04: b1=b2=b3=b4=0	2.209667	(43, 84)	0.0010
H03: b1=b2=b3=0	2.269852	(35, 92)	0.0010
H02: b1=b2=0	2.725369	(23, 104)	0.0003
H01: b1=0	3.184456	(12, 115)	0.0006

The H0i test uses the i-th order Taylor expansion (bj=0 for all j>i).

Null Hypothesis	Terasvirta Sequential Tests F-statistic	d.f.	p-value
H3: b3=0	1.247564	(12, 92)	0.2637
H2: b2=0	b3=0	1.919129	(11, 104)	0.0449
H1: b1=0	b2=b3=0	3.184456	(12, 115)	0.0006

All tests are based on the third-order Taylor expansion (b4=0).
Original model is rejected at the 5% level using H03.
Recommended model: first-order logistic.
. Pr(H1) <= Pr(H2)

Null Hypothesis	Escribano-Jorda Tests F-statistic	d.f.	p-value
H0L: b2=b4=0	1.960838	(16, 87)	0.0249
H0E: b1=b3=0	1.799142	(16, 87)	0.0439

All tests are based on the fourth-order Taylor expansion.
Original model is rejected at the 5% level using H04.
Recommended model: exponential with nonzero threshold.
. Pr(H0L) < Pr(H0E) with Pr(H0E) < .05

Based on these estimates briefly comment on the hidden non-linear characteristics of the USD_JPY daily exchange rates returns between the period 1 January 2020 and 22 July 2020 in your report.

Note: Estimates includes: USD_JPY daily exchange rates returns graph; Descriptive statistics with histogram; ADF Test estimates; BDS Independence tests estimates; TAR and STAR estimates; SSR diagrams for TAR & STAR; Threshold weight function plot; STAR linearity and remaining non-linearity tests.

REFERENCES

Bai, J., & Perron, P. (1998). Estimating and testing linear models with multiple structural changes. *Econometrica, 66*, 47–78.

Broock, W. A., Scheinkman, J. A., Dechert, W. D., & LeBaron, B. (1996). A test for independence based on the correlation dimension. *Econometric Reviews, 15*(3), 197–235.

Chen, H., Li, Y., Lin, M., & Zhu, Y. (2019). *A regime shift model with nonparametric switching mechanism* (No. 2019-07-03).

Dickey, D. A., & Fuller, W. A. (1979). Distribution of the estimators for autoregressive time series with a unit root. *Journal of the American Statistical Association, 74,* 427–431.

Hansen, B. E. (2000). Sample splitting and threshold estimation. *Econometrica, 68*(3), 575–603.

Hansen, B. (2011). Threshold autoregression in economics. *Statistics and its interface, 4,* 123–127.

Li, W. K., & Lam, K. (1995). Modelling asymmetry in stock returns by a threshold autoregressive conditional heteroscedastic model. *Journal of the Royal Statistical Society: Series D (the Statistician), 44*(3), 333–341.

Maiti, M., Grubisic, Z., & Vukovic, D. B. (2020). Dissecting tether's nonlinear dynamics during COVID-19. *Journal of Open Innovation: Technology, Market, and Complexity, 6*(4), 161.

Maiti, M., Vyklyuk, Y., & Vukovič, D. (2020). Cryptocurrencies chaotic co-movement forecasting with neural networks. *Internet Technology Letters* (e157).

Teräsvirta, T. (1994). Specification, estimation, and evaluation of smooth transition autoregressive models. *Journal of the American Statistical Association, 89,* 208–218.

Thanh, S. D., Canh, N. P., & Maiti, M. (2020). Asymmetric effects of unanticipated monetary shocks on stock prices: Emerging market evidence. *Economic Analysis and Policy, 65,* 40–55.

Tong, H. (1990). *Non-linear time series: A dynamical system approach.* Oxford University Press.

Vukovic, D., Lapshina, K. A., & Maiti, M. (2019). European Monetary Union bond market dynamics: Pre & post crisis. *Research in International Business and Finance, 50,* 369–380.

Vukovic, D., Vyklyuk, Y., Matsiuk, N., & Maiti, M. (2020). Neural network forecasting in prediction Sharpe ratio: Evidence from EU debt market. *Physica A: Statistical Mechanics and its Applications, 542,* 123331.

CHAPTER 9

Introduction to Wavelets

Key Topics Covered
- *Fourier transform*
- *Windowed Fourier transform*
- *Wavelet transform*
- *CWT & DWT*
- *Scaling & Shifting function*
- *Wavelet coherence & clustering*
- *R Illustrations on Wavelet analysis*

9.1 BACKGROUND

The financial time series is often asymmetric and non-linear (Maiti et al. 2020a, 2020b; Thanh et al., 2020; Vukovic et al., 2019; 2020). These abrupt changes in the time series may be resulting from the several issues such as structural breaks, regime switching, conditional volatilities, and others. Unexpected changes in the time series have important information regarding its characteristics. The Fourier transform is considered to be one such powerful tool for data analysis. However, previous studies emphasized that Fourier transform is not fully capable in capturing those unanticipated changes in the time series features. The reason is that the Fourier transform characterizes time series only as the summation of sine

© The Author(s), under exclusive license to Springer Nature Singapore Pte Ltd. 2021
M. Maiti, *Applied Financial Econometrics*,
https://doi.org/10.1007/978-981-16-4063-6_9

waves that oscillates endlessly and are not localized in time or space. The Fourier transform of the time series $F(t)$ represents only the function of frequency (ω) as shown in Eq. 9.1.

$$F(\omega) = \frac{1}{2\pi} \int_{-\infty}^{\infty} F(t)e^{-i\omega t} dt \qquad (9.1)$$

The above issue related to the Fourier transform is significantly overcome by the windowed Fourier transform. The windowed Fourier transform introduced a local windowing function into the Fourier transform equation. By doing so, the windowed Fourier transform represents the time series $F(t)$ both into the time and frequency localized space. The windowed Fourier transform of the time series $F(t)$ is shown in Eq. 9.2.

$$F^{Window}(\omega, t) = \int F(s)G(s-t)e^{-i\omega t} ds = \int F(s)G^{\omega,t}(s)ds \qquad (9.2)$$

where, $G^{\omega,t}(s)$ is the windowing function.

Thus, for fully capturing the time series asymmetric and non-linear characteristics, there is a need for the transform function that is localized in both the time and frequency space. It is true that the resolution problem is certainly reduced in case of windowed Fourier transform over the Fourier transform. But both of them (Fourier & Windowed Fourier Transform) lack the property of multi levels resolution analysis. Figure 9.1 shows the illustrations for the time and frequency domain localized characteristics of the Fourier and Windowed Fourier transforms.

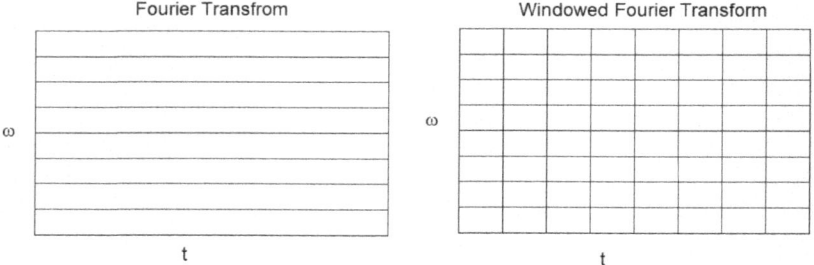

Fig. 9.1 Illustration of the time and frequency domain localized characteristics of the Fourier and Windowed Fourier Transforms

At this point emanates the importance of the wavelets analysis that allows multi levels of resolution for different time and frequencies regions. The wavelets basically are the rapidly decaying wave like oscillation with zero means. The greatest strength of a wavelet is that it can take different shapes and sizes. Some of the widely used wavelets are as follows: Coiflets, Daubechies, Haar, Morlet, and others. The wavelets exists for a finite period of time unlike the sinusoids. The wavelet transform of the time series $F(t)$ can be represented as shown in Eq. 9.3. Equations 9.2 and 9.3 are pretty identical.

$$F^{Wavlet}(a, b) = |a|^{-1/2} \int F(t)\psi\frac{t-b}{a}dt = \int F(t)\psi^{a,b}(t)dt \qquad (9.3)$$

where, $\psi^{a,b}(t)$ is the wavelets function, and mother wavelets function are represented by the $\psi(t)$ notation.

Based on the applications, different types of wavelets are used. Scaling and shifting are the two important terms related to the wavelet transform. The term scaling refers to the stretching or shrinking of the original series in time as shown in Eq. 9.4.

$$Scaling\,Function = \psi\left(\frac{t}{scaling\,factor}\right) \qquad (9.4)$$

Scaling factor can take any positive values (scaling factor > 0) and inversely proportional to the frequency. Thus, in wavelet transform, there exists a reciprocal relationship between the scaling factor and frequency with a constant of proportionality (also known as the centre frequency of the wavelet). Notably, the wavelet transform has a band pass feature in the frequency domain and mathematically equivalent frequency can be represented as shown in Eq. 9.5.

$$F_{equivalent} = \frac{Center\,frequency\,of\,the\,wavelet\,(C_f)}{Wavelet\,scale(s) * Sampling\,interval(\Delta_t)}) \qquad (9.5)$$

This means scaling the wavelet by a scaling factor of two will be resulting into reduction of the equivalent frequency by an octave. Similarly, for other wavelet scaling factors, (2^i) equivalent frequency will be reduced accordingly as shown in Table 9.1.

A larger value of the wavelet scaling factor indicates stretched wavelet with a lower frequency. Likewise, a smaller value of the wavelet scaling

Table 9.1 Wavelet scaling factor and equivalent frequency

Wavelet scaling factor (2^i) Where i = 1, 2, …, n	2	4	8	16	32	…	2^n
Equivalent frequency reduction by the following factor	1/2	1/4	1/8	1/16	1/32	…	$1/2^n$

factor represents shrunken wavelet with a high frequency. Hence, the shrunken wavelets are useful for studying the slowly varying features of the time series. Similarly, the stretched wavelets are advantageous while reviewing the abrupt varying structures of the time series.

The shifting of the wavelet means either advancement or postponement of the onset of the wavelet along the length of the time series. Mathematically it is represented by the following notation: $\phi(t - k)$. In a whole Fig. 9.2, highlights the key differences between the Fourier, Windowed Fourier, and Wavelet transform of the time series. The Continuous Wavelet Transforms (CWT) and Discrete Wavelet Transforms

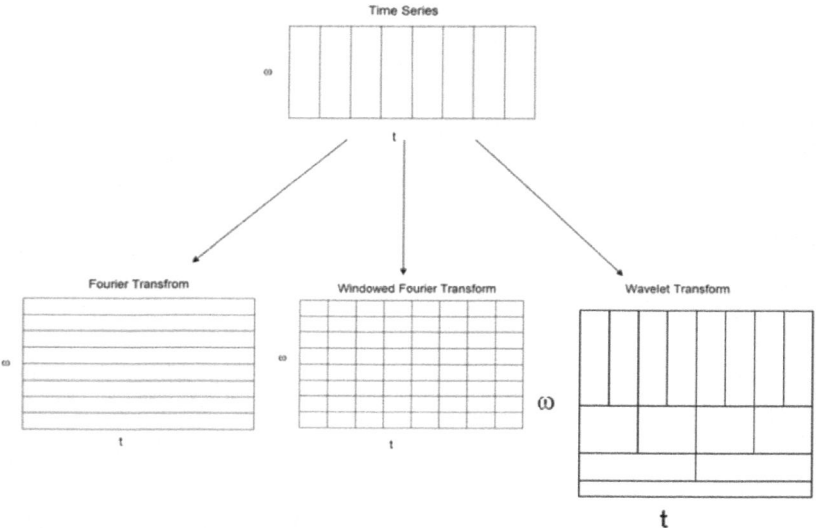

Fig. 9.2 Time series transform using the Fourier, Windowed Fourier, and Wavelet transform

(DWT) are the two most commonly used wavelet transforms method for the wavelet analysis. These two wavelet transform methods differ in terms of how the wavelets are scaled and shifted. The Continuous Wavelet Transforms (CWT) is useful for studying the intermediate scales by allowing fine scaling of the series. Mathematically, the CWT function is represented as shown in Eq. 9.6.

$$C(\tau, s) = \frac{1}{\sqrt{s}} \int F(t)\psi'\left(\frac{t - \tau}{s}\right)dt \qquad (9.6)$$

where,
   $C(\tau, s)$ represents the CWT function of the time series $F(t)$.
   τ is translation parameter, measure of time
   s is scale parameter, measure of frequency
   Similarly, the inverse CWT function can be represented by the Eq. 9.7.

$$F(t) = \frac{1}{\sqrt{s}} \iint_{\tau s} C(\tau, s)\psi\left(\frac{t - \tau}{s}\right)d\tau ds \qquad (9.7)$$

On the other hand, the Discrete Wavelet Transforms (DWT) is quite advantageous in denoising the time series. The greatest advantage lies with the Discrete Wavelet Transforms (DWT) method is that it yields less number of coefficients and uses lesser amount of memory for computation. The Discrete Wavelet Transforms (DWT) method uses base scale as the order of two. Other scales are obtained by raising the base values as 2^i. Where, i can take any positive integer values from one to n. Fundamentally, the Discrete Wavelet Transforms (DWT) method follows the process of dyadic scaling and shifting for translation. Mathematically, it can be represented by the following notation: $2^i m$. Where, m can take any positive integer values from one to n. Mathematically, the Discrete Wavelet Transforms (DWT) can be represented as shown in Eqs. 9.8a, b.

$$a_{jk} = \sum_t F(t)\psi^*_{jk}(t) \quad - Forward\ DWT \qquad (9.8a)$$

$$F(t) = \sum_k \sum_j a_{jk}\psi_{jk}(t) \quad - Inverse\ DWT \qquad (9.8b)$$

where, $\psi_{jk}(t) = 2^{\frac{j}{2}}\psi(2^j - k)$. Mathematically, multi resolution conditions can be represented by the equation no. 9.9a, b).

If a set of functions can be represented by a weighted sum of $\psi(2^j t - k)$ then a larger set including the original can be represented by a weighted sum of $\psi(2^{j+1}t - k)$.

$$V j \, [Span \, of \, \psi(2^j t - k)] : F_j(t) = \sum_k a_k \psi_{jk}(t) \tag{9.9a}$$

$$V j + 1 \, [Span \, of \, \psi(2^{(j+1)}t - k)] : F_{(j+1)}(t) = \sum_k b_k \psi_{(j+1)k}(t) \tag{9.9b}$$

Where, $V_j \subseteq V_{j+1}$.

Thus, the wavelet decompositions involve a linear combination of scaling function $\phi(t - k)$ and wavelet function $\psi(2^j t - k)$. If $F(t) \in V_{j+1}$ then $F(t)$ can be represented as shown in Eq. 9.10.

$$F(t) = \sum_k c_k \phi(t - k) + \sum_j \sum_k d_{j,k} \psi\left(2^j t - k\right) \tag{9.10}$$

Conceptually, the Discrete Wavelet Transforms (DWT) process is performed as shown in Fig. 9.3.

The original time series is initially decomposed following the Nyquist criterion into two groups, namely Low Pass and High Pass filter as shown in Fig. 9.3. Then similar process is followed to obtain the Low Pass and High Pass filter sub bands at different levels.

Thus, the wavelet analysis provides an important tool for the time & frequency localized study. Choosing the correct filter is very important as the shape of the wavelet is essential for performing the wavelet analysis. The wavelet transform can be accomplished in O(n) time. The wavelet analysis is well applied in many fields since last few decades. However, last decade seen significant application of the wavelet analysis in the field of finance (see Maiti et al.,2020c; Vukovic et al., 2021; & others).

Wavelet Coherence

The wavelet coherence measures the local correlation of two time series in time-frequency domain. The wavelet transform of the two time series $x(t)$ and $y(t)$ can be represented by the $W_x(u, s)$ and $W_y(u, s)$ following functions, respectively. Then the cross wavelet function $|W_{xy}(u, s)|$ can be obtained from the below expression as shown in Eq. 9.11.

$$W_{xy}(u, s) = W_x(u, s)W_y^*(u, s) \tag{9.11}$$

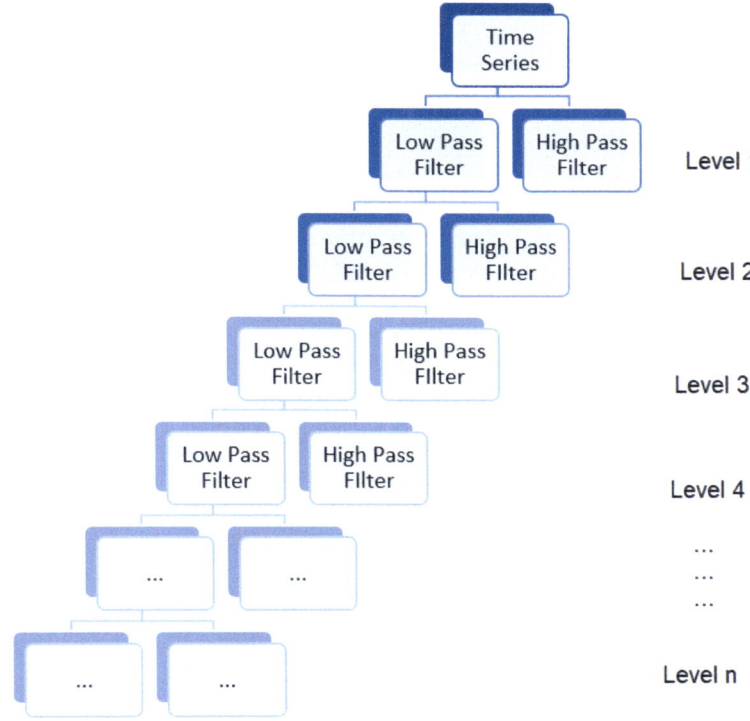

Fig. 9.3 Multi Scale Wavelet Decomposition

where,

> u represents position index
> s represents the scale
> * represents a complex conjugate.

The wavelet coherence is defined as the squared absolute value of the smoothed cross wavelet spectra normalized by the product of the smoothed individual wavelet power spectra of each series as represented in Eq. 9.12.

$$R^2(u, s) = \frac{\left|S(s^{-1}W_{xy}(u, s))\right|^2}{S\left(s^{-1}|W_x(u, s)|^2\right)S\left(s^{-1}|W_y(u, s)|^2\right)} \tag{9.12}$$

where, S is the smoothing operator. In absence of smoothing, the wavelet coherence is unity for all scales. The values of the squared wavelet coherence coefficient range between 0 and 1 [$0 \leq R^2(u, s) \leq 1$]. A value closer to zero represents a weak correlation, whereas a value closer to one represents a strong correlation. Thus, the wavelet coherence is powerful tool for analysing the co-movement across financial time series in time frequency domain.

The phase difference in the wavelet coherence diagram can be obtained by this expression (9.13).

$$\phi_n(s) = \tan^{-1}\frac{imaginary[S(s^{-1}W_n^{xy}(s))]}{real[S(s^{-1}W_n^{xy}(s))]} \tag{9.13}$$

Direction of the arrows in the wavelet coherence diagram represents following evidences for the time series x and y:

$\rightarrow$: x and y are in-phase
$\leftarrow$: x and y are anti-phase
$\downarrow$: x leading y by 90°
$\uparrow$: y leading x by 90°

Wavelet Clustering

The Ward's minimum variance criteria is often used for calculating the squared Euclidian distances between the two objects. The initial cluster's squared Euclidian distance between the two objects can be obtained using the following Eq. 9.14.

$$D_{ij} = d[X_i, X_j] = |X_i - X_j|^2 \tag{9.14}$$

Next, for an instance, assume that the clusters C_i and C_j are going to merge. Likewise, D_{ij}, D_{ik}, and D_{jk} represent squared Euclidian distance between the clusters C_i, C_j, and C_k. Then the squared Euclidian distance between the clusters $C_i \cup C_j$ and C_k can be represented by $D_{(ij)k}$. The value of $D_{(ij)k}$ can be estimated by the following Eq. 9.15.

$$D_{(ij)k} = \alpha_i D_{ik} + \alpha_j D_{jk} + \beta D_{ij} + \gamma \left| D_{ik} - D_{jk} \right| \qquad (9.15)$$

Where

$$\alpha_i = \frac{n_i + n_j}{n_i + n_j + n_k}$$

$$\alpha_j = \frac{n_j + n_k}{n_i + n_j + n_k}$$

$$\beta = -\left(\frac{n_k}{n_i + n_j + n_k} \right)$$

$$\gamma = 0$$

Note: n_i, n_j, $and n_j$ represent the cluster sizes (C_i, C_j, $and C_k$).

9.2 FINANCE IN ACTION

Illustration 1: To detect the seasonality in the Stellar daily returns between the period 1st January 2015 to 31st December 2017. Then display the two highest power frequencies.

R Code:

```
library("TSA1")
p = periodogram(Series)
dd = data.Frame(Freq = p$freq, Spec = p$spec)
order = dd[order(-dd$spec),]
top2_frequencies = head(order, 2)
top2_frequencies
Time = 1/top2_frequencies [Convert frequency to time periods]
time
```

[1] https://cran.r-project.org/web/packages/TSA/TSA.pdf.

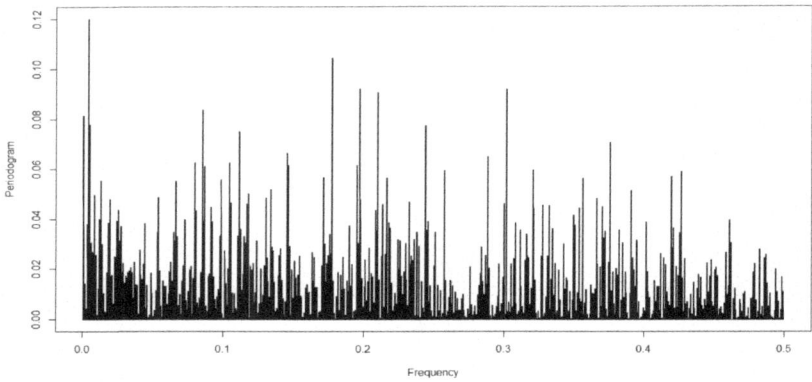

Fig. 9.4   Periodogram Plot for Stellar

Output:

freq spec
5 0.004444444 0.1200697
200 0.177777778 0.1042636
[1] 225.000 5.625

	freq	spec
5	0.004444444	0.1200697
200	0.177777778	0.1042636
[1]	225.000	5.625

The periodogram plot is very useful in detecting the seasonality in the time series as shown in Fig. 9.4. The seasonalitys are detected at the frequencies 0.004444444 and 0.177777778. The primary seasonality detected is 225 days, whereas the secondary seasonality of 5 days is also detected. Thus, the Stellar series has both annual and weekly seasonality.

Illustration 2: To decompose the Stellar daily returns using MODWT between the period 1st January 2015 and 31st December 2017.

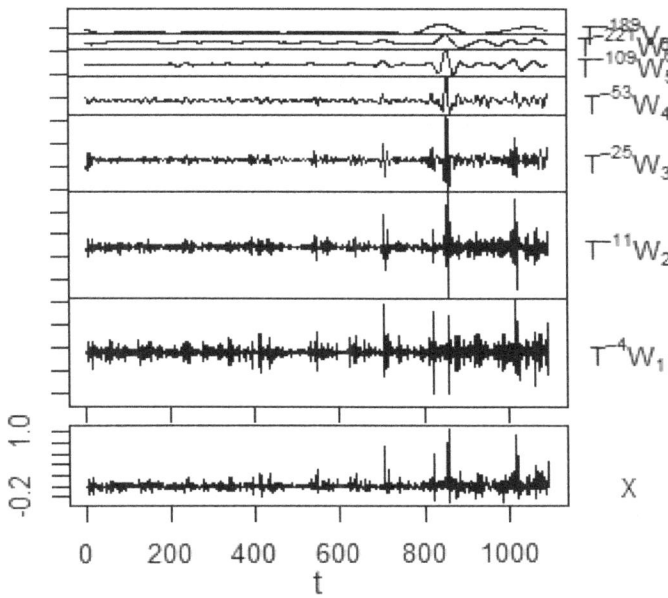

Fig. 9.5 MODWT decomposition of the Stellar daily returns

R Code:

```
library(wavelets²)
modwtobj < - modwt(Series_Name)
plot.modwt(modwtobj, levels = number_of_levels)
```

Output:

Figure 9.5 shows the MODWT (maximal overlap Discrete Wavelet Transform) decomposition of the Stellar daily returns between the period 1st January 2015 and 31st December 2017. It is clearly noticed that at the higher scales time series is more stressed with lower frequency. At different scales of the wavelet decomposition the shape of the time series varies. The varying shape of the time series at different levels of

---

² https://cran.r-project.org/web/packages/wavelets/wavelets.pdf.

the wavelet decomposition conveys different information about the time series.

Illustration 3: To plot the wavelet coherence diagram between the Stellar and XBP daily returns between the period 1st January 2015 and 31st December 2017.

R Code:

```
library(biwavelet³)
attach(Dataset_Name)
t1 = cbind(Series_1)
t2 = cbind(Series_2)
nrands = 500
wtc.ab = wtc(t1, t2, nrands = nrands)
par(oma = c(0, 0, 0, 1), mar = c(5, 4, 5, 5) + 0.1)
plot(wtc.ab, plot.phase = TRUE, lty.coi = 1, col.coi = "grey", lwd.coi = 2,lwd.sig
= 2, arrow.lwd = 0.03, arrow.len = 0.12, ylab = "Scale", xlab = "Period",plot.cb
= TRUE, main = "Wavelet Coherence: Stellar_Monero").
```

Output:

Figure 9.6 shows the wavelet coherence diagram between Stellar and Monero daily returns. The U shaped white curve in the diagram represents the region of significance or cone of influence. Y axis represents different wavelet scales. Whereas X axis represents the time periods. Brighter colours (Shades in red) represent higher coherence among the two time series. Whereas lighter spectrum (Shades in blue) represents lower coherence among the two time series. At lower scales, short contagion effects are observed which last for a few days. At the higher scales (256 and above), wavelet coherence is higher among the two series that lasts for a longer period. Stronger wavelet coherence represents higher co-movement among the two time series. The direction of all the arrows in the wavelet coherence diagram are right oriented ($\rightarrow$). It indicates that the two time series are in-phase. Further, the direction of the arrow heads (Upward or Downward) are not constant across the different wavelet scales. Upward ($\uparrow$) direction of the arrow represents XBP leading Stellar by 90°. Likewise, downward ($\downarrow$) arrow direction represents Stellar is leading XBP by 90°. The wavelet coherence diagram is a very powerful

---

³ https://cran.r-project.org/web/packages/biwavelet/biwavelet.pdf.

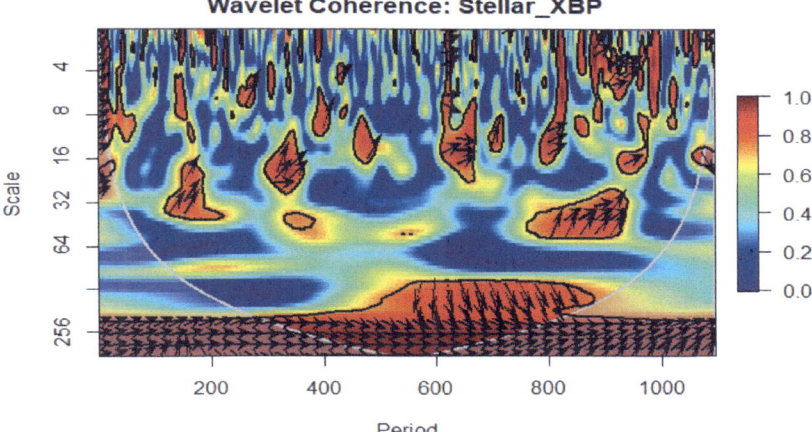

Fig. 9.6 Wavelet Coherence diagram between Stellar and Monero daily returns

tool for analysing the co-movements among the time series in both the time and frequency domains. Then the presence of the contagion effects can easily be detected by studying the wavelet coherence diagram.

Illustration 4: To plot the wavelet clustering diagram between the four cryptocurrencies (Stellar, Monero, XBP, and Bitcoin) daily returns between the period 1st January 2015 and 31stDecember 2017.

R Code:

```
library(biwavelet)
attach(Dataset_Name)
t1 = cbind(Series_1)
t2 = cbind(Series_2)
…
…
…
tn = cbind(Series_n)
wt.t1 = wt(t1)
wt.t2 = wt(t2)
…
…
…
```

```
wt.tn = wt(tn)
w.arr    =    array(NA,    Dim    =    c(Number_of_series,    NROW(Wt.T1$wave),
NCOL(Wt.T1$wave)))
w.arr[1„] = wt.t1$wave
w.arr[2„] = wt.t2$wave
...

...

...

w.arr[N„] = wt.tn$wave
w.arr.dis = wclust(w.arr)
plot(hclust(W.arr.dis$dist.mat, method = "ward.D2"),sub = " ", main = " ",ylab =
"Dissimilarity", hang = -1)
```

Output:

Figure 9.7 represents the wavelet clustering diagram for the four cryptocurrencies. The wavelet clustering diagram shows that the Monero has the highest dissimilarity value among the four cryptocurrencies. If an investor invests only in the XBP and Bitcoin, then the investor will not get any benefits of the portfolio diversification. As the dissimilarly values are same for both the XBP and Bitcoin. However, including Stellar into the portfolio that contains the XBP and Bitcoin. The investor will get an extra amount of the portfolio diversification benefits. The wavelet clustering

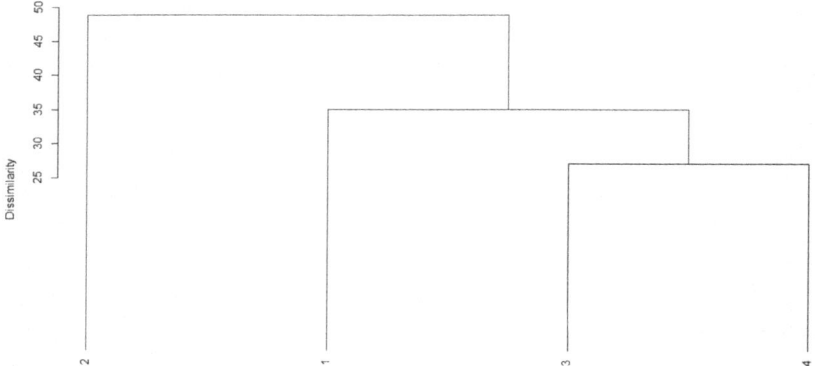

Fig. 9.7 Wavelet Clustering diagram for four cryptocurrencies (*Note* 1. Stellar, 2. Monero, 3. XBP, and 4. Bitcoin)

diagram is considered to be one of the very powerful tools to decide on the portfolio composition.

Summary

This chapter briefly introduced the wavelets and its applications in finance. Time series can be transformed using the Fourier transform, Windowed Fourier transform, and Wavelet transform. Among these three techniques, wavelet transform is superior for time and frequency domain analysis. The wavelets analysis allows multi levels of resolution for different time and frequencies regions. The greatest strength of a wavelet is that it can take different shapes and sizes. The two properties of a wavelet, namely scaling and shifting function are important for wavelet transform. Based on the applications either the Continuous or Discrete Wavelet Transform can be used. The wavelet coherence diagram and clustering diagram are very powerful tools for analysing the time series. R stepwise implementations and estimation interpretations of the different wavelet analysis are discussed plausibly.

Analysts/Investors Corner

It is quite often that the financial times series is asymmetric, non-linear, and chaotic in nature. To deal with such time series, wavelet analysis is a powerful tool. The wavelet analysis provides an important tool for both the time and frequency localized study. It is very important to choose the correct filter in wavelet analysis. As the shape of the wavelet is essential for performing the wavelet analysis. The compressed wavelets are useful for studying the slowly varying features of the time series. Likewise, the stretched wavelets are advantageous while reviewing the abrupt varying structures of the time series. The wavelet coherence is one of the powerful tools for analysing the co-movement across the financial time series in time and frequency domain. Then the wavelet clustering diagram is useful in selection of the assets for the investment-optimum portfolio development.

9.3   EXERCISES

9.3.1   *Multiple Choice Questions*

1. These abrupt changes in the time series may be resulting from the several issues such as

   (a) structural breaks
   (b) regime switching
   (c) conditional volatilities
   (d) All of the above

2. The Fourier transform of the time series represents the function of

   (a) frequency
   (b) time
   (c) either frequency or time
   (d) both frequency and time

3. The Windowed Fourier transform of the time series represents the function of

   (a) time
   (b) frequency
   (c) either time or frequency
   (d) both time and frequency

4. The Windowed Fourier transform is also referred as the

   (a) short time Fourier transform
   (b) medium time Fourier transform
   (c) long time Fourier transform
   (d) None of the above

5. Which of the following does not belong to any wavelet families?

   (a) Daubechies
   (b) Haar
   (c) Morlet
   (d) TAR

6. A larger value of the wavelet scaling factor indicates

   (a) Shrunken wavelet with a lower frequency
   (b) Stretched wavelet with a lower frequency

(c) Shrunken wavelet with a higher frequency
(d) Stretched wavelet with a higher frequency

7. A lower value of the wavelet scaling factor indicates

(a) Shrunken wavelet with a lower frequency
(b) Stretched wavelet with a lower frequency
(c) Shrunken wavelet with a higher frequency
(d) Stretched wavelet with a higher frequency

8. The Discrete Wavelet Transforms (DWT) method usually follows which of the following translation process for scaling and shifting?

(a) Monodic
(b) Dyadic
(c) Triadic
(d) Harmonic

9. The values of the squared wavelet coherence coefficient ranges between

(a) −1 and 1
(b) 0 and 1
(c) −2 and 2
(d) −1.5 and 1.5

10. The wavelet transform can be accomplished in

(a) $\Theta(n)$ time
(b) $O(n)$ time
(c) $\Theta(n.\log(n))$ time
(d) $O(n.\log(n))$ time

9.3.2   Fill in the Blanks

1. The wavelet analysis provides an important tool for the _____ and _____ localized study.
2. The _____ transform introduced a local windowing function into the Fourier transform equation.
3. The wavelets basically are the rapidly decaying wave like oscillation with _____ means.

4. The Discrete Wavelet Transforms (DWT) is quite advantageous in _____ the time series.

5. The Discrete Wavelet Transforms (DWT) method uses base scale as the order of _____.

6. The shifting of the wavelet means either _____ or _____ of the onset of the wavelet along the length of the time series.

7. MODWT stands for _____.

8. In wavelet transform, there exists a reciprocal relationship between the _____ and frequency with a constant of proportionality.

9. The wavelets analysis allows _____ of resolution for different time and frequencies regions.

10. The wavelet coherence is powerful tool for analysing the _____ across financial time series in time and frequency domain.

9.3.3   Long Answer Questions

1. Define Fourier transform and its implications with suitable examples?

2. Define Windowed Fourier transform and its implications with suitable examples?

3. Define wavelet transform and its implications with suitable examples

4. Explain briefly how windowed Fourier transform is different from wavelet transform?

5. What are the advantages and disadvantages associated with the Fourier transform?

6. Explain briefly how CWT is different from DWT?

7. Briefly explain the process of DWT taking suitable examples.

8. Briefly explain the scaling and shifting functions with respect to the wavelet transform.

9. Briefly explain the importance of wavelet coherence diagram taking suitable examples.

10. Discuss various application of wavelet analysis in finance and its implications with suitable examples.

11. Briefly explain the importance of wavelet clustering diagram taking suitable examples.

12. What is mother wavelet function and its implications in wavelet transform?
13. What is multi resolution analysis and its significance in finance ?
14. Comment on the phase difference in the wavelet coherence diagram and its significance.

9.3.4   Real-World Tasks

1. A professor asks his/her student to conduct a comparative wavelet analysis during the COVID-19 and subprime crisis on the European stock markets. Assume yourself as the student and perform the task. Then prepare a detailed report of the analysis to be submitted to the professor.
2. A researcher wants to examine the wavelet coherence and clustering among the top seven cryptocurrencies returns during the noble Corona virus pandemic. Assume yourself as the researcher perform the mentioned task in details and develop the analysis report.
3. An analyst wants to examine the short and long-term contagion effect between the world indices before, during, and after the subprime crisis. Help him/her to perform the said analysis and prepare the report.
4. A student needs to conduct multi-resolution analysis among the five major currency pairs daily exchange rate during the last three years as his/her project dissertation. Help the student to complete his/her project dissertation successfully and satisfactorily.
5. A senior manager of the Reserve bank of Australia asked his/her junior to conduct wavelet analysis for all the technological and pharmaceutical securities traded in the Australian Securities Exchange during the first phase of COVID-19 pandemic. Help the junior in analysing and developing the final report for timely submission to the senior manager.
6. An investor is evaluating his/her investing option as the hedge funds during early 2020. Help the investors to examine the hedge fund with respect to the multi-resolution analysis and help him/her to make investment decision.
7. A student needs to detect seasonality in the five major currency pairs daily exchange rate during the COVID-19 pandemic as

his/her project dissertation. Help the student to complete his/her project dissertation successfully and satisfactorily.

8. An analyst wants to examine the short and long-term periodicity or cyclicality among the precious metals before and during the COVID-19 pandemic. Help him/her to perform the said analysis and prepare the report.

9. An investment banker wants to examine the short and long term contagion effect among the ASEAN markets for making investment decision. Help him/her to perform the said analysis and prepare the report.

10. An investment banker wants to conduct multi-resolution analysis for making investment decision on the following: commodity market, gold, silver, crude oil, and VIX. Help him/her to perform the said analysis and prepare the report.

9.3.5   Case Studies

1. The figures below show the Periodogram plot for the Monero, XBP, and Bitcoin between the period 1st January 2015 and 31st December 2017. Then the obtained two highest power frequencies and time periods are also represented. Based on these information comment on the seasonality incidence in the Monero, XBP, and Bitcoin.

Monero

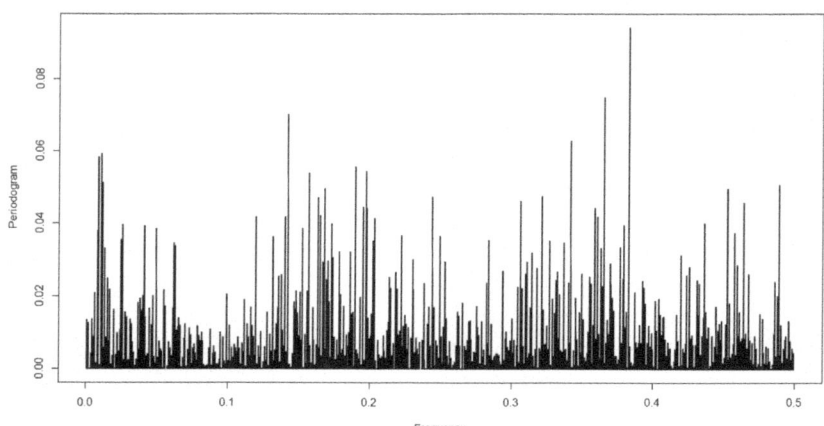

Xbp

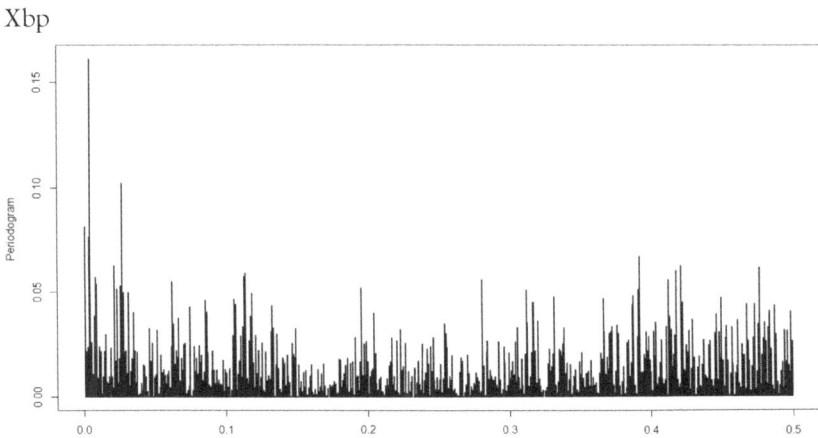

Bitcoin

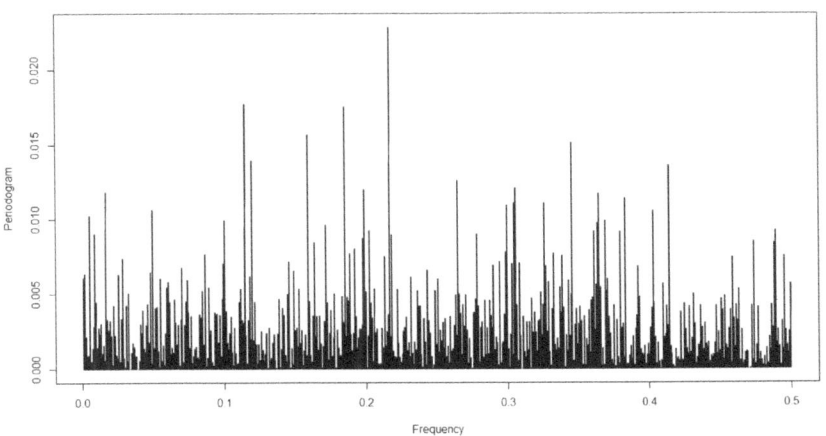

Frequencies and time periods estimates:

Monero	XBP	Bitcoin
freq spec	freq spec	freq spec
0.3831111 0.09425539	0.004444444 0.1608538	0.2168889 0.02287820
0.3653333 0.07489229	0.026666667 0.1022776	0.1146667 0.01772995
Time	Time	Time
2.610209 2.737226	225.0 37.5	4.610656 8.720930

2. The figures below show the MODWT decomposition diagram for the Monero and Bitcoin between the period 1st January 2015 and 31st December 2017. Based on these information comment on the series characteristics.

Monero

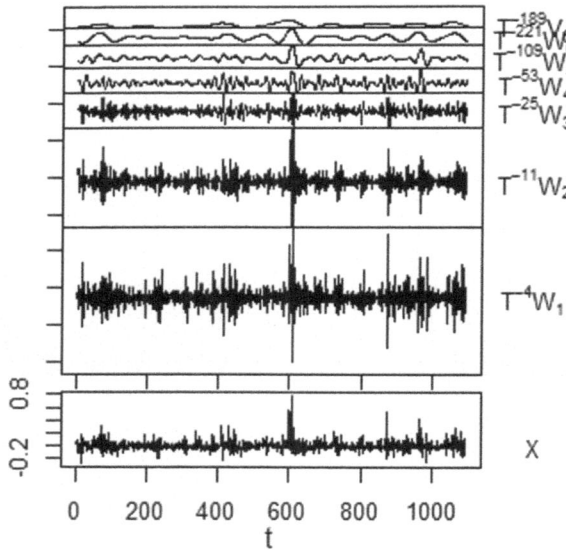

Bitcoin

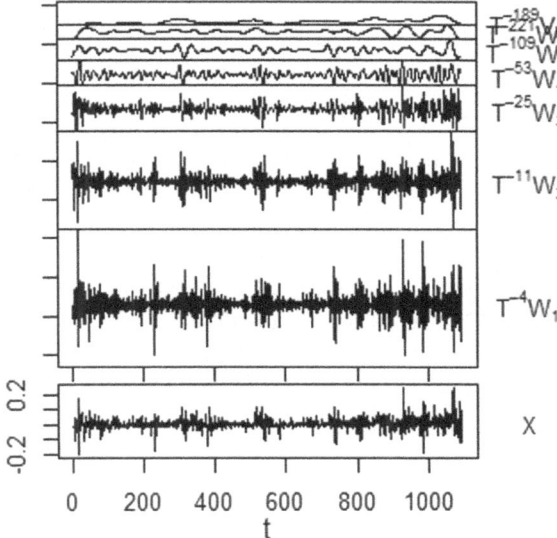

3. The figures below show the wavelet coherence diagram between the Monero, XBP and Bitcoin between the period 1st January 2015 and 31st December 2017. Based on these information comment on the contagion effects and co-movements among the series.

Wavelet Coherence: Monero_XBP

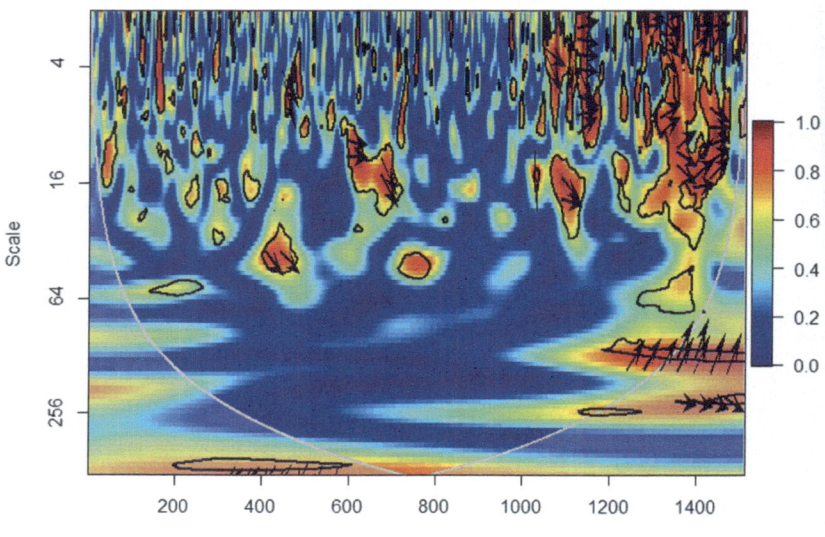

Wavelet Coherence: Monero_Bitcoin

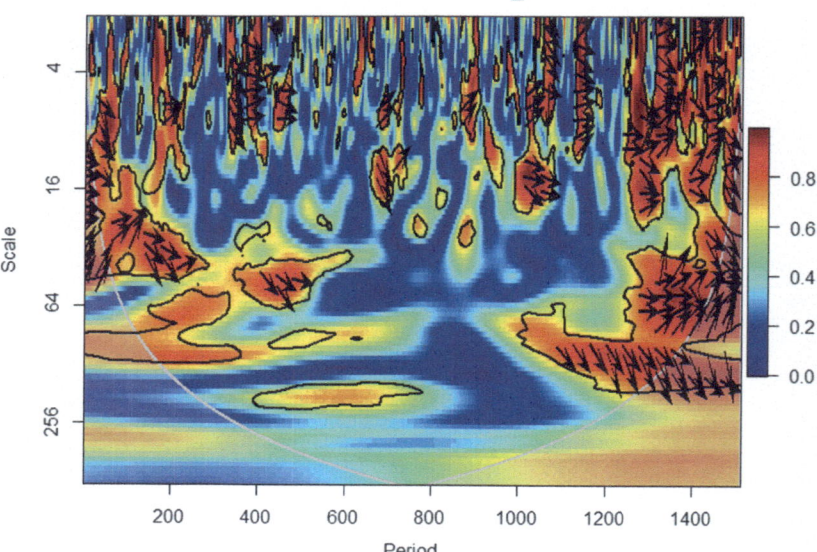

Wavelet Coherence: XBP_Bitcoin

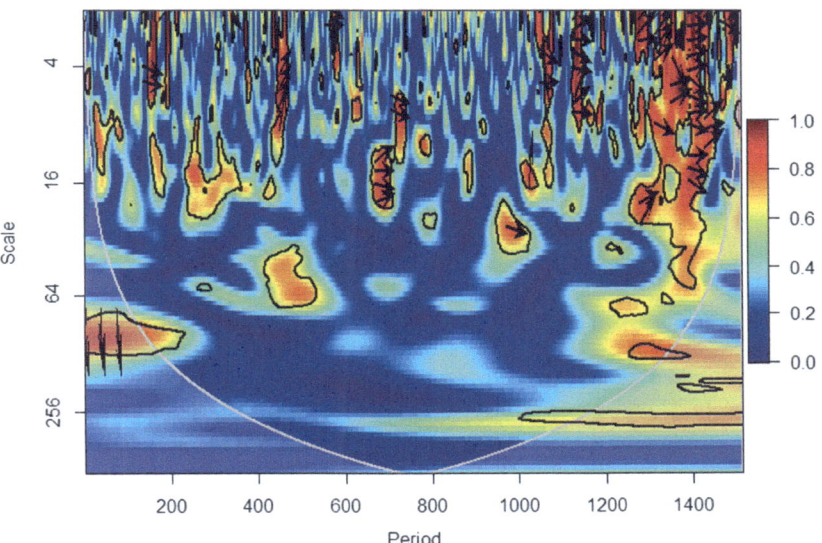

4. The figures below show the wavelet clustering diagram for four
   financial assets (1, 2, 3, and 4). Based on these information
   comment on the portfolio diversification opportunities.

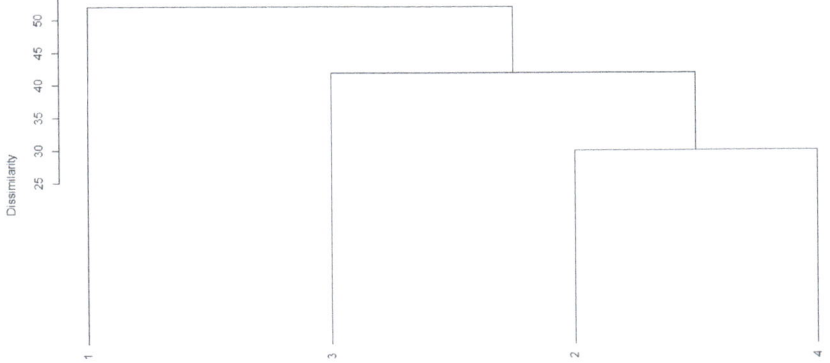

REFERENCES

Maiti, M., Grubisic, Z., & Vukovic, D. B. (2020a). Dissecting Tether's nonlinear dynamics during COVID-19. *Journal of Open Innovation: Technology, Market, and Complexity, 6*(4), 161.

Maiti, M., Vukovic, D., Krakovich, V., & Pandey, M. K. (2020b). How integrated are cryptocurrencies. *International Journal of Big Data Management, 1*(1), 64–80.

Maiti, M., Vyklyuk, Y., & Vukovi´C, D. (2020c). Cryptocurrencies Chaotic Co-movement forecasting with neural networks. *Internet Technology Letters*, e157.

Thanh, S. D., Canh, N. P., & Maiti, M. (2020). Asymmetric effects of unanticipated monetary shocks on stock prices: Emerging market evidence. *Economic Analysis and Policy, 65*, 40–55.

Vukovic, D., Lapshina, K. A., & Maiti, M. (2019). European monetary union bond market dynamics: Pre & post crisis. *Research in International Business and Finance, 50*, 369–380.

Vukovic, D. B., Lapshina, K. A., & Maiti, M. (2021). Wavelet coherence analysis of returns, volatility and interdependence of the US and the EU money markets: Pre & Post Crisis. *The North American Journal of Economics and Finance*, 101457.

Vukovic, D., Vyklyuk, Y., Matsiuk, N., & Maiti, M. (2020). Neural network forecasting in prediction Sharpe ratio: Evidence from EU debt market. *Physica A: Statistical Mechanics and its Applications, 542*, 123331.

INDEX

The manufacturer's authorised representative in the EU is Springer
Nature Customer Service Centre GmbH, Europaplatz 3, 69115 Heidelberg,
Germany. If you have any concerns regarding our products, please
contact ProductSafety@springernature.com

Printed and bound by CPI Group (UK) Ltd, Croydon, CR0 4YY
29/04/2026
02099471-0011